# Advances in African Economic, Social and Political Development

Africa is emerging as a rapidly growing region, still facing major challenges, but with a potential for significant progress – a transformation that necessitates vigorous efforts in research and policy thinking. This book series focuses on three intricately related key aspects of modern-day Africa: economic, social and political development. Making use of recent theoretical and empirical advances, the series aims to provide fresh answers to Africa's development challenges. All the socio-political dimensions of today's Africa are incorporated as they unfold and new policy options are presented. The series aims to provide a broad and interactive forum of science at work for policymaking and to bring together African and international researchers and experts. The series welcomes monographs and contributed volumes for an academic and professional audience, as well as tightly edited conference proceedings. Relevant topics include, but are not limited to, economic policy and trade, regional integration, labor market policies, demographic development, social issues, political economy and political systems, and environmental and energy issues.

All titles in the series are peer-reviewed. The book series is indexed in SCOPUS.

Kenneth Mahuni · James Zivanomoyo ·
Puruweti Siyakiya · Simba Mutsvangwa

# Zimbabwe's Economy

## Four Decades in Perspective (1980–2020)

Springer

Kenneth Mahuni
University of Mauritius
Reduit, Mauritius

Puruweti Siyakiya
National University of Lesotho
Roma, Maseru, Lesotho

James Zivanomoyo
Great Zimbabwe University
Masvingo, Zimbabwe

Simba Mutsvangwa
Bindura University of Science Education
Bindura, Zimbabwe

ISSN 2198-7262 ISSN 2198-7270 (electronic)
Advances in African Economic, Social and Political Development
ISBN 978-3-031-81587-4 ISBN 978-3-031-81588-1 (eBook)
https://doi.org/10.1007/978-3-031-81588-1



This Springer imprint is published by the registered company Springer Nature Switzerland AG
The registered company address is: Gewerbestrasse 11, 6330 Cham, Switzerland

# Foreword

Why are Zimbabwe's economic problems seemingly unending? This is a question which baffles any inquisitive mind which is so much acquainted with Zimbabwe's economic history. The narrative of Zimbabwe over the past four decades is one which can be described as paradoxical. Despite the vast latent potential in the human and material resources, the crushing weight of poverty continues to haunt the country. After over 40 years of independence, the economy continues to battle many challenges manifesting in one form or the other.

*Zimbabwe's Economy: Four Decades in Perspective (1980–2020)* is a book on Zimbabwe's economic history over the four decades which starts immediately after independence from erstwhile colonisers when she inherited a *jewel* of an economy. According to the authors, the independence euphoria created a bubble pregnant with expectations for the masses—it was a dawn of a new era.

Donning oversized robes, Zimbabwe dazzled in her early days as correctly captured by the authors in Chap. 2 when she took over and gloated over the 'residuals' of the jewel economy from the former colonial masters. Substantial gains made in education, health and agriculture among other sectors then made Zimbabwe a model economy ranking ahead most of her peers in the region and beyond. Sadly, like morning dew, this did not last. The glory days vanished. *WHAT THEN WENT WRONG ALONG THE WAY?* In part, this book aims to bring closer to the reader what went wrong along the four-decade arduous and melodramatic journey.

Much of the story of the narrative of the economy is intricately weaved in the themes which precede each part of this interesting book which I give a brief overview shortly as they unpack the central theses of this book. I present the selected paraphrased themes in italics. From Chap. 3 onwards, deftly combining solid economic facts and evidence across the length and breadth of the economy over the four decades, the authors skilfully trace the journey of Zimbabwe unpacking what *stoked the fires of economic turbulence.* Like the 'Biblical *writing on the wall*', the signs of turbulence were ignored resulting in them coalescing into a fully-fledged crisis pushing the economy to the *edge of a cliff*, most of it *breaking the economy.*

According to the authors, a *crisis begets a crisis.* The economy continuously lurches from one crisis to another. In the process, numerous blunders were created as Chap. 6 elucidates. The jewel was the greatest casualty. It was peeled. With little respite along the way, the economy further *sank into turbulence*, the central theme of Chap. 7.

The authors have solid backgrounds and experience in economics amassed over many years. They know the appropriate prescription required by Zimbabwe to come out of the intensive care unit so as for her to reclaim her glory of the days gone by. Beyond the turbulence of the four decades, the authors see hope for the economy. Thus, the other part of the book is to also educate other developing economies with a similar disposition to Zimbabwe on how to sustainably progress. The narrative by the authors is also laced with examples from the continent and beyond drawing similarities and differences with Zimbabwe.

Despite the challenges, the authors see endless possibilities of trumping turbulence by the economy of Zimbabwe. They deliberately take stock of some of the attempts at the present at getting over turbulence and the economic headwinds ahead which still pose a threat to the economy.

The book is therefore a product of an in-depth exegetical detail of Zimbabwe's journey in the attempt to transform the economy. The book compliments other books about the Zimbabwean narrative although it is extensive in its coverage specifically about the mixed experience of the post-colonial state.

Professor Albert Makochekanwa,
(Ph.D.)
Department of Economics
and Development
University of Zimbabwe
Harare, Zimbabwe

# Preface

'You have inherited a jewel. **KEEP IT THAT WAY**!' These were the famous words of Tanzania's founding president, the late Julius Kambarage Nyerere in a speech on Zimbabwe's independence, in 1980 to be precise. That was a long time ago. The message was *loud* and *clear*!

In as much as it was a congratulatory message, it carried with it powerful words of advice and a *stern* warning—KEEP IT THAT WAY! That was very strong a piece of counsel to Zimbabwe on her newly found independence. It still baffles the mind to digest what was in the revered statesman's mind especially when he affirmed: *Keep it that way !* What was really racing through his mind about Zimbabwe's capabilities with respect to the jewel? Possibly the warning had been motivated by what he had seen in other states that had gained their freedoms earlier.

We can deduce that the underlying bigger message in those words was that greater responsibilities lay ahead so as to ensure that the jewel remains unblemished. In addition, at least if you may not succeed in taking it to another level at least, *keep it that way*, do not defile it. Further enhancing the jewel to the next higher level of glory proved a herculean task, not only for Zimbabwe but for other states which have had a dalliance with the colonial past. Was the jewel *kept that way?* If so, for how long? If not, what went wrong along the way for the former model economy which was an envy of many?

Over the past few years, I have travelled around a number of countries in Africa as well outside the continent I have often come across the question, '*How is Zimbabwe now?*' from different people. Some have been friends whereas others being college professors. I have always tried to answer as much as possible to explain in detail the socio-economic successes as well as the challenges. In an attempt to give detailed answers, a book idea was thus born!

So approximately after four decades when the beautiful words were spoken by Julius Nyerere, a lot has changed for the jewel of Africa. Whether the country changed for the better or worse can be a raging debate of unprecedented intellectual ferment. Thoroughly examining the journey Zimbabwe has traversed so far, too many questions popped up. In the process of trying to carry an exegesis of the advice of Nyerere, the book idea became even clearer. There was a need to closely have a look at how

Zimbabwe has survived over the past four decades. However, we battled with the title with which to give our book in relation to what we continuously observe and experience in our beloved motherland.

After a strong conviction that the narrative of Zimbabwe can illuminate beautiful lessons to other post-colonial states in Africa, we settled for the title *Zimbabwe's Economy: Four Decades in Perspective (1980–2020).* We saw it befitting as a comprehensive answer to most questions we had about Zimbabwe's economic journey. How then to put flesh to this skeletal title in order to intricately weave a narrative of our country was another mammoth task. We however got solace from the fact that plenty of countries especially those developing have a lot of things in common in terms of the challenges and suitable solutions to transform them.

Serious work on the book commenced when the coronavirus (COVID-19) struck across the world. The global economy was caught unawares and was shaken to its very foundations. Upon seeing how suddenly livelihoods of people had been impacted by the pandemic across many poor countries on top of their pre-existing precarious conditions, the pieces of the jigsaw puzzle began to come together. The book began to take shape. Given differential impacts of COVID-19, deep rooted problems for struggling economies were being unmasked. With very little coping mechanisms in place, weak economies were devastated. Since most countries had shut their physical borders, the lives of ordinary people as they came to terms with local realities in the new normal made it easier for us to relate with our country—specifically the achievements, the past glory and the challenges which lay ahead. These became crucial subject matter and mortar binding our diverse ideas culminating into this beautiful book about our country.

Executed with vitality, this book is a varied mine of exegetical details providing an objective analysis of Zimbabwe's economic experiences during the first forty years after independence. It will be folly for the reader to quickly point a finger at political actors especially about '*who did what*' and '*when*' resulting in the difficult journey of forty years. To us, this will be a discourse of no merit. To borrow words from a Lebanese economist, Badaro during an interview with the New York Times, 'There are many sins and many sinners' in reference to the turmoil gripping Lebanon. The same can relate to Zimbabwe if we look at her economic history with an objective lens.

In writing this book therefore, we were not much concerned about the *sinners* as Badaro would put it but to look at the *sins.* These are the bolts and nuts defining Zimbabwe's four decades of mixed fortunes. Focusing on the 'sinners' will only foment disunity among people, a common problem of most developing countries which has become an albatross for sustainable progress.

With this book, we also aimed to show how Zimbabwe's own experience can be a great lesson to other economies. In addition, Zimbabwe has a great deal of learning points from her very own story as she labours along to enhance her people's capabilities in hot pursuit of real development right through to its poorest poor.

The book caters for a broader spectrum of readers. We made every effort to use simple and understandable language and useful everyday metaphors to make the narrative solid without throwing facts away. To scholars keen on acquainting themselves with much of Zimbabwe's economic history, it provides a solid information base laden with facts. On the other hand, for development enthusiasts, the policy-makers and academics, the book is a useful guide and an example of how post-colonial African states often struggle going past *residual economies* inherited from the colonial past in their quest to create new and sovereign economies addressing present realities.

Reduit, Mauritius Kenneth Mahuni

# Acknowledgements

For this book to be a success, we are greatly indebted to Springer Nature for the immense faith they showed in our potential to deliver this book. Dr. Glaeser, Mr. Vijay Kumar Selvaraj and the entire team, we thank you for your support and guidance from the beginning of this beautiful project to its successful completion.

Special thanks to Associate Professor Taruna Shalini Ramessur[1] and Moses Changa[2] for contributions in the development and shaping Chap. 11. It remains a special feature of this book chronicling *Migration, Empowerment and Zimbabwean Women* in the context of the Zimbabwean economy from 1980 to 2020. Their insights helped us to situate women in the economy of Zimbabwe. Success also of solving the problems of Zimbabwe will also depend on profound understanding of issues which impact them—migration in relation to their empowerment is also key as elucidated in the book. A lot of valuable contributions helped to shape this book.

[1] Department of Economics and Statistics, University of Mauritius.

[2] Department of Peace and Security Midlands State University.

# About This Book

This book is a product of valuable, relevant and timeless facts playing out for post-colonial Zimbabwe spanning over four decades. Using their diverse experience and profound knowledge about the economic history of Zimbabwe, the authors provide a powerful and informative book that is not only useful to economic historians but a broader spectrum of readers as well. In the book, the authors journey with the reader through four decades of Zimbabwe in its quest to transform like any other post-colonial developing state. In the process, the book lays bare the numerous short-lived post-independent achievements as reflected in key macroeconomic indicators. The book explores how the achievements slowly faded paving way for multi-layered problems which compounded challenges for an economy which still has latent potential in its human and natural resources. Quite a number of books on Zimbabwe have been written. However, this book stands out in three ways.

Firstly, the book uses simple, accessible language yet it is juxtaposed with critical facts and figures which have played out for Zimbabwe post-independence. This way, it appeals to a wider audience. In the process, the book helps to also educate in a simple way any reader who may not be so much skilled in economics.

Secondly, the book takes the reader through the journey of Zimbabwe using powerful metaphors. Simple as the metaphors may appear, the message conveyed is however priceless. The purpose by the authors in doing so is to allow soul searching and find meaning by every reader beyond everyday simple objects. This reflection helps to unlock the understanding of complex realities confounding a number of post-colonial states in Africa.

Lastly, not only does the book dissect through post-independent Zimbabwe's critical challenges, but also poses *Eight Fundamental Questions* with respect to the narrative of the economy once regarded as a Jewel of Africa. For instance, the authors ask the hard-hitting question number 2: *Will Zimbabwe be able to salvage lost decades of development?* This is the main question to those acquainted with Zimbabwe's narrative can relate to.

A special feature of the book is material included in Chaps. 10 and 11. In Chap. 10, the authors explore the issue of Zimbabwean women with respect to migration and empowerment in the four decades. Drawing from other contexts, the book highlights the importance of empowering women as part of broader strategies of solving Zimbabwe's challenges.

In Chap. 11, the book looks into further issues. Understanding them helps to appreciate Zimbabwe's multi-layered challenges post-independence. Other post-colonial states can also relate to these issues.

Beyond the problems and troubles of the years, the book challenges everyone in Zimbabwe's development journey to play a special role. In retracing the steps towards rebuilding the jewel, the book proffers simple yet invaluable lessons. In addition, the solution set also appeals to other post-colonial states which are struggling to set themselves on a sustainable development trajectory.

Associate Professor Taruna Shalini Ramessur
Department of Economics and Statistics
University of Mauritius
Reduit, Mauritius

# Contents

# About the Authors

**Kenneth Mahuni** is a multi-award-winning Ph.D. student at the University of Mauritius and co-author of book, '*Africa's Incomplete Cycles of Development*', and several peer reviewed papers and policy briefs. He has presented at prestigious research and policy forums such as International Economic Association (IEA), COMESA, Academics Stand Against Poverty (ASAP) Global Financial Integrity Program as well as South Korea's Official Development Assistance (ODA) forum. He has a wealth of experience acquired from working in academic and policy environment as well as through years of travelling in many countries.

**Dr. James Zivanomoyo** is a senior lecturer with over twenty-one years' experience teaching and supervising graduate and postgraduate students. He has published over twenty peer reviewed papers and presented in over twelve international conferences. He is a co-editor of one book and has over fourteen book chapters.

**Dr. Puruweti Siyakiya** has over ten years of work experience. He has a Ph.D. in Economics from Turkey and a Masters in Economics and Development from Erasmus University of Rotterdam, the Netherlands. He is an expert in development economics, international trade, industrialisation and industrial. Currently, he is a senior lecturer at National University of Lesotho.

**Dr. Simba Mutsvangwa** is a research economist with experience in research and policy analysis. He holds a Ph.D. in International Economics (Yokohama National University, Japan), and M.Sc. and B.Sc. Honours Degrees in Economics (University of Zimbabwe). He has over ten years of researching in both government and university environment.

# Abbreviations

| | |
|---|---|
| ACR | African Consolidated Resources |
| AfDB | Africa Development Bank |
| CCPR | Convention on Civil and Political Rights |
| CEDAW | Convention on the Elimination of all Forms of Discrimination Against Women |
| CIs | Cluster Initiatives |
| COMESA | Common Market for Eastern and Southern Africa |
| COPAC | Constitutional Parliamentary Select Committee |
| DDCP | Diarrheal Disease Control Programme |
| ECD | Early Childhood Development |
| ECEC | Early Childhood Education and Care |
| ESAP | Economic Structural Adjustment Programme |
| FAO | Food and Agriculture Organisation |
| FEEB | Further Education Examination Board |
| FELOCS | Foreign Exchange Licensed Oil Companies |
| FEWSNET | Famine Early Warning Systems Network |
| FOLIWARS | Foreign Exchange Licensed Warehouses |
| FOLOPADS | Foreign Exchange Licensed Outlets for Petrol and Diesel |
| FTLRP | Fast Track Land Reform Programme |
| GFPs | Gender Focal Persons |
| GNU | Government of National Unit |
| GoZ | Government of Zimbabwe |
| HPC | High Potential Centres |
| LPC | Low Potential Centres |
| LRRP | Land Reform and Resettlement Programme |
| MFEPD | Ministry of Finance, Economic Planning and Development |
| MSMEs | Micro Small to Medium Enterprises |
| MWAGCD | Ministry of Women Affairs, Gender and Community Development |
| NAC | National AIDS Council |
| NGO | Non-Governmental Organisation |
| NGP | National Gender Policy |

| | |
|---|---|
| ODA | Official Development Assistance |
| POTRAZ | Postal and Telecommunications Regulatory Authority of Zimbabwe |
| PTC | Posts and Telecommunications Corporation |
| RBZ | Reserve Bank of Zimbabwe |
| SACCOs | Savings and Credit Cooperative Societies |
| SADC | Southern African Development Community |
| SIP | Smallholder Irrigation Programme |
| STERP | Short-Term Emergency Recovery Programme |
| TNDP | Transitional National Development Plan |
| UDACIZA | Union for Development of Apostolic Churches in Zimbabwe |
| UNICEF | United Nations Children's Fund |
| UZ | University of Zimbabwe |
| VFU | Victim Friendly Unit |
| WHO | World Health Organisation |
| ZACH | Zimbabwe Association of Church-related Hospitals |
| ZEC | Zimbabwe Electoral Commission |
| ZEPI | Zimbabwe Expanded Programme for Immunisation |
| ZETDC | Zimbabwe Electricity Transmission and Distribution Company |
| ZIMCHE | Zimbabwe Higher Council for Education |
| ZIMDEF | Zimbabwe Development Fund |
| ZIMSTAT | Zimbabwe National Statistics Agency |
| ZIPSHAW | Zimbabwe Private Sector HIV/AIDS and Wellness Coordination Board |
| ZMF | Zimbabwe Miners Federation |
| ZPC | Zimbabwe Power Company (ZPC) |

# List of Figures

# List of Tables

# Part I
# Becoming a Sovereign State

# Chapter 1
# 18 April 1980, Dawn of a New Era?

**Keywords** Corruption · Currency stability · Debt · Post-independence · Zimbabwe

## 1.1 Introduction

Jubilations, wild celebrations and tears of joy were the hallmarks of 18 April 1980 as people united to celebrate dawn of a new era. On this day, Zimbabwe as a sovereign state was born. Whatever lay ahead no one could tell. The most important thing at that particular moment however was looking forward to a brilliant future filled with good fortunes where everyone was going to partake in the rebuilding of a nation towards prosperity whereby the national cake would be shared by everyone to achieve an egalitarian society built on the ethos of unity, equality and a shared vision.

The eighteenth of April 1980 will remain engraved in our hearts as the day out great nation Zimbabwe was born, signalling a new journey of self-rule and determination. It marked the day when the voice of the trampled conquered. The long-cherished dream of freedom had become a reality. Beautiful stories are often told by some of the people who witnessed this transition of how the enemy had been defeated. It had been a long wait they say, for the majority to be free at last after having lived under the shadow of the oppressor. Independence meant that as a once marginalised people we now have unfettered access to our resources.

The above synopsis is just a glimpse of the state of affairs in particular the mood (opening paragraph) of people of this great nation approximately four decades ago. The economy in its present state tells a different narrative. There are many challenges. Ordinary people continue to endure the crushing weight of the ever-imploding economy.

Socio-economic challenges characterised by closure of companies, high inflation levels, economy getting too informalised, infrastructure decay, epileptic power

 
K. Mahuni et al., *Zimbabwe's Economy*, Advances in African Economic, Social and Political Development, https://doi.org/10.1007/978-3-031-81588-1_1

supplies, successive droughts, deterioration of health delivery system, escalating cost of living have shattered dreams of many people. Life savings and pensions have been lost by some; on the other hand, getting a formal job in particular for graduates is increasingly becoming a nightmare. The informal sector is largely supporting hand to mouth survival. For a country churning thousands of graduates annually against the backdrop of company closures and a shrinking formal job market struggling to open new opportunities, ordinary people continue to face many problems.

Over the last four decades, the narrative of transformation of Zimbabwe brings despair than hope, it's a disturbing narrative. Given the immense potential the country exhibits and the mismatch between what has been attained over the years against actual potential, one can only wonder as to when then the fruits of real development be sustainably enjoyed by Zimbabwe. Furthermore, if Zimbabwe's time is not now, then when?

Zimbabwe is struggling to gather as much momentum for real transformation. At some stage strong momentum for progress can be gathered only to suddenly dissipate. The country starts over again. In confused circles, the country continues to saunter ahead.[1] Heading where? No one knows. The ordinary poor and vulnerable who make up the majority of the over 16 million population and continuously dine and wine with poverty on a daily basis are quite convinced that the journey is still long way and the future may not be as bright. Instead of seeing light of hope at the end of the tunnel, they are seeing dazzling light of an oncoming *goods* train travelling at an incredible speed.

Independence marked the end of minority rule so as to pave way for self-determination by the black majority. Since then, the path to transform the lives of the masses has not been a stroll in the park. To date, the journey is still not filled with roses.

Up to now what makes big powers such as the Great Britain and America continue to make a lot of noise about the state of affairs of Zimbabwe than they will do about say South Sudan, the continent's youngest state? The reader should note that the authors are not in any way belittling South Sudan. Zimbabwe is of a unique disposition. Despite lying on vast resources and amazing talent, she is still among the poor nations, still struggling on the lowest rungs of the development. The majority of its inhabitants are still rubbing shoulders with abject poverty, while at the same time a few inhabitants are swimming in opulence.

Besides the above, Zimbabwe is not progressing very much. More is expected of her yet she has disappointed in a majority of instances for the greater part of her four decades of existence as an independent state. Zimbabwe still scores poorly on most global indicators reflecting a sluggish progress on efforts to grow and develop not only its territorial space but its inhabitants as a whole. Here is a look at how the country has performed on a number of indicators over the years. The bulk of our analysis is with respect to regional peers as they are closer to Zimbabwe. Moreover,

---

[1] *Saskam Express*, a title of a novel by Lilian Masitera. The phrase, 'saskam' can imply crazy, usually when used in common or street language. Then the whole phrase can be understood to mean a journey where nothing is predictable or secure.

historical conditions are quite similar. The fairly homogenous conditions will also help the reader appreciate further Zimbabwe's economic history.

## 1.2 A Brief Survey of Macroeconomic Indicators

In brief, we examine the performance of Zimbabwe over the years in five key macroeconomic indicators. These are corruption, ease of doing business, foreign direct investment, debt and currency.

### *1.2.1 Zimbabwe Corruption Ranking Over the Years*

Over the years, corruption has become a developmental challenge in Zimbabwe just like in other countries. Trading Economics (2024) gives a timeline of corruption rankings of Zimbabwe dating back to the 1990s. From around 1999, Zimbabwe out of 180 countries was ranked number 45. A rank of number 1 for any economy is the best and implies minimum corruption. As ranks move away from number 1 towards 180, it implies increase in corruption. Advanced countries normally score very well as they have made great strides in controlling corruption. From the statistics, starting from the year 2000 onwards, the country has been performing badly as corruption gradually increased in the economy reaching an all-time high of 166 out of 180 countries in the year 2008. From the year 2009 up to 2023, the country has averaged three digit ranking hovering above 150. In the year 2020, the rank was 157. In the years to come up to 2022, the country remained at 157. Corruption has cost Zimbabwe a lot of resources including also undermining of key developmental institutions. The country loses on average USD 1.8 billion annually due to corruption (The Herald, 2022). Corruption has been rampant in the public sector through tenders in which procedures are not properly followed. Notable avenues for corruption include sectors such as transport, health, energy and agriculture. In local authorities across the country, corruption has been a major issue affecting overall service delivery. Not decisively dealing with corruption will pose a lot of challenges to Zimbabwe. A study by Bonga and Mahuni (2018) showed that most African countries have corruption as an albatross and this blights the prospects of success and efficacy of Africa Free Trade Zone (AFTZ). How Zimbabwe will perform also on AFTZ will also be linked to how corruption and other related challenges are dealt with.

### *1.2.2 Ease of Doing Business Indicators*

The World Bank publishes ease of doing business indicators for countries across the globe to show how they perform on 10 categories. These range from issues such as trading across borders, getting credit, electricity and permits. A country is then ranked depending on how it performs. Zimbabwe given its numerous problems has been performing poorly compared to most countries showing a difficult business environment. A time series analysis of ease of doing business indicators of Zimbabwe with respect to FDI by Mahuni and Bonga (2017) showed that certain key ease of doing indicators are important for gauging FDI flows for Zimbabwe. These were enforcing contracts, paying taxes, dealing with construction permits and getting electricity. The study implied that as long as there is no serious effort at addressing these and other related factors, then FDI inflows will not be much for the country. So, alongside corruption explored above, the business environment gets murkier.

### *1.2.3 Foreign Direct Investment*

Table 1.1 shows that FDI flows to Zimbabwe have been steadily increasing from the selected periods. Despite the figures implying 'positivity' and a country making milestones, the reality on the ground tells a different story. Unemployment levels continue to rise given the dwindling formal sector. From the statistics also, Zimbabwe performs poorly when compared to other economic powerhouses such as Kenya and South Africa receiving low FDI for the greater part of the time period. Other economies in question despite posting low figures e.g. Rwanda and Botswana in other years as depicted in Table 1.1, they have economies which are however robust and resilient. The point is Zimbabwe has latent potential to at least match or surpass these.

Given the above analysis of indicators, it should not come as a big surprise to the reader that in some instances Zimbabwe has been compared with states such as Venezuela, for not so good reasons of cause. Again, the authors are not looking down upon Venezuela. Just like Zimbabwe, Venezuela has also experienced hyperinflation. For example, in 2019 annual inflation rate for Venezuela reached approximately

**Table 1.1** Annual foreign direct investment inward flows for selected countries (in US dollars at current prices in millions)

| Country | 1980 | 1985 | 1990 | 1995 | 2000 | 2005 | 2010 | 2015 | 2018 |
|---|---|---|---|---|---|---|---|---|---|
| Botswana | 111.55 | 53.61 | 95.9 | 70.41 | 61.24 | 421.38 | 218.38 | 378.55 | 228.71 |
| Kenya | 78.97 | 28.85 | 57.1 | 33 | 110.90 | 21.21 | 1197.55 | 619.72 | 1625.92 |
| Malawi | 9.48 | 0.52 | 23.3 | 5.64 | 39.63 | 99.14 | 46.08 | 509.67 | 101.61 |
| Rwanda | 16.42 | 14.62 | 7.66 | 2 | 8.1 | 7.96 | 250.50 | 379.80 | 398.47 |
| South Africa | – 10.3 | – 448 | – 78.45 | 1241.21 | 887.34 | 6646.92 | 3635.59 | 1729.37 | 5333.99 |
| Zambia | 61.75 | 51.53 | 202.78 | 107 | 121.7 | 356.94 | 1729.3 | 1304.9 | 568.95 |
| Zimbabwe | 1.6 | 2.9 | 12.2 | 117.7 | 23.2 | 102.8 | 165.9 | 421 | 744.64 |

*Source* Authors compilation using UNCTAD data base

345 000%.[2] Zimbabwe has been in a similar corner before with highest recorded inflation figure being 89.7 sextillion %.[3] Zimbabwe has thus struggled a lot in spite of the abundant resources to transform herself, just like Venezuela who continues in turmoil regardless of abundant oil. Due to globalisation, economies are becoming more connected than before. This phenomenon has seen the rise and rise of other economies which have taken advantage of the globalisation tide. Those that have been frail have not gone unscathed. We borrow a passage from Shakespeare's Julius Caesar, when he speaks of the need for people to take advantage of situations/opportunities which can come their way. Failure to utilise such moments often leads to regret:

> There is a tide in the affairs of men, which taken at the flood, leads on the fortune; Omitted, all the voyage of their life is bound in shallows and in miseries.[4]

The context of the quote related to military strategy of characters in Julius Caesar which is nevertheless important in helping us analyse how globalisation has impacted on economies. The above quotation helps us to illustrate a point. The tide of the sea we can take it to mean the wave of globalisation. Plenty of countries in the continent have taken advantage of the tide and have obtained amazing results for their people. Countries such as Botswana and Rwanda, for instance, are currently enjoying favourable and relatively stable economies due to positioning themselves strategically to take advantage of networking with other global economies, all which have been accelerated by globalisation. Botswana for instance due to her investor friendly policies has managed to create a better functioning economy anchored mostly by the diamond sector. Her largely arid conditions do not favour much of agriculture. Zimbabwe on the other hand has plenty of minerals including gold, diamond, platinum, etc. Moreover, she has a favourable climate favouring thriving agriculture when compared to Botswana. When the two economies are compared, Botswana is performing much better despite the fact that Zimbabwe has abundant chances of being a diversified and robust economy.

Has Zimbabwe taken advantage of the tide too over the four decades? Is she also riding high on the crest of success? Whatever her standpoint, has it led to fortune for her general populace? For a country like Rwanda for example, globalisation has meant a lot in terms of quality of FDI she is receiving, the nature of friends and partners she is currently associating with, the resulting positive spillover effects to her people, etc. The benefits accruing to Rwanda have been tremendous. For instance, the quality of business environment has greatly improved over years. For example, in 2008 Rwanda was ranked 143/190 in terms of ease of doing business. As at 2019, the country had improved to 38/190,[5] signifying a lot of progress.

---

[2] See Trading Economics: https://tradingeconomics.com/venezuela/inflation-cpi#:~:text=Inflation%20Rate%20in%20Venezuela%20averaged,percent%20in%20February%20of%201973.

[3] See: Hanke and Kwok (2009). Available at: https://www.cato.org/sites/cato.org/files/serials/files/cato-journal/2009/5/cj29n2-8.pdf.

[4] Julius Caesar by William Shakespeare. Full explanation of the quotation available on https://www.enotes.com/homework-help/what-is-the-meaning-of-the-following-quote-from-522799.

[5] See Trading Economics. Available at: https://tradingeconomics.com/rwanda/ease-of-doing-business.

Can impactful investments be attracted to a location which has problems with stability? It's not easy. At the current, Zimbabwe is expected to enjoy less and less of the kind of investments Rwanda is enjoying relative to the immense potential the country has. Rwanda embraced globalisation and is riding the tide much to the benefit of the greater Rwandan economy.

Why comparing Zimbabwe with Rwanda? Are we not over using Rwanda as an example of what Zimbabwe could have attained? Zimbabwe is very much capable of also fitting into the same shoes. Rwanda's story is somehow a low hanging fruit moreover at a reasonable height within Zimbabwe's grasp. It will be folly to compare Zimbabwe in terms of development with countries such as say USA, UK, Japan and Norway. They are worlds apart with Zimbabwe! While it is the dream of most developing countries to be like the USA and UK of this world development wise, it may not be an easy feat. So much as it may be desirable, it may not be attainable by most developing countries like Zimbabwe if we scan with objective lenses respective development trajectories.

### 1.2.4 Domestic and External Debt

According to World Bank (2022), Zimbabwe is classified as, 'in debt distress'. Zimbabwe Treasury (2023) shows that as of September 2023, Zimbabwe's Domestic Debt Stock was Z$27.4 trillion whereas External Debt Stock was USD 12.7 billion. The report shows that since the year 2000, Zimbabwe has struggled in terms of payment of arrears resulting in accumulation of penalties resulting in the increase of external debt. Debt does matter for an economy. World Bank (2022) showed that Zimbabwe's debt had '*breached the thresholds in both the baseline and shock scenarios*'. In other words, the debt level is unsustainable. The implications of this are that the country is not able to access fresh lines of credit internationally. Domestically with excessive government borrowing resulting in accumulation of domestic debt, the private sector investment is reduced. This phenomenon is called 'crowding out effect' by economists. The overall impact is that the national cake (GDP) will not grow much.

### 1.2.5 Currency Strength and Stability

From 2009 to 2024, it marks approximately 15 years. Over this period, Zimbabwe has changed currency six times. In 2009, Zimbabwe started using a basket of foreign currency which saw the Zimbabwean dollar which had been ravaged by inflation losing public confidence. The major issue has been the lack of public confidence in the numerous currencies. The currency woes have been a manifestation of underlying structural issues on the broader economy. From history of economies, it is difficult for a country after having dollarised to successfully de-dollarise. It remains to be seen if Zimbabwe will be able to also successfully de-dollarise. But successful de-dollarisation will require a lot of honest hard work across the economy so as to build the much-needed trust.

## 1.3 The Media and the Narrative of Zimbabwe

Role of media in any society's developmental journey is crucial. The following text from Wilbur Schramm aptly captures how media aids development:

> By making one part of a country aware of other parts, their people, arts, customs, and politics; by permitting the national leaders to talk to the people, and people to the leaders and to each other; by making possible a nation-wide dialogue on national policy; by keeping the national goals and national accomplishments always before the public, thus modern communication, widely used, can help weld together isolated communities, disparate subcultures, self- centred individuals and groups, and separate developments into a truly national development.[6]

Thus, media helps to bring out to the public domain issues which would otherwise not be known. Zimbabwe's journey of transformation has also been captured. How it has featured especially in local and international media has been intriguing. The most important feature of the reportage to any critical reader reflects also the difficult economic terrain the country has been through.

While tabloid sensationalism at times cannot be ruled out in some of the reportage, the bulk of headlines from the different tabloids have also presented compelling evidence as far as the story of Zimbabwe is concerned. They point to a nation which is continuously burning whereas some would want to downplay the turbulence. The headlines reflect on the deep-seated challenges embedded in different facets of the economy—for instance power supply, food security, health, industry, etc., all of which are a barometer of the general health of an economy. Here is a glimpse of some of the headlines which have trended over the years from both local and international media (Table 1.2).

Headlines from different media be it print or electronic cannot be exhausted. Everyday stories are written so as to keep people informed as pointed by Wilbur Schramm we quoted earlier. From the few headlines we highlighted above, we can posit that Zimbabwe's journey over the last four decades has been difficult.

The first headline speaks of masses facing hardship as the economy is heading to a 'meltdown'. This is in sync too with The Economist's observation in the second headline. The third headline speaks of an economy in a currency crisis by the BBC. It further talks also of there being *'no bread'* in Zimbabwe. Interestingly whether or not there is bread in the country as alluded to in the headline, the answer at times depends on which politician you come across and ask at a given time. Furthermore, the varying responses are likely to point to a deeply polarised society.

---

[6] See: SOLUTION: Media developments role in social economic and political progress literature review—Study pool.

**Table 1.2** Local and international media trending headlines for Zimbabwe

| Media and date | Headline |
|---|---|
| The Guardian-Sunday 21 July 2019 | Millions face hardship as Zimbabwe comes close to 'meltdown'. Source: (The Guardian, 2019) |
| The Economist-August 15 2019 Edition | Zimbabwe faces its worst economic crisis in a decade. Source: (The Economist, 2019) |
| BBC-October 2018 | Zimbabwe currency crisis: no cash, no bread, no KFC. Source: (BBC, 2018) |
| Newsday-June 4 2019 | 4 Mysteries of Zim's Economic Crisis. Source: (Newsday, 2019) |
| The Herald-17 February 2020 | Industry capacity to drop 27%<br>No plans to exit Zim: StanChart. Source: (The Herald, 2020) |
| The Herald-11 October 2019 | Impact of sanctions on Zim, region. Source: (The Herald, 2019a) |
| The Independent-13 December 2019 | Energy crisis sinking Zim economy. Source: (The Independent, 2019) |
| The Financial Gazette-24 December 2024 | Zim dollar not about to return: RBZ<br>Struggling Zim workers vow massive strikes in 2016. Source: (The Financial Gazette, 2024) |
| The Financial Gazette-24 December 2024 | Zimbabwe faces huge infrastructure deficit. Source: (The Financial Gazette, 2024) |
| The Herald-09 August 2018 | Land reform: The World Bank finally sees the light. Source: (The Herald, 2018) |
| The Chronicle-01 April 2019 | Zimbabwe's economy on recovery path. Source: (The Chronicle, 2019) |

*Source* Authors' compilation from electronic media and news channels

Related to the currency is headline number 8 when the exchequer assures Zimbabwe that the dollar is not about to return. Why is it so dreaded as a currency? What memories does it invoke? What has brought its demise? Similarly, what could make workers vow to protest in 2016 as pointed by headline number 10? Partly it could be the issue of currency among other grievances. Why is the said currency associated with doom and gloom? Closer to the points just mentioned is headline number 4:

> '*4 mysteries of Zim's crises*'. What has brought these mysteries?

As the challenges unfold, industry is not spared either. The fifth and sixth headlines reflect all this. Industry capacity indeed is projected to drop by 27%, obviously owing to a bleak outlook. Then, StanChart hints on not exiting Zimbabwe despite having operated for over a century. Why did they contemplate exiting in the first place? What have they experienced in the operating environment?

Headline 11 speaks of a country in massive infrastructure deficit. This possibly in part explains why energy crisis is sinking Zimbabwe as in headline number. The land question is addressed in headline number 12. Why is the World Bank now seeing light as is alleged by the headline? Why was *there no* light at first? Maybe it was due to the turbulence alluded to earlier.

The final headline assures of an economy under recovery. Recovering from where or what? Arguably from turmoil of over the years. Full recovery entails then addressing the energy crisis, currency, land reform, infrastructure gaps, confidence deficit, industry concerns as well as alleviating hardships of the masses.

Another interesting component of the media is how the story of Zimbabwe's journey is often portrayed in comic strips. So simple some of the caricatures may appear but to any inquisitive reader they are worth a thousand words when related to Zimbabwe's journey in four decades. The following are a few examples we present in the box.

**Example 1** ***'The Dilapidated House'***

In this comic strip, a seemingly derelict house nearing the point of disintegration located on the edge of a cliff is depicted. On its sides, there are a few props precariously *trying hard* to support the house from being completely decimated. A few partly obscured, seemingly petrified faces with bulging eyes crammed on one corner of the house are starring outside a window with horror filled eyes. It seems the only support left for this giant building are the few struts on its sides. Why would a big building need propping with struts? Possibly it has been through a lot structurally. Weakened by all the compression and tension forces, it can hold fort no more hence the struts are 'trying hard' to offer this support albeit with little success. Now the fate of the house occupants lies on the few supports that are outside.

**Example 2**

***'Overloaded bus facing a steep road ahead'***

In another cartoon strip, we come across an overloaded bus approaching a steep gradient. The appearance of the bus itself is striking. Firstly, there are too few windows given the size of the bus. It only makes one wonder if the passengers can properly breathe in the absence of enough ventilation. Secondly, the main body of the bus has patches all over, a testimony that it has seen too much of panel beating. Given the too many patches on the main body, even the name of the bus is difficult to tell. (In Zimbabwe, buses do have names in most cases for easy identification. It is easy to identify them and distinguish between buses from different companies. The identity is very important in the transport industry because of the powerful brand image which is created.)

The numerous makeovers only make the bus look not so good. It also makes one wonder whether any of the passengers can be proud to be identified with the bus. In fact, many stories are written all over it.

Thirdly, the bus seems to be divided into two partitions. These types of buses were common in the early 1980s through 1990s in Zimbabwe. The driver separated from the rest of the passengers will be in an office like compartment/

cage whereas the rest of the bus is in another section. You would hardly see the driver from his *little office* where he directs the rest of the operations of the bus. Occasionally he would be engaging with his other crew members.

Growing up, we marvelled at how buses travelled, we always had the curiosity of wanting to get a glimpse of the driver from his little office as he was always separated from the rest of the bus albeit with little success. The gulf between the driver and the passengers makes one wonder whether the driver was fully aware of the agony and distress of the passengers he is carrying. Lastly in the cartoon, the bus has very small tyres compared to its size. You wonder if it would last the journey. Besides the disturbing general appearance of the bus, one other thing seems wrong also. Although the body of the bus seems to be sitting on its body properly, it looks like the whole bus is awkwardly tilted to one side giving the impression that it can land on its side any time. It could be that it is overloaded hence it seems to be losing its balance.

On the other hand, the passengers in the bus appear weary with long faces as they ponder possibly whether the driver will be able to safely manoeuvre the intimidating gradient. Besides being overloaded with passengers inside, the bus is also overloaded on its rooftop with an assortment of 'branded' luggage. Some of the tags on the luggage include Eskom debt, water crisis, unemployment, inflation, power crisis, drought, corruption, etc. All this luggage is 'unwanted' for an economy. It exacerbates challenges. In essence to use traffic safety language, the bus will be labelled *a road unworthy vehicle.* It is not supposed to be travelling, let alone carry passengers as it endangers their lives. Lives matter when it comes to road safety regulations.

## 1.4 The Art of Music to Communicate About the Economy and Country in General

On the other hand, Zimbabwe is a musical country. Music is part of our culture. As a country we do have a rich and diverse musical landscape. The country boasts of some of musicians who have toured the globe. Music is one such powerful way of communicating which human beings are gifted with. Through music, sorrow, anguish, joy among other feelings can be expressed. During the colonial days in our country, music was also a powerful tool used by musicians to urge on those on the battlefront to persevere with the struggle. As a result of music also, the enemy could be easily outwitted. Music too featured when an enemy was defeated in the war of liberation; thus, it was used to celebrate demise of the enemy. Some would also like to label musicians as 'prophets' or 'visionaries' as some of their lyrics would speak about the future.

The journey of four decades of Zimbabwe has also been expressed directly or indirectly by musicians. Musicians have often sung about the imploding economy and struggles of the people. Numerous themes which have been tackled by especially yesteryear musicians involve hard-hitting songs juxtaposed with lyrics ranging from themes such as corruption, general suffering of ordinary people, rising prices, joblessness, corruption, struggling of the working class and loss of value of local currency, etc. Musicians live among people. They communicate about people's lived experiences.

A growing crop of contemporary musicians especially Zimbabwe Dancehall genre is not to be out done also. Their music often gives insights into struggles faced especially in the numerous sprawling ghettos across the length and breadth of Zimbabwe. The story of raw poverty and general suffering is often encountered in most lyrics where some of these artists hail from. Most singers of this genre are youthful as such there is a tendency for them to sing about their experiences. What is often outstanding is how the struggling youths in the ghettos are often profiled in the music as they try hard day to day to outsmart hardships.

While there are plenty of musical offerings which have related to Zimbabwe's journey, in this book we will only give one example of a track by Edwin Hama, one of Zimbabwe's finest musicians to emerge in the 1990s. One song most people would remember about him is titled, '*Today's paper*'. The song is laced with lyrical richness speaking of various problems facing the economy of the day back in the 1990s. The singer speaks about rising prices and cost of living, unemployment against rising population, doubling of taxes, corruption and scandals. These very issues have been part and parcel of the narrative of Zimbabwe over the years.

## 1.5 Outline of the Book

This book is divided into five parts. Each part has chapters under it and their respective themes. Part I contains Chapter 1. Chapters 2 and 3 are contained in Part II of this book and focus on post-independence early Zimbabwe. Then, the country used to be a shining beacon not only to its citizens but the continent at large. The leftover/residual economy from the colonial masters modestly firing from all cylinders buoyed by largely agriculture and manufacturing sectors. Zimbabwe was an envy of many. At independence Julius Mwalimu Nyerere the then Tanzanian president had a piece of advice to the country and remarked that the country had inherited a '*a jewel of Africa, **do not tarnish it***'. What had Nyerere seen which sparked his powerful remark which people reminisce even to this day? Probably, he had witnessed the beautiful roads, vibrant rail networks, clean streets, well-planned urban settlements, functioning factories, etc. Do they still exist in the present? If so, are they in a desired state? If not, why then? The speech by Nyerere acknowledged the context under which independence was attained. Ground work had been prepared so as to usher in the first economy. Under this section, Chap. 2 will look at how various indicators were like during early years of independent Zimbabwe so as to justify the jewel of Africa status Zimbabwe was known for due to her newly found freedom.

In Chap. 3, we focus on the milestones Zimbabwe accomplished as she began her journey of self-determination. Globally, for instance Zimbabwe's education system has been known to produce some of the most competent graduates. The country has churned luminaries who have even impressed at top institutions like Harvard, Oxford, etc. The chapter will look at these and other remarkable things this great nation has done over the years mostly in the short-lived first economy.

Part III of the book is made up of Chaps. 4 and 5. Various policy missteps and shortcomings are captured vividly in Chap. 4 where we briefly carry an exegesis of various policies of early post-independent through the years. Chapter 5 is explosive. Forty years of existence of Zimbabwe as a sovereign state have seen several issues (both positive and negative) unfolding which in turn shaped the trajectory the nation has followed. We focus on the different issues which either positively shaped the nation or contributed to even much more turbulence. Economic programmes such as ESAP with its not so pleasant consequences come to mind. The 1991–2 droughts which pummelled the vulnerable agriculture-dependent economy inflicted damage to the economy which triggered another round of poverty for the already burdened people. In a nutshell, we carry out an in-depth analysis of events/ phenomena which occurred from 1987 through 2020 which we believe have been defining moments in our history of turbulence firmly entrenching the second economy. As you read the chapter through the events under this period, you will indeed appreciate the turbulence thesis which dominates this book.

Chapters 6 and 7 make up Part IV of the book. When challenges had taken firm root, it became a crisis within a crisis. While there are positives as explored in Chap. 3, the blunders blighted most of the accomplishments reducing the nation into a pariah state. We look at how the blunders contributed to trashing of the jewel of the nation we inherited the greater part of Chap. 6.

Relatedly, one blunder begets another. The blunders explored in Chap. 6 did fuel turbulence over the years. In Chap. 7, we explore how the economy continues to sink further in problems. For instance, the millennial generation the country has not made use of very much means lost opportunities not only for the generation but for the entire nation and beyond. It is not only in Zimbabwe where the millennial generation has had few opportunities but in the bulk of the continent. Failure to reap demographic dividends out of this comparative advantage will cost countries of this continent. Issues highlighted under this chapter only show how the country will keep on sinking further in turbulence.

Part V of the book contains Chaps. 8–11 and a concluding section coming in as Chap. 12. As alluded to earlier, Zimbabwe is a great nation despite the many challenges. Chapter 8 examines some of the visible spirited efforts at solving the challenges despite the strong headwinds to be manoeuvred. The book captures invaluable lessons which can be learnt by other countries that still struggling to develop. Chapter 9 explores key lessons other states can also learn from the journey Zimbabwe has travelled so far. At the same time, Zimbabwe can learn from her shortcomings and can still claim her *jewel status* where she rightfully belongs.

Chapter 10 is a special feature committed to discussing women issues with special reference to migration and empowerment in Zimbabwe's four decades. They have also not been spared from the challenges of the past four decades. How have they been empowered or disempowered? Chapter 11 explores further issues which are also important in the history of the country. We conclude the book by Chap. 12 when we tie together the rest of the chapters. Specifically, we explain how Zimbabwe's economic turbulence is a product of a continuum of problems confluencing together. The major highlight of the conclusion is a revisit of the overloaded bus, a very powerful metaphor we use in this chapter.

## References

BBC (2018). Zimbabwe currency crisis: No cash, no bread, no KFC. Available at: https://www.bbc.com/news/world-africa-45822166

Bonga, W. G., & Mahuni, K. (2018). Assessing the impact of ease of doing business and corruption on economic growth for Africa Free Trade Zone (AFTZ) member states. *MPRA Paper* (88932).

https://www.herald.co.zw/industry-capacity-to-drop-27-percent/#:~:text=The%20manufacturing%20sector%20capacity%20utilisation,of%20Zimbabwe%20Industries%20(CZI)

Hanke, S. H., & Kwok, A. K. (2009). Measuring hyperinflation in Zimbabwe. Cat Journal, 29, 353.

Mahuni, K., & Bonga, W. G. (2017). Nexus between doing business indicators and foreign direct investment for Zimbabwe: A time series analysis. *Journal of Economics and Finance, 2*(2), 1–8.

NewsDay (2019). 4 Mysteries of Zim's Economic Crisis. Available at: https://www.newsday.co.zw/opinion-amp-analysis/article/55570/4-mysteries-of-zims-economic-crisis

The Chronicle (2019). Zimbabwe's economy on recovery path. Available at: Zimbabwe's economy on recovery path. Available at: https://www.chronicle.co.zw/zimbabwe-economy-on-recovery-path/

The Economist (2019). Zimbabwe faces its worst economic crisis in a decade https://www.economist.com/middle-east-and-africa/2019/08/15/zimbabwe-faces-its-worst-economic-crisis-in-a-decade

The Financial Gazette (2024). Breaking News. Available at: https://fingaz.co.zw/category/breaking-news/

The Financial Gazette (2024). Top Stories. Available at: https://fingaz.co.zw/category/s1-news/c25-top-stories/page/206/?yop_poll_tr_id&yop-poll-nonce17_yp597d8d056235f=c9f6d0421c

The Guardian (2019). Millions face hardship as Zimbabwe comes close to 'meltdown'. Available at: https://www.theguardian.com/world/2019/jul/21/millions-face-hardship-as-zimbabwe-comes-close-to-meltdown

The Herald (2018). Land reform: The World Bank finally sees the light. Available at : https://www.herald.co.zw/land-reform-the-world-bank-finally-sees-the-light/

The Herald (2019a). Impact of sanctions on Zim, region. Available at: https://www.herald.co.zw/impact-of-sanctions-on-zim-region/

The Herald (2020). https://www.herald.co.zw/industry-capacity-to-drop-27-percent/#:~:text=The%20manufacturing%20sector%20capacity%20utilisation,of%20Zimbabwe%20Industries%20(CZI)

The Herald (2022). Zimbabwe losing USD 1.8 billion to corruption annually. Available at: https://www.herald.co.zw/zimbabwe-losing-us18-billion-to-corruption-annually/

The Zimbabwe Independent (2019). Zimbabwe: Energy Crisis Sinking Zim Economy. Available at: https://allafrica.com/stories/201912130682.html

Trading Economics (2024). Zimbabwe Corruption Rank. Available at: https://tradingeconomics.com/zimbabwe/corruption-rank

World Bank (2022). Zim Joint World Bank IMF Debt Sustainability Analysis. Available at: https://documents1.worldbank.org/curated/en/342191656080358057/pdf/Zimbabwe-Joint-World-Bank-IMF-Debt-Sustainability-Analysis.pdf

Zimbabwe Treasury (2023). Public Debt Report. Available at: www.zimtreasury.gov.zw/wp-content/uploads/2024/01/Public-Debt-Report-2023.pdf

# Part II
# Unpacking a New Zimbabwe and Taking Charge

# Chapter 2
# Early Years of Post-independence Zimbabwe

## 2.1 Introduction

For the past four decades after full attainment of independence by Zimbabwe, a lot is still expected of this beautiful Southern African state. The ecstasy we explained briefly in Chap. 1 invoked great expectations among the multitudes of 'milk and honey' to be savoured in the first republic as the journey which had been ignited by the liberation fires had finally delivered us to the promised land. The greater part of this chapter focuses on how the Government of Zimbabwe took charge of various aspects of the economy, notably education, health, agriculture among others. As the reader shall notice, in one way or the other this later on influenced the overall path the country will traverse. Recall also that we are examining a country which was a model economy during her early years of independence. As such, it is befitting for us to explore issues such as education, health care, urbanisation among other factors as they played out so as to shape the development path of Zimbabwe. In addition, this background is essential material for later sections of the book.

## 2.2 Education

Investment in human capital and provision of education has been recognised as central to quality life. The provision of education and literacy for all, the cornerstone for quality life, have been recognised at national policy level. This is in accordance with the United Nations Declaration on Basic Human Rights (Mubika & Bukaliya, 2011). In this section, we review the experiences of Zimbabwe in the implementation of education for all during its first decade of independence. We also examine the causes and consequences and challenges of educational expansion. Furthermore, we explore policy dilemmas that were faced by the Zimbabwean government in its attempts to provide universal primary and secondary education.



K. Mahuni et al., *Zimbabwe's Economy*, Advances in African Economic, Social and Political Development, https://doi.org/10.1007/978-3-031-81588-1_2

The colonial educational system had excluded the majority of blacks from formal education through a series of educational policies and practices which ensured that as few blacks as possible attended primary school and that even fewer proceeded to secondary and higher education. Under the colonial system, access to education for blacks was further inhibited by the unavailability of school places, parental inability to pay user fees and a series of selective terminal examinations which were designed to create severe school-progression bottlenecks of black pupils (Nhundu, 1992).

Colclough (1990) observed that a dual system of education existed in Zimbabwe during the colonial period, one system for whites and the other one for blacks. Each system's aims and purposes were designed to prepare children for their predetermined status in life: that of employer/master for the white status in life; that of employer/master for the white child; that of labourer/servant for the black child. While the white education system offered each child 11 years of free education, the black system was voluntary, highly restricted and not free at any level.

### 2.2.1 Post-independence Education Expansion

The main orientations of the post-colonial education reforms have been guided by democratisation of access to education and localisation of curriculum and examinations. Realising that the majority of black citizens were deprived of formal education during the colonial era, Zimbabwe embarked on an extensive education drive to provide the marginalised citizens with the much-sought education. Zimbabwe experienced a boom in the enrolment figures as schools were established within a walkable distance from the children's homes (Mubika & Bukaliya, 2011; Nhundu, 1992). Key policy initiatives of the new government included the introduction of free and compulsory primary education, the removal of age restrictions to allow over-age children to enter school, the encouragement of community support for education and automatic schooling progression, especially for primary-grade school children entering secondary school. Other policy initiatives by the new government include the decentralisation of education administrative and management structures; the localisation of curricula including the vocationalisation of the secondary school curriculum; the localisation of examinations; the introduction of the single teaching service; and Ministry of Education and Culture's assumption of direct control of primary school per capita grant disbursements (Colclough, 1990).

In order to accommodate the large numbers of Zimbabwean children seeking school places, the government introduced a massive reconstruction programme to reopen and expand nearly 90% of the rural schools that had been decimated by the war as well as construct new ones. The active participation of local communities in these endeavours resulted in a 186% increase in the number of primary schools, from 2401 in 1979 to 4471 in 1988. The number of secondary schools increased by an incredible 838%, from 177 to 1484 during the same period (Nhundu, 1992). Government-run schools were established in rural areas, and by 1981, 40 public rural secondary day schools existed where previously there were none. Community input greatly boosted the expansion programme; 400 community built, rural secondary day schools were opened by the end of 1981. Thus, a total of 440 secondary schools were opened in rural areas in 1981 alone compared to 57 in non-rural areas. Government continued to give priority to the development of rural education by allocating US $13.75 million towards capital development of rural schools in the 1982–83 fiscal year compared to US $0.6 million for urban schools.

The 1987 Education Act provides for the establishment of schools by government itself, local authorities, organisations and individuals, but government is not completely involved in the establishment of new primary schools. The Ministry of Education and Culture assumed full responsibility for pre-school education and adult literacy from the Ministry of Community Development and Women's Affairs in 1988. The development of pre-schools, particularly in rural areas, is provided through the Early Childhood Education and Care (ECEC) programme which was funded jointly by the government and UNICEF. The target is to establish a pre-school facility at each of the 6000 villages in the rural areas plus 3000 in the urban centres.

In 1989, less than 13% of the around 1500 secondary schools were operated by government. Total enrolment was a little more than 650,000 pupils taught by more than 24,500 teachers (pupil: teacher ratio: around 27:1), half of whom were formally qualified. During the 1980s, teacher education was serviced by 14 colleges, four of which train secondary school teachers while the rest train primary school teachers. In addition, the Cuba Teacher Training Programme trained secondary school mathematics and science teachers. All teachers' colleges are associated with the University of Zimbabwe through the Department of Teacher Education. In 1989, there were 8 government plus 105 privately owned technical colleges offering a wide range of subjects. Government technical colleges offered local courses examined by Further Education Examination Board (FEEB) while the majority of private colleges still offer external courses. There were also two vocational training centres offering upgrading training courses to skilled workers and help them gain craftsman certificates. Under the apprenticeship scheme, companies took on young men/women as apprentices for 3–5 years depending on trade. Apprentices received on the job training supervised by skilled workers and gained theoretical knowledge at technical colleges through full-time block or day release schemes. Successful apprentices graduated to be journeymen.

All colleges in Zimbabwe experienced acute staff shortages which adversely affected their effectiveness and size of intakes. Despite the recruitment of expatriates, colleges continued to operate with high vacancy ratios. The main causes of staff shortages were poor salaries and conditions of service offered by the Public Service as opposed to those offered by the private sector. The University of Zimbabwe (UZ) was the only state university in the country during the first decade of independence. In 1989, UZ had a total of 7900 undergraduate students in ten faculties. By 1990, the government approved the establishment of a second state university.

While significant strides and positive results were realised, towards the attempt to make education readily available to all those in need through the policy of 'Education for All', a number of challenges were met. The rapid increase in pupil and student enrolments meant corresponding increases in the number of teachers and lecturers, and the number of schools and training institutions. However, rural schools and schools in the former African townships continue to be under-staffed while those in the former European areas and in the high-fee-paying schools have the best qualified teachers because these schools top up the government salaries (Dzvimbo, 1991). Therefore, such privileges continue to exist despite the socialist rhetoric of the transition state.

### 2.2.2 Consequences of Education Expansion

Nhundu (1992) pointed out that government's attempt to universalise Zimbabwean education by providing all children with 11 years of schooling created some negative consequences that threatened to undermine the educational gains that had been achieved. Some of these consequences included rising unemployment for the educated youths, declining educational quality, teacher shortages and huge educational budget. Opportunities for professional training in Zimbabwe were highly competitive as few places were available for training in areas such as medicine, law, engineering, economics and accountancy. Entry into technical colleges, teachers' colleges and agricultural colleges was also very competitive as the demand for enrolment into these colleges outstripped supply. The combined enrolment capacity for Zimbabwe's technical, agricultural and teachers' colleges in 1988 was 41,688. This falls short to meet the professional and career needs of its 146,181 'O'-level school leavers who could not proceed to 'A' level. The prospects for going to university were equally bleak. By 1990, 6000 students had completed 'A' level studies could all not be absorbed at the University of Zimbabwe as only 1937 places were available.

The only alternative left for the majority of 'O'-level graduates who fail to progress academically or enter training institutions was to enter the labour market. However, prospects for employment were also bleak. Since 1981, unemployment had steadily worsened due to general economic stagnation and decline. The annual average increase in total formal employment between 1980 and 1981 was only 2.7%, while economic growth averaged 12%. Over the five-year period from 1980 to 1984, the average increase in annual employment was 1.1%; for the four-year period from 1981 to 1984, the average increase fell to 0.7%. From 1980 to 1984, a total of 30,000 additional jobs were created in the formal sector, giving an annual average of around 7000 jobs, well below the 70,000 projected annual additions to the labour market. Even in 1985, when the nation experienced good economic performance, the government admitted that unemployment remained at unacceptably high.

The MFEPD's first five-year national development plan cited the flooding of the labour market by school leavers (mostly 'O'-level graduates) as one of the major causes of the nation's unemployment. This suggests that the massive unemployment experienced in Zimbabwe during the 1980s was, in part, directly attributed to massive educational expansion.

### 2.2.3 *Issues in Education During the Early Years of Independence*

The critical issues confronting education policymakers arose from the remarkable post-independence expansion of the system. Although this represents a major achievement, it stretched resources to the limit and created shortages which threaten the system's viability. One area of concern has been the argument that the policy of education for all has resulted in the erosion of quality education in favour of quantity. Fears abound that the unsustainable teacher–pupil ratios have demotivated the teachers. The expansion in enrolment figures has further strained the existing resources and facilities. Thus, the rapid expansion of primary and secondary education appeared to have precluded integrated central planning resulting in problems related to the control of the expansion process, allocation of resources, shortages of manpower, accommodation, equipment and materials. There was evidence of uneven distribution of the available human and material resources in favour of the more developed areas. Government spent much more on the urban child than on his/her rural counterpart. Equally, within urban areas there were highly disadvantaged schools and pupils. Therefore, the pattern of provision of education in Zimbabwe can be described as being highly unequal and it discriminates much more strongly in favour of the richer groups in society than is compatible with the longer-term social and economic objectives of government. Also, the mushrooming of 'high-fee' or 'trust' schools initiated mainly by whites resulted in furthering elitism in education contrary to declared government intentions.

The bussing of pupils from high-density areas to schools in the low-density areas, in an attempt to utilise more efficiently space and equipment in former Group A secondary schools, worked well for a while but has since been unwelcomed by most of the parents concerned as they cannot afford the levies, school and sports uniforms, bus fares, lunch money and other incidentals demanded by this arrangement. Such parents preferred that government provides adequate schools in their own areas. In addition, the abolition of primary school tuition fees in 1980 made primary schooling cheaper for many families, but did not succeed in making it free. Parents were still expected to build and maintain schools, pay general purpose fees, sports, building and other types of fees.

The establishment of government day secondary schools in each rural district was a plausible idea. However, these schools benefited only those pupils within walking distances of the schools. Also, government boarding secondary schools located in disadvantaged areas were servicing more children of the richer families mainly from the urban centres and only a few of the intended beneficiaries as the majority cannot afford the fees. More so, government paid the salaries of teachers at all registered schools and authorised secondary schools and per capita giants for each school pupil. The government was also paying boarding giants for secondary schools and disadvantaged pupils like those with visual impairment who were boarders and provided all secondary schools with building grants covering only 5% of the total capital cost of each facility. The per capita grant was insufficient to purchase books and equipment required by schools. Thus, unless parents were able and willing to supplement school resources by buying additional materials, the quality of education available to their children would be seriously affected.

The policy position favouring day secondary schools as against boarding secondary schools was based on the realisation that boarding schools are expensive institutions to put up, maintain, operate as well as restrictive in terms of high fees and carrying capacity. In urban centres where student population densities are high and distances short, double sessioning of tutorial facilities, but not of teachers, was being encouraged thereby increasing enrolments and reducing costs by maximising the use of these facilities. The provision of schools, particularly secondary schools, in the remote sparsely populated areas remained problematic. Schools were still too few, far apart and hardly viable enrolment wise. They were also generally depressing: pupils learning under trees, self-help shades, old tobacco barns, storerooms, etc., and teachers living in huts or sharing accommodation. It is in these areas that illegal boarding was prevalent with the pupils concerned living in appalling conditions. The financial burden of providing school facilities in rural areas has fallen upon individual households who have been contributing 100% of primary school construction costs and 95% of secondary school capital development costs with only 5% coming from government in the form of grants. In urban areas, primary schools have been provided by local authorities and secondary schools by government. The localisation of the secondary school examination system was on course, and by end of the 1990s, the government has fully achieved this object.

UZ, which was the only state university during the 1980s, was funded by means of a direct recurrent grant from the Ministry of Higher Education; UZ students were fully funded by government through a grant and loan arrangement and so were student teachers. In the vocational training sector, a large part of the cost was funded through ZIMDEF. Expansion at the tertiary level was much slower compared to that at the lower levels of the education system. However, teacher education expanded quickly in response to the pressure to provide trained teachers for the expanding school system.

## 2.3 Healthcare System

Zimbabwe's independence in 1980 witnessed increased government responsibility in the provision of social services for the majority who had been marginalised under British colonial rule. In particular, education and health were key areas of government focus and agents for economic development (Mhike & Makombe, 2018). In line with the new policy changes, the government expanded existing infrastructure and increased capital investments in social services. However, Bate et al. (2007) assert that Zimbabweans benefited from a functioning and efficient public health system which was a legacy of the colonial and post-unilateral declaration of independence (UDI) government. Moreover, government policy realignments and financial investment in key sectors of the economy engendered an overarching narrative that overshadowed the function of non-state actors in the development agenda (Agere, 1990, pp. 31–38). Indeed, under the government's socialist policies of the 1980s, scholars analysed the development strategy largely within the confines of government programmes. This dominant narrative precluded a nuanced picture that characterised partnerships between government and other private players in achieving set targets (Mhike & Makombe, 2018). Although the government was clearly the single largest investor in social services, the history of Zimbabwe's public health system will be incomplete without acknowledging the role of mission hospitals.

After independence in 1980, the government continued to support and fund the public health system (Mhike & Makombe, 2018). Life expectancy at birth rose by nearly a decade from 54.9 years in 1980 to 63 years in 1988. The government's healthcare policies ensured that the rate of child immunisation nearly tripled between 1980 and 1988. Childhood immunisation for diphtheria, pertussis and tetanus (DPT) increased to 75% coverage in 1986, 80% in 1994 and 81% in 1999, compared with an average of 32%, 51% and 48%, respectively, for sub-Saharan Africa as a whole. The improvements in primary health care ensured that between 1980 and 1998 infant mortality rates fell by 80% to 49 deaths per thousand by 1988 (Bate et al., 2007). Historically, Zimbabwe boasted a thriving teaching hospital network, a strong primary healthcare system installed in the 1980s by the government.

### 2.3.1 *Major Interventions*

As alluded earlier, the health service delivery is the most publicly visible building block of any health system. Zimbabwe has a long track record of delivering comprehensive services across the country, dating back to structures and institutions created during the pre-independence and immediate independence era. The flagship policy of post-independence Zimbabwe, 'Growth with Equity', was a framework which entailed, inter alia, the improvement and expansion of social services and consumption levels in the local economy. Equity in health entailed improved distribution of and access to health services. The majority of the neglected African population gained access to basic care and government launched a range of cost-effective preventive health programmes. This involved improvement of allocative efficiency by directing more funds into child immunisation, safe motherhood, family planning, water and sanitation. At hospital level, government improved inward efficiency through staff deployment, drug consumption and vehicle usage, among other things. Overall, government sought to augment the urban-based curative approach by emphasising preventive care in rural areas, where '90 per cent of the cases of disease was preventable' (Agere, 1990). In this regard, health sector reforms became one of many instruments for social equality and poverty reduction.

The Zimbabwean government supported policy changes with capital investment, human resources and infrastructural development. The improvement of health service delivery was largely financed through an expansion of government spending. Between 1980 and 1990, the Zimbabwe government consistently provided an average of four to six per cent of its total expenditure to health provision. The Ministry of Health became the largest provider of health care and employed about 23,000 health personnel by 1987, and provided funding to local authorities and other voluntary organisations. The base for the delivery of comprehensive primary health care was the provision of healthcare centres and 273 were constructed between 1980 and 1989, giving a total of about 927, including local government, mission and industry-owned facilities. This improvement in infrastructure fed into government health policy and strategy for the period 1980–1990, aimed at building and upgrading district-level hospitals and clinics. These healthcare centres were largely located in rural areas for the benefit of some of the poorest and vulnerable sections of Zimbabwean society.

However, the structure of the health delivery system could not be changed overnight. Health infrastructure still remained inadequate at a time when government's development thrust was gathering momentum. Similarly, increased health funding did not translate to any radical shift in health policy. Government spent about 12% of health funding on preventive services and 82% on medical care services, which bears evidence that government policy reflected continuity of the largely curative orientation in health policy. The system also remained top-heavy and urban-oriented, given the large financial allocations to tertiary institutions in the urban areas. For example, in the 1980/81 financial year, government allocated 44% of its health budget to urban-based central hospitals serving about 15% of the population, while 24% was allocated to primary- and secondary-level rural services for the majority of the population. In view of this fact, the new policy thrust was not being effectively implemented, partly due to the reality of infrastructural inadequacy in rural areas. In order to close this gap, government had to partner with mission hospitals which were strategically located, in order to serve hard-to-reach areas and meet the health needs of the rural populace.

### *2.3.2 Health Policy*

Zimbabwe's health policy was informed by two main factors. First, the health sector was characterised by inadequate health infrastructure, and provision of such consumed a considerable part of the available resources to the extent that government, by the mid- to late 1980s, was financially hamstrung to effect a paradigm shift from curative to preventive health. Second, the rhetoric of socialism and the euphoria of independence had a bearing on health policy. Government considered healthcare provision as one avenue through which it could alleviate poverty and, therefore, decisions on health became entangled in the political cycle. Hammer and Berman (1995) argue that governments, trapped in five-year electoral cycles, are increasingly driven by short-term pressure and considerations. A health agenda as mediated, partly, by preventive health programmes demands a longer-term horizon, and there are risks in expecting too much short-term progress. This process pushes governments to be consumed by a search for short-term palliatives to problems that may, in fact, require a longer time frame and a wholly different approach. Owing to the crisis of expectation, as mediated by the socialist experiment of the post-independent state, the public was impatient for results and expected immediate relief from decades of poor health delivery. Given the paternalistic and populist orientation of the Zimbabwe government and its sensitivity to the media, curative health offered an opportunity for them to appear successful and to be regarded as high achievers. While preventive health ensured a sound human capital base, the reverse was true for political capital.

The Plan for equity in health was the first health policy intervention by government in 1980. The major drivers of this intervention were the dictates of the Alma Ata Declaration of 1978 which emphasise the need for primary health care and that health care is a fundamental human right that needs to be prioritised as a social worldwide goal and the unacceptability of inequality in health care on both grounds. Additionally, the International Conference on Primary Health Care calls for urgent and effective national and international action to develop and implement primary health care throughout the world and particularly in developing countries.

The Government of Zimbabwe implemented various programmes to deal with the aspects of equality, mortality human workforce, finance and service delivery among others. First, free health care was implemented in September 1980 especially to those earning less than Z$150, hospitals and healthcare building programmes. By June 1987, 224 rural health care had been completed. In addition, provincial health care facilitities had been upgraded. Further, immunisation programmes against six killer diseases, and by 1984, percentage of children between 12 and 23 months fully immunised rose from 25 to 42 in rural areas and in urban areas rose from 56 to 80. National nutrition programmes, diarrhoea disease control programmes, national village health worker programmes and child spacing programmes were also implemented in the first decade under the Plan for equity in health. Under this policy, positive changes were noted particularly to mortality rate which reduced from estimated 120–220 per 1000 in 1980 to 83 per 1000 by 1983, with an estimate of 23%. Morbidity and malnutrition were also reduced from 1980 to 1983. However, despite having positive outcomes, these programmes had implications particularly on the fiscus. Health budget rose to 5.1% and doubled by 1982, and preventive services rose from 7 to 9 in 1980 to 14% by 1986, the reason being that the Plan required donor funding which contributed towards increase in foreign debt. Overall, the intervention had limited success.

### *2.3.3 State and the Zimbabwe Association of Church-Related Hospitals (ZACH)*

As part of its development drive, the post-colonial government fostered partnerships with non-governmental organisations (NGOs) including religious ones in an effort to harness resources in order to create a sound economic base. In particular, government recognised the work that the church accomplished in socially beneficial functions (Gundani, 1988, p. 217). Mission health institutions under the Zimbabwe Association of Church-related Hospitals (ZACH) became a strategic partner of government in the running of national programmes to expand on both preventive and curative health services. Their geographical location and referral level in the health structure were especially important in driving the new policies. In addition, ZACH was not wholly financed by the government and sometimes instituted own programmes that augmented those run by the state. ZACH is an NGO founded by the Heads of Christian Denominations (HCD) in 1973 with a mandate to assist and support member institutions in providing good quality health care, especially to the vulnerable rural population. The HCD comprise the Evangelical Fellowship of Zimbabwe (FZ); the Zimbabwe Council of Churches (ZCC); Zimbabwe Catholic Bishops Conference (ZCBC); and Union for Development of Apostolic Churches in Zimbabwe (UDACIZA). ZACH was formed as the secretariat which would oversee the operations of the mission health institutions.

It sought to achieve a sustainably high-quality health care through a holistic approach to health and healing, which encompasses principles of equity, equality and accessibility. The organisation, while sometimes working with government, remained autonomous and kept its philosophy and independent sources in financing its hospitals. Indeed, mission institutions had provided health care in colonial Zimbabwe for the greater part of the twentieth century, but the post-independence era ushered in a new period of closer cooperation with government. ZACH was a strategic government partner in health because its formation was an attempt to plug the gaps in financing, infrastructure development and other key needs of mission hospitals, which the government was not able to immediately work on. The secretariat coordinated cooperation between its member institutions and the Ministry of Health and other partners. It worked in line with the Ministry of Health's National Strategic Plan on priority objectives and its values of equity and accessibility dovetailed with the thrust of 'Equity in Health' which government set to achieve after 1980.

In addition, the organisation sourced for funding for its member institutions and was involved in advocacy. ZACH operations were financed through various sources, which included external partners, a government grant, well-wishers and member subscriptions. This move strengthened the coordination of the operations of mission hospitals, while at the same time improving their image and capacity to engage the donor community and government.

The government sought to harness the decades' long experience of mission hospitals as well as their strategically located health institutions as a counter weight to rural infrastructure limitations. The institutional make-up of Zimbabwe's health sector was highly heterogeneous, with the central government, municipal and local authorities, church missions and other NGOs, industries and mines, private practice and traditional healers all playing a role. Of infinitely greater significance is the fact that Zimbabwe operated on a four-tier system in healthcare provision. Level four comprised the five central hospitals (including a specialised psychiatric hospital) located in Harare and Bulawayo and these served as national referral facilities. Level three consisted of eight provincial and four general hospitals. At level two were 55 designated district hospitals (Ministry of Health and church mission run, of which 26 met the regulations, providing a first line of referrals). Level one comprised 86 rural hospitals and 927 health centres (122 Ministry of Health; 510 local governments; 70 missions; 35 urban; and 160 industry-owned facilities) providing a range of curative care as well as some preventive services. In the light of government policy, the health institutions in tier one and two were most critical, given the primary healthcare drive that it had adopted and the need to have efficient first-line-of-referral health institutions. The mission health institutions were concentrated in tiers one and two, providing services throughout about 97 clinics and 70 clinics/hospitals, and 13 of the country's 42 designated district hospitals. More significantly, all but two of the 126 mission health hospitals were in the rural areas, with the exception St Anne's Hospital in Harare and Mater Dei Hospital in Bulawayo.

Mission health institutions became a primary vehicle for preventive health programmes in Zimbabwe. The critical role of the mission health institutions to government policy goals became apparent in the early 1980s. They spearheaded national programmes such as the Zimbabwe Expanded Programme for Immunisation (ZEPI), Diarrheal Disease Control Programme (DDCP) and the National Nutrition Programme. The strategic location of rural mission hospitals made them a fundamental partner to government in providing health care to the remote areas of the country, which had suffered neglect prior to independence. ZACH was also involved in human resources development. Nurse training in church hospitals started in the early 1900s with the training of nursing orderlies by white nuns. Training programmes expanded to include state-registered nurses and midwifery.

In the 1980s and 1990s, the church was also actively involved in the fight against the emergent HIV and AIDS scourge at a time when treatment of the disease was not standardised. Zimbabwe recorded its first HIV case in 1985 and missionaries were some of the leading advocates of behavioural change. At their 1987 and 1990 Interdenominational Aids Conferences, the church emphasised the preaching of morality to prevent infection, abstinence among the youth and fidelity in marriages, and they condemned other sexual unions that did not amplify God's name. When the HIV/AIDS treatment became standardised in the 1990s, the government chose mission hospitals to run awareness campaigns and dispense drugs in affected rural communities.

The ZEPI, DDCP and the HIV/AIDS programmes were central to the new preventive health development initiative adopted after independence. Mission institutions provided healthcare facilities which were points of access to the health system in rural and other remote areas of Zimbabwe. Following a zero national economic growth rate in 1982, negative growth in 1983 and inflation, the grants given to health institutions fell in real terms (Mandaza, 1986). The net effect was that in the 1984/85 financial year, mission hospitals had to limit their outreach work following financial constraints, which particularly affected their travel. Although the reduction in grants constrained service delivery in the outlying areas, most mission hospitals continued running these programmes because they had an obligation to provide service to people in need. In this respect, under a constrained national budget, the existing infrastructure in mission hospitals was critical for national programmes in preventive health.

Mission hospitals' religious and spiritual connection attracted patients from areas beyond their areas of service. In addition to receiving medication, the faithful believed that mission hospitals' daily routine of morning prayers and hymns was spiritually uplifting and added to the process of physical healing. Often, the terminally ill would choose to spend their last days at a mission hospital where they could receive prayer, talk to a priest and attend church services. Even non-believers sometimes requested to be taken to a mission hospital in the hope that whatever miracles of healing were said to exist at these hospitals would also help them overcome illness. In view of this fact, mission hospitals became the institutions of choice because they offered their patients physical healing and spiritual upliftment.

The relationship between government and these mission establishments was complicated. The former was the policymaker and single largest financier of health services up to the late 1990s, and the latter occupied a strategic position in the implementation and delivery of set targets, but at the same time remained semi-autonomous. Government undertook to pay for the salaries of qualified personnel and those in training programmes in mission health institutions as well as the purchase of drugs (Medical, Dental and Pharmacy Act 1927). Individual missions received significant financial assistance from government for the purchase of drugs and some of them worked with the National Health Service. However, government financial support did not translate to the Ministry of Health's control over the missions. This was, in large measure, a result of the fact that mission establishments continued to rely on church funding and were partly subsidised by external charities. Additionally, some donors did not accept the conditions of employment regulations of the public sector, making it difficult for the government to entirely control mission institutions' activities. The Ministry of Health was in charge of the national health policy framework, and implementation of activities in the public sector was organised through provincial medical directorates and district health bodies, public and private care providers. Interestingly, mission healthcare providers were officially regarded as part of the 'private medical sector' but in practice they functioned as part of the public health sector.

To this end, a 1992 World Bank report recommended that government should seek to induce non-governmental institutions to assume greater responsibility for providing and paying for health services, by encouraging church missions, in particular, and other private practitioners, commercial enterprises and health insurance. This recommendation was made in the light of the fact that church missions accounted for a significant share of health services nationally, especially in the rural areas, and did so at relatively low cost. Allowing them more initiative would augment government efforts for fiscal stability and enhance service delivery. Notwithstanding this call, the Zimbabwe government had by 1996 not formalised its relationship with mission health institutions. Mission hospitals also worked as alternative sources of public health financing. The private public nature of mission hospitals was expedient for government. During the first decade of independence, the government received up to 12% of its health expenditure from donors intended for mission.

Second, government conveniently weaned-off mission institutions in times of financial strain because it was not under any legal obligation to support these institutions. For example, due to low economic growth rate in the late 1980s and a high expenditure in social services, the government was forced to adopt fiscal austerity in the form of Economic Structural Adjustment Programmes (ESAPs) between 1990 and 1996. Social services expenditure in health, social welfare and education was severely reduced. This rolled back the existing levels of staffing, salaries and conditions of service for professionals in the health sector. The situation also triggered a health personnel haemorrhage as doctors and nurses left government service for the private sector, while others left Zimbabwe altogether (Gaidzanwa, 1999). Mission institutions were not spared, since their doctors and nurses were on the government pay roll. In addition, there was a shortage of drugs and equipment that had debilitating effects on service delivery. Notwithstanding these developments, government continued to peddle the rhetoric of its socio-political commitment to providing 'free' medical and health care for all, but in practice it backed out on its financial and other commitments to the health sector, in general, and particularly to mission establishments. This was based on the premise that missions were semi-autonomous and, therefore, could stand alone.

The meagre government resources were now being directed towards critical areas in government-administered health institutions. From the above analysis, one can deduce a number of realities that build a nuanced appreciation of the development of Zimbabwe's public health system and the nature of church-state relations during this period. ZACH constituted 35% of the public health infrastructure, so much that they were, in reality, public institutions. In addition, partnership in health was testimony of a steady cooperation and interdependence between the state and church-based NGOs. However, the relations between mission institutions and the state did not really mature in terms of the legal provisions and obligations that could have further strengthened their cooperation. To the extent that church institutions remained semi-autonomous, the state was not legally obliged to conveniently 'weaned-off' these 'private' entities to fend for themselves. Invariably, the Zimbabwe African National Union Patriotic Front (ZANU-PF) government and its populist approach to development of the 1980s claimed credit for the strides made in health delivery and rarely acknowledged its partners. This attitude undermined the mutual trust and closer cooperation that could have further enhanced efficiency in public health delivery.

The absence of a legally binding agreement between the state and ZACH on such a critical partnership is as surprising as it is worrying. A manipulative relationship of patronage emerged where the government used NGOs and other entities not directly under its control as tools in pursuing its developments goals. While the government provided the overall policy framework in which these entities operated, legally these institutions could not demand anything from government. The government co-opted organisations as junior partners in the national development agenda. There were no assured funding commitments from government and involvement of the church with health policy development. Health service provision could have been more efficient and effective if there had been a greater focus on strengthening the partnership between national governments and church health service providers. The government's treatment of its development partners was reflective of an aggressive hegemonic discourse advanced by the ZANU-PF government designed to control everything. In the same fashion, the state also sought to control labour, students and civic forces. As a result, state utilisation of mission health institutions became haphazard and inconsistent. Clearly, the government found it convenient to maintain an ambivalent relationship with its development partners, although these partnerships could have been used to improve service delivery even during years of good fiscal balance.

Conclusively, the church in Zimbabwe has been an important cornerstone in the development of the health delivery system. Beyond providing spiritual well-being, the church has healed Zimbabwe through its mission health institutions, in order to satisfy the teachings of and reflect on the life of Jesus Christ as a Healer. Thus, this book demonstrates that contrary to their 'invisibility' in Zimbabwe's health development literature, missionaries were a strategic ally of the government and their activities in health were critical to the development agenda. Their contribution in health was at different levels, including providing the necessary infrastructure in remote rural areas, development of a healthcare human resource base and provision of private health financing. Indeed, the success story of Zimbabwe's health delivery system—and indeed its development agenda during the first 15 years of independence—was partly a product of the church's call to meet physical human needs.

### 2.3.4 Policy Implications

Makochekanwa (2012) drew important policy implications with respect to developments on the healthcare front. First, although the health policies were on paper sound, the state needed to intensify their implementation. The other policy implication is that the complexity of health delivery system in Zimbabwe, coupled with limited government resources to adequately intervene, called for collaborative work between government and all stakeholders working in this sector.

Makochekanwa (2012) further recommended that the government should put in place strategies to lure back health professionals who left the country to come and work in the health facilities in the country. Government should also ask the help of well-wishes, friends and donors in addressing some of the challenges in the health sector including shortage of health personnel, drugs and problem of old or dysfunction medical equipment. One way could be through lobbying for assistance from UNICEF, WHO as well as other donor agencies.

In conclusion, from the health front in the decade following independence in 1980, Zimbabwe experienced some of the most rapid improvements in HNP indicators in all of sub-Saharan Africa. Infant mortality declined from 90 per thousand in 1980 to 53 per thousand in 1988. Household incomes increased only modestly during this period, however, suggesting that the government's strong emphasis on basic health and family planning services, health education and community outreach, bolstered by a strong focus on prevention, were responsible for the improvements. Sadly, however, the government's failure to control the budget deficit and its financing of that debt by borrowing domestically at high interest rates led to escalating interest rate payments. Johnston (1999) had a reasonable concern for this development. The World Bank was concerned that increasing debt as well as fiscal deficits would continue to work against progress of the Health Sector.

## 2.4 Agriculture and Land Reform

Agriculture is the backbone of Zimbabwe's economy and underpins the economic, social and political lives of the majority of the people of Zimbabwe. Furthermore, Zimbabwe possesses rich agricultural resources. About two-thirds of Zimbabweans work in agriculture and many Zimbabweans, directly or indirectly, depend on it. Food security in Zimbabwe is intimately linked to agricultural production, especially of maize which is the staple food. The sector is at the centre of the economy, accounting for about 20% of Gross Domestic Product (GDP), supplying 60% of the raw materials required by the industrial sector and contributing about 40% of total export earnings (Government of Zimbabwe, 1995; World Bank, 2019).

Zimbabwe has a total land area of over 39 million hectares, of which 33.3 million hectares are used for agricultural purposes. The remaining 6 million hectares have been reserved for national parks and wildlife, and for urban settlements. The distinguishing characteristic of Zimbabwe agriculture during the first two decades of independence was its dualism. There were two major subgroups based on the size of landholdings. The larger group was comprised about 7.1 million smallholder and communal farmers occupying a total of 21 million hectares. The communal and smallholder farmers occupied areas of lower natural potential for agriculture in terms of rainfall, soils and water for irrigation. In addition, these areas were of lower economic potential because of the distances from markets and poor communication and social infrastructure. The other group comprised about 4000 large-scale farmers with very sophisticated production systems and occupies about 11 million hectares of prime land, primarily located in the areas of high agricultural and economic potential.

### 2.4.1 *Crop Production*

Communal and commercial farmers are distinguished by the fact that the former produce mainly for own consumption, and the latter produce mainly for commerce. The principal crops produced in the Zimbabwean communal areas are maize, cotton, sugar, groundnuts, beans, vegetables, meat and milk. Commercial farmers concentrate on cash crops such as tobacco, horticultural products, coffee, sugar cane, maize, groundnuts, sorghum, soya beans, sunflowers, cattle, pigs, goats and sheep. More often than not, the significant part of the crops that are produced commercially is being exported to other countries. On the other hand, most of the crops that are produced in the communal area are for household consumption. Although the initial post-independence period saw a major boom in commercial crop production in communal areas, the trend went down later. Cotton is one of the major crops produced for commercial purposes in both the communal and commercial lands. Cotton production has grown considerably in communal areas since 1985 with the area dedicated for cotton cultivation more than doubling from 115,000 ha to 353,000 ha in 2001, and similarly, production more than doubling. In contrast, cotton production in commercial areas has declined considerably, with the area for cotton cultivation falling from 76,617 ha to 37,473 ha in the 2000/01 cropping season with corresponding production of 11,000 tonnes and 51,713 tonnes, respectively.

Furthermore, maize is another major crop in Zimbabwe. The Grain Marketing Board of Zimbabwe receives 75% of its grain from small holder/communal farmers. Thus, maize is a very important income earner in the rural areas. From 1980 to 2001, the annual production of maize in Zimbabwe had been well above 200,000 metric tonnes with the exception of 1990 when it fell drastically to 1,585,800. This drastic reduction was mainly accounted by the low production in the commercial sector. The communal sector, however, continued to witness a general expansion in maize production despite annual fluctuation and inefficient production methods. Maize is not only a basic crop for household food security but also an important source of household cash income. Therefore, any trade arrangements, which allow the import of cheap subsidised maize at prices that undermine local prices, will depress rural household incomes.

## *2.4.2 Animal Production*

There is a long history of commercial cattle ranching, and that landowners have the right to commercially use wildlife on their lands. In semi-arid African savannas, multispecies wildlife communities tend to use heterogeneous vegetation more completely than cattle alone. Wildlife production has been ecologically the most rational form of land use in semi-arid areas. Hence, wildlife that is common in Zimbabwe areas consists mainly of plains game species but a few larger herbivores, like elephant, rhino, hippopotamuses, giraffe and buffalo. However, the most valuable game species are leopard, eland, water buck, kudu, tsessebe, zebra, baboons and different types of antelope (Kreuter & Workman, 1996). The livestock production division supports animal production and is the livestock outreach arm while livestock development and schemes division link up with technology transfer, multiplication and breeding of animals and forage, responsible for breeding nucleus heads, gene banks for fodder and grass as well as new initiatives.

### 2.4.3 Land Reform and Resettlement

The post-independence land reform in Zimbabwe started with the Lancaster House Agreement, in which it was agreed that land should change hands through a willing-seller willing-buyer mechanism with the white framers who wanted to continue farming being free to do so. At independence in 1980 about 70% of Zimbabwe's landmass, including communal areas, was owned by the state and 24% owned by large-scale commercial farmers. In 1980, the targeted number of households for resettlement was 18,000 on 1.5 million hectares of land over five years, which was revised in 1982 and 1990 to include 162,000 farming families on 8.3 million hectares of land.

When Zimbabwe became independent in 1980, reversing historical inequalities became a primary development objective. The land reform programme was targeted at the landless, war veterans, the poor and commercial farm workers. Land reform in Zimbabwe can be classified into two main phases, the Land Reform and Resettlement Programme I (LRRP 1) from 1980 to 1998 and LRRP II, commonly referred to as the Fast Track Land Reform Program (FTLRP), since 2000. The Government of Zimbabwe undertook its land redistribution programme to address the socio-economic injustices of the colonial era. The LRRP I was at first carried out under the principle of willing-buyer willing-seller. However, the requirement that land be acquired through the market, coupled with lack of funds and legal constraints, gave rise to the FTLRP, which fundamentally altered the production structure of agriculture. In this chapter, we consider LRRP 1.

After independence, agricultural policy was directed to reducing inequality and to supporting smallholders. The supply response by smallholders was dramatic, and they became the largest suppliers of maize and cotton to formal markets within the first five years of independence. The focus on stimulating and supporting smallholder agriculture was also seen as a means towards achieving food self-sufficiency and food security among communal farmers. At the same time, government instituted a land resettlement programme and charged all key public sector institutions to give a high priority to smallholder agriculture.

As part of their overall plan, sophisticated agricultural institutions were made available to black farmers and a land resettlement programme enacted. Due to constitutional constraints, international pressure, fears about restructuring the economy too rapidly and a class alliance between white farmers and an emerging black bourgeoisie, limited arable land was reallocated and large-scale commercial farmers maintained their historical privileges. When land reform began in the 1980s, resettlement was carefully planned, focusing on small-scale farming, communities and cooperatives, with redistribution of land managed through the national budget on a willing-buyer willing-seller basis or through public expropriation of the land that had been abandoned during the liberation war. Support was relatively well targeted, with resettlement focusing on victims of the preceding war, landless peasants and people with inadequate land to sustain themselves. Although the process was slower than intended, by 1989 about 52,000 families had been resettled (World Bank, 2019).

However, there was a stumbling block in the form of the Lancaster House Agreement of 1979, which required that all land be acquired on a 'willing-buyer willing-seller' basis and that compensation for any land seized was to be denominated in foreign currency. Donor support for this programme was poor, and disbursements were relatively small. As a result, land was costly, and since it was purchased under the 'willing-seller willing-buyer' rule, it was available mainly in marginal production areas and on an ad hoc basis. Despite the passing in 1985 of the Land Acquisition Act, which gave the government the first option to purchase land that was put on the market, it did not redress the problem of the lack of large blocks of land for resettlement.

The major significant change in the agriculture sector was increased capital intensity of production. Small-scale black farmers with access to good land and productive resources responded remarkably to new production opportunities. Tekere and Kuda (1999) observed that during the first seven years after independence, black production of maize and cotton more than doubled and marketed contributions rose from less than 10% to approximately half of national sales. The pattern of agricultural development, however, was spatially and socially limited during the first decade of independence. The majority of rural blacks still had inadequate land and off-farm income resources to insure subsistence levels of consumption on an annual.

In 1986, government took measures to stimulate production through export incentives, introducing the Export Retention Scheme and the Export Revolving Fund and foreign exchange allocations in favour of exporters. Air transport was improved, the Horticultural Promotion Council was formed, and the communal areas management programme for indigenous resources (Operation Campfire) was established towards the end of the 1980s. In addition, government policy indirectly stimulated export production through the relatively low government-set producer price for maize, which made many commercial farmers diversify into cash crops destined for the more lucrative export markets.

### 2.4.4 Export of Agricultural Commodities

In 1980, Zimbabwe joined the African, Caribbean and Pacific countries (ACP) group and acceded to the Lome Convention. Since then, the country has been considering to benefit from the nonreciprocal trade preferences extended by European Union to ACP countries under the provision of the Cotonou Agreement. Indeed, EU is the major trading partner for Zimbabwe, accounting for about 35% of the country's export revenue. Zimbabwe has also benefited from the financial resources under the European Development Fund, for trade development projects targeting both regional and European markets. In addition, between 1980 and 1997 Zimbabwe was one of the 5 most successful ACP countries in taking advantage of the trade preferences made available under the Lomé Convention. At a point in time, Zimbabwe had problems in exporting its textile to South Africa, and consequently, the EU provided an important alternative market for the product.

#### 2.4.4.1 Zimbabwean Agricultural Exports to the European Union

Furthermore, it was observed that the most important trade preferences for Zimbabwean exporters have been in the fields of agricultural, horticultural (fruit and vegetables) and floricultural (cut flowers) exports. During the period from 1992 to 1996, Zimbabwean agricultural, horticultural and floricultural exports accounted for 53.7% of exports to the EU. Therefore, it was estimated that output in the sugar sector alone provided an income transfer to Zimbabwe in 1998 of over 18 million EURO, an amount greater than the annual aid allocation to Zimbabwe under the Lomé Convention.

The production of both fruit and vegetables on the one hand and that of cut flower on the other hand have steadily increased over the years. Hence, these products are being exported year in year out and they have been important source of foreign exchange earnings. Cut flowers are produced on both large-scale and small-scale commercial farms, although export of quality flowers comes almost exclusively from large-scale commercial farms.

The production of export quality cut flowers on communal area farms is not feasible, given the investments required and production methods used. Consequently, around 5% of land in the commercial farming sector is used for cut flowers, with a high concentration of cut flower farms in Mashonaland Central. In tonnage terms, horticultural exports grew 25 folds and there was corresponding 40-fold increase in the exchange earning. For example, cut flower alone grew 40-fold in terms of both tonnage exchange earnings. Between 1985 and 1999, the cut flower sector expanded and rose from 88th most important export product to the 11th position. In a relatively short period, Zimbabwe has become one of the major suppliers of cut flowers to the EU market. Remarkably, Zimbabwe was the second largest cut flower exporter in Africa and the third largest supplier of cut flowers to the EU in the world. The factors which have contributed to this growth include significant margins of trade preference, favourable climatic conditions, a relatively well-educated work force, improvements in airfreight and private sector initiative.

Another important agricultural product was beef, the bulk of which was being exported to the EU market. Under the Beef Protocol of the Lomé Convention and subsequent Cotonou Agreement, Zimbabwe was allocated a quota of 9100 tonnes for the export of frozen and chilled de-boned beef. The utilisation of this quota has varied considerably, from 5 to 178%. Traditionally, this has been a consequence of two main developments: drought and the outbreak of animal diseases, with periodic foot and mouth disease outbreaks resulting in the complete closure of the EU market to Zimbabwean beef exports and drought affecting the availability and quality of beef cuts.

### 2.4.5 Agricultural Trade Developments

A number of salient features characterised Zimbabwe's agricultural trade. First, there was a marked shift from cereal production and exports to cash crops. Second, export performance was directly a function of rainfall pattern, as is the case with import performance. Third, agricultural exports are relatively diversified by African standards. Fourth, agricultural imports are concentrated in cereals.

The agricultural sector was the largest single source of export earnings, contributing about 40–45% of total exports in most years. The single largest foreign currency earner is tobacco, even in years of very serious drought. Until the fast land reform, other rising stars in terms of exports were horticulture and beef. Without disturbances on farms and depending on the rainfall pattern, Zimbabwe is generally a net food exporter rather than an importer.

One of the main features of Zimbabwe's agriculture was the marked shift from production and exports of cereals to cash crops. There has been a general decline in cereal production in the country ever since 1985. Commercial farmers realised that they could reap higher profits by producing more of other cash crops like tobacco and the highly demanded horticultural products in the international market. This scenario has brought about a change in the export composition of the county. However, it resulted in increased importation of cereal commodities, an unhealthy situation from the viewpoint of the country's food security. It is also interesting to note that there has been a steady increase in citrus fruit production from the 1980s through to the year 2001. This increased production has been brought about because of the increased demand for citrus fruits in the international market, which has seen exports of citrus fruits becoming one of the dominant exports in the country's export basket. Zimbabwe has experienced a continuous deterioration in its terms of trade for agricultural commodities over a long period, which has adversely affected its agricultural trade performance.

### 2.4.6 Agricultural Exports

Zimbabwe exports a wide variety of agricultural products, ranging from cash crops and cereals. The major agricultural exports include tobacco, cotton, tea, coffee, beef sugar, horticultural products and maize, depending on the rainfall pattern. After 1995, there was considerable diversification away from tobacco to horticultural products. The industry experienced increased exports in four main categories: fresh produce (mostly vegetables), citrus and subtropical fruits, deciduous fruits and flowers. This was mainly because the tariff harmonisation brought about by trade liberalisation under the foreign exchange liberalisation under ESAP offered new options and enabled growers to penetrate previously impenetrable markets.

#### 2.4.6.1 Tobacco

Zimbabwe is one of the top producers of tobacco. It follows countries such as China, Brazil, Indonesia and USA. Tobacco is often known by the moniker 'golden leaf' in Zimbabwe. It plays an important role in the export sector of the country, the world's third largest tobacco producer after the USA and Brazil. Tobacco has always dominated the agricultural export composition, with the largest shares of 78% and 67% in 1992 and 1993, respectively. Low labour costs and high yields make Zimbabwe a more competitive producer of quality tobacco than its Brazilian and American rivals. Tobacco production is mainly for export, with the domestic market consuming around 2–3% of the total. The bulk of Zimbabwe's tobacco crop is exported to the EU and China. Tobacco exports have been growing since the 1980s. Flue-cured tobacco dominates tobacco exports, and its price started to rise in 1994 and peaked in 1996 at US $2.94 in response to a world shortage. Statistics from Food and Agriculture Organisation (2001) show upward trend in the value of exported tobacco from 1985 to 2000 by Zimbabwe.

#### 2.4.6.2 Cotton

Cotton contributes 10–22% of agricultural exports. The introduction of an input credit scheme and deregulation of cotton marketing have resulted in a massive surge in production. Zimbabwe produces high-quality cotton because it is hand-picked, thus helping it secure and establish a niche market. Exports of cotton increased from 18,797 tonnes in 1993, peaked at 92,769 tonnes in 1997 and declined to 79,671 tonnes in 1998 because of low yields.

#### 2.4.6.3 Sugar

Sugar is one of Zimbabwe's major exports and Zimbabwe is a beneficiary of the sugar protocol under the ACP-EU Cotonou Agreement. Exports of sugar to the EU are within two arrangements: the normal ACP EU duty free annual quota and the special preferred sugar arrangement. The problem with sugar in Zimbabwe is that it is reliant on irrigation, which also depends on the rainfall pattern. As such, there have been fluctuations in the contribution of sugar to exports, with a significant drop experienced during the drought years of 1992–1993. The industry recovered in the ensuing years, and this enabled the country to negotiate an above-quota allocation under the special preferred sugar arrangement, which came into effect in 1995 and provided enhanced market access for Zimbabwe's sugar exports (Fig. 2.1).

Figure 2.2 shows the trends in exports of raw and refined sugar between 1985 and 2000. After 1985, there was a gradual decline in the exports of sugar, with the lowest levels being reached between the drought years 1992 and 1993. There was a rapid increase in sugar exports in 1994 caused by an improved market access condition following autonomous liberalisation of trade in 1992 and enlargement of

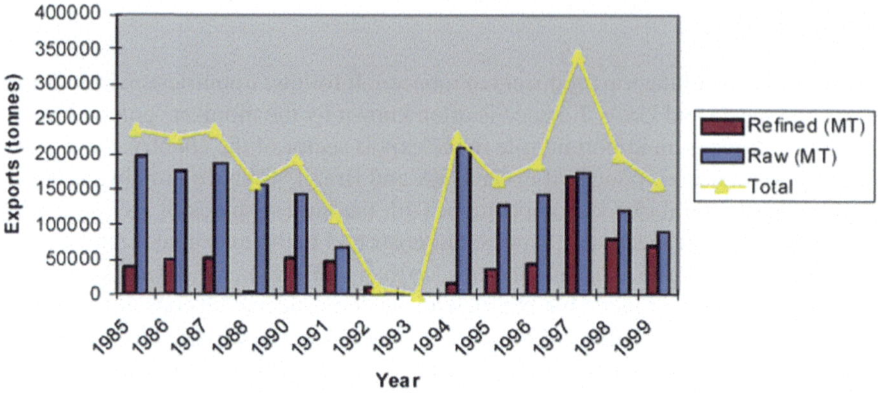


Fig. 2.1 Exports of sugar 1985–1999. *Source* Authors compilation

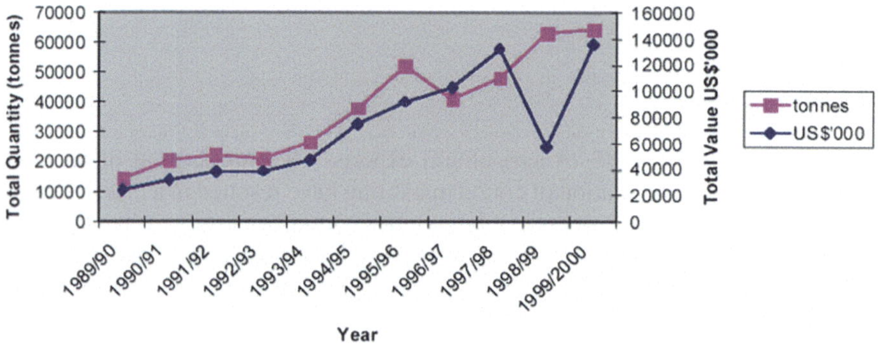


Fig. 2.2 Horticultural exports: 1989–2000. *Source* Authors compilation

the EU market in 1995. The peak was reached in 1997, and since then, there has been a gradual decline in exports of sugar mainly as a result of the decline in world commodity prices and the current land redistribution programme in the country.

### 2.4.7 Horticultural Exports

The horticulture industry is the fastest growing export sector in Zimbabwe. Before the Fast Track Land Reform, it was ranked number six in the agricultural sector in terms of its contribution to foreign currency earnings after tobacco, cotton, cereal and grain, sugar, tea and coffee. Zimbabwe's horticultural products used to enjoy a competitive cost advantage in the international market, deriving from low costs, good climate, vast availability of land suitable for horticulture, export processing zone status and the number of airlines servicing the industry. There was a drastic fall in the export value of horticultural commodities in the 1998/1999 season of about 57%, despite the continuous increase in quantity produced resulting from depressed flower markets and prices and withdrawal of several airlines from Zimbabwe as well as the introduction of exchange rate controls. However, exports recovered again in 1999/2000. Figure 2.2 shows performance of the agriculture exports from 1989 to 2000.

### 2.4.8 *Agricultural Imports*

During the 1980s, Zimbabwe has been largely self-sufficient in the provision of agricultural goods. From 1985, imports have been growing because of the increased shortages of cereals caused by drought, population growth, increased urbanisation and the shift of production from cereals to cash crops. Before the reform programme, emphasis was on food security through self-reliance in cereal production rather than through trade. As such, food imports were minimal. The implementation of the structural adjustment programme in 1990 saw a shift from self-reliance towards trade.

### 2.4.9 *Food Security Dimensions*

In Zimbabwe, food security, defined in terms of availability of maize as the staple food product, has remained an issue of great concern in view of the increased incidence of drought-related hunger. For a number of years, agricultural food imports have constituted a large proportion of food trade. Further, the food security situation has been seriously threatened by the increased production of cash crops by commercial farmers in the country. The fall in returns from food crops has led farmers to increase their production of non-food cash crops, which are usually grown on large farms in the country. However, small-scale farmers have moved in to grow food crops for subsistence, with surpluses being sold. As such, the area under food crops has been increasing, although at a lower rate than for cash crops (Mangoyana & Meda, 2001).

Cereals supply in Zimbabwe is largely dependent on domestic production, especially when the rainfall pattern is not erratic. Cereals are at the heart of food security of Zimbabwe covering maize as the staple and other grains as well.

## 2.5 Trends in Poverty and Under-Nutrition

In Zimbabwe, post-independence (1980) agricultural policies focused on developing a high degree of food security through production while improving the welfare of the long-marginalised rural population. Government directly stimulated agricultural production by way of policies and measures on land, water, infrastructure, credit and technology. These measures include irrigation development, input support, provision of tillage services, credit availability and strengthening of research. It also established depots and collection points, and ensured guaranteed prices and markets. Indirect stimulants in the form of subsidies and income policies were employed to stimulate production and demand. During the same period, food insecurity at both household and national levels fell.

## 2.6 Infrastructure Development

In its summary report of 2001, AfDB said 'Infrastructure is considered a key component of the investment climate by reducing the costs of doing business and enabling people to access markets. Investments in infrastructure are critical to advances in agriculture and fundamental to human development, including the delivery of health and education services to poor people. Infrastructure is an enormous untapped potential for the creation of productive employment'. Economic growth and development cannot be achieved without the availability of appropriate economic and social infrastructure. The need to improve the quality of infrastructure services in Zimbabwe is, therefore, the cornerstone of the Government of Zimbabwe's policy, strategy and programmes to promote sustained and shared economic growth in the country.

Infrastructure consists of both economic and social components. Economic infrastructure refers to public utilities and works that promote economic activity, such as roads, highways, railroads, airports, sea ports, electricity, telecommunications, water supply and sanitation. Social infrastructure is the infrastructure that promotes the health, education and cultural standards of the population. It consists of schools, libraries, universities, clinics, hospitals, courts, museums, theatres, playground and national parks (Yoshino & Nakahigashi, 2000).

Zimbabwe benefited substantively from the colonial infrastructure stocks and made significant progress in infrastructure development following the attainment of independence in 1980. During the early years of independence, the country's infrastructure backbone was very impressive compared to other countries in the Southern Africa region. Zimbabwe managed to put in place a national electricity network and establish regional interconnection in the power sector; to build an extensive network of roads for countrywide accessibility and integration into the regional transport corridors; to lay the water and sewerage system; and to make progress on building dams and tapping the significant irrigation potential.

The provision of good infrastructure is a prerequisite for achieving economic growth and development and also for enabling other sectors of the economy to function properly. Investment potential exists in the expansion and modernisation of the existing infrastructure as well as the construction of new infrastructure such as modern highways and associated tollgates linking key cities, power generation, dam construction, water reticulation and budget hotel chains in the tourism industry.

### 2.6.1 Roads Network

At independence, Zimbabwe inherited road and rail transport systems that were well developed and efficient by African standards, but which only covered the central parts of the country that are urban areas and the commercial farms (Pedersen, 2004). After independence in 1980, one of the most important actions of the new government was to extend and upgrade the road system into the more densely populated areas of African settlement in order to increase their market access. Thus, during the late 1980s, a large proportion of the state road network was upgraded from earth to tarred or gravel roads. This meant that the share of the 18,400 km of state roads which were tarred increased from 38% to 45% between 1985 and 1990, and the proportion of gravel roads increased from 27% to 35%. At the same time, many new agricultural marketing depots were established in the African rural areas in order to encourage production for the market. This resulted in a rapid increase in the smallholder production of, especially, maize and cotton for the market during the 1980s. There were also plans to upgrade some of the existing feeder and secondary roads in the rural areas, but that only occurred to a limited extent before the economy tightened in the late 1980s, while the structural adjustment policies in the early 1990s stopped further improvements of both rural and state roads almost entirely.

Zimbabwe road network is managed by a number of authorities, namely the State, Rural District Councils and Municipalities. The Ministry of Transport, Department of Roads is responsible for the primary and secondary roads, which links cities and towns as well centres of growth and development. District Councils are responsible for tertiary roads which account for about 40% of the total road network. Municipalities are responsible for servicing about 9% of total road network in urban areas.

### 2.6.2 Railway System

The railway system in Zimbabwe is made up of 2760 km of narrow-gauge main track lines, of which 313 km is electrified, about 2500 km of branch lines and sidings. Rail falls under the responsibility of the National Railways of Zimbabwe which is a statutory board of government with the exception of the Bulawayo-Beitbridge line. A giant leap in the development of the rail transport system of Zimbabwe was made in 1983 with the electrification of the busy mainline, a distance of 305 km between Harare and Dabuka marshalling yard near Gweru in the Midlands Province. In 1987, the NRZ relinquished ownership of the Botswana section of the railway line and this gave rise to the formation of the Botswana Railways. September 1992 saw the arrival of Diesel Electric (DE) 11 class of locomotives, thereby boosting the main line fleet and enabling the NRZ to cope with greatly increased traffic volumes.

### 2.6.3 *Electricity*

The power sector is crucial in that it plays a strategic role in enabling and promoting economic activity in all sectors of the economy. There is state monopoly in the generation, transmission and distribution of electricity through the Zimbabwe Electricity Supply Authority (ZESA). ZESA Holdings a state-owned company holds the government share of four of its subsidiaries, namely the Zimbabwe Power Company (ZPC), Zimbabwe Electricity Transmission and Distribution Company (ZEDTC). The installed capacity is about 1960 MW while the demand varies between 1600 and 2100 MW. Electricity consumption per capita in Zimbabwe was 738 kWh in 1995, when the average for low-income countries around the world was 414 kWh per capita and the average for sub-Saharan Africa.

### 2.6.4 *Telecommunications*

Zimbabwe has made some institutional reforms such as the creation of the Postal and Telecommunications Regulatory Authority of Zimbabwe (POTRAZ). When Zimbabwe attained independence in 1980, Post and Telecommunication Corporation (PTC) was a state enterprise. After the unbundling of the corporation during the 1990s, Telone now runs the fixed telecommunication network. However, there are three mobile telecommunication companies, namely; Netone, Econet Wireless and Telecel Zimbabwe. During the 1980s, the coverage and quality of the basic infrastructure of Zimbabwe were among the best in the region, the SSA.

## 2.7 Informal Sector—The Shadow Economy of Zimbabwe

The term *informal sector* is considered to mean very small-scale goods and services production and distribution units which consist of both employed workers and independent self-employed persons in both rural and urban areas (Bagachwa & Naho, 1995). Their informality comes from the fact that they are for the most part unregistered, unrecorded in official statistics, and participants have little or no access to organised markets, to credit institutions, to formal education and training or to many public services. *Parallel market* activities involve illegal production and trade of goods and services that are legal in themselves, and therefore have an alternative legal market. The informal economy thrives in the context of high unemployment, underemployment, poverty, gender inequality and precarious work, the very circumstances we have in Zimbabwe. It plays a significant role in income generation due to of the relative ease of entry and low requirements for education, skills, technology and capital. However, most people enter the informal economy by necessity rather than by choice, in order to access basic income-generating activities as a means of survival.

The informal economy is marked by acute decent work deficits and a disproportionate share of the working poor. Workers in the informal economy face higher risks of poverty than those in the formal economy. Although some activities offer reasonable livelihoods and incomes, most people engaged in the informal economy are exposed to inadequate and unsafe working conditions. Illiteracy levels are high, skill levels are low and training opportunities are inadequate. Incomes are also lower, less certain and less regular and working hours are longer. There are no opportunities for collective bargaining and representation rights and their employment status is usually ambiguous or disguised. These workers are also physically and financially more vulnerable because work in the informal economy is either excluded from, or effectively beyond, the reach of social security schemes and safety and health, maternity and other labour protection legislation.

### *2.7.1 The Background of Informal Sector in Zimbabwe*

At independence in 1980, Zimbabwe inherited an economy that exhibited both extreme characteristics of a relatively developed economy and economic backwardness. This dualism had arisen from the policy of white supremacy that underlined the colonial era. The relative strength of the economy lay in its diversified formal sector, with no overwhelmingly dominant sector. They further state that despite the relatively developed nature of the economy that the government inherited in 1980, ‘the Zimbabwean economy had a dark side to it: the underdeveloped, deprived and marginalised non-formal sector which constituted about four fifths of the populations’ (Chiripanhura & Makwavarara, 2000). This however assertion contradicts to the 1980 statistics which states that the informal economy was relatively small, accounting for less than 10% of the labour force. As a result of the more relaxed post-independence environment, reserve labour found it easy to migrate into urban areas, as evidenced by the growth of the urban population from 13% of the total in 1960 to 23% by 1980. However, the lack of employment in the formal sector meant that these migrants had to make do with secondary jobs in the informal economy.

### *2.7.2 Zimbabwe Informal Sector in the 1980s: Development of the Sector and Challenges*

The informal economy in Zimbabwe has been on the increase since independence in 1980. Chirisa (2009) states that from 1980 to 1990, ‘the formal sector was booming immensely such that the informal sector had very little role to play, especially in the urban centres’. The government policy to promote the idea of growth points in the countryside was aimed towards encouraging micro-entrepreneurialism. It was hoped that the new entrepreneurs would be established at the same time taking the small established entrepreneurs to greater heights of investment. Thus, within this decade, it can be said that government supported the informal sector in the form of home-based industries and growth points, but due to large public sector employment, the informal sector during this decade was very small in size. In addition, government did not seem to pay much attention to the informal sector during this time as it was seized with redressing past injustices and reconfiguring economic, political, social and cultural structures. However, the economy did not perform as anticipated and this meant that 'there was less investment to create more employment opportunities while at the same time, inflation was rising. The end result was that employment became output constrained'. The final outcome of government's policies was that even though public sector employment had been relatively high, it was not sustainable. By 1989, the rate of unemployment was approximately 26% from about 12.5% in the mid-1980s.

Contrary to Chirisa (2009)'s earlier argument that government promoted micro-entrepreneurs or informal sector initiatives, Chiripanhura and Makwavarara (2000) argue that, 'the policies that were in place during the 1980s did not'. However, when the prospects of employment creation in the formal sector were good, government's attitude towards the informal sector was hostile, with stiff and oppressive regulations. The central and local authorities hoped that this sector would one day disappear. However, the downturn in formal employment growth, high levels of rural–urban migration and public and private sector retrenchments under structural adjustment led to a change in attitude. Therefore, by the end of the first decade of independence the country was treading on a precarious road of recession. This saw the rationale for adopting the economic reform programme, which was in the form of Economic Structural Adjustment Programme (ESAP) which was synonymous with the rapid growth of the informal sector. By the end of the first decade, the hope after a legacy of colonialism was grim and marked with scepticism. The informal sector which had been a rare feature during this decade was beginning to grow rapidly and become a prevalent feature of the macroeconomic environment.

Small enterprises in Zimbabwe have mostly been small by nature. In addition, they are generally family organised, informalised, unregulated and subject to high levels of competition. The other characteristic of informal enterprises is that they relate directly and personally to their clients and they use local materials and are efficient at recycling materials. More so informal sector experiences a serious scarcity of capital and does not have access to credit from financing institutions. These characteristics of the informal sector are widely accepted by Mupedziswa (1991). In Zimbabwe, the informal sector can be said to have emerged by default and not by design. The colonial regime attempted to control the spread of the informal sector in urban areas. This had the effect of making it a shadow feature of the economy. They point out that the Town and Country Planning Act (1946), the Vagrancy Act (1960), the Urban Councils Act and the Vendors and Hawkers By-laws (1973) are some of the pieces of legislation that were enacted to frustrate the growth of informal sector activities. Local authorities had the unenviable task of enforcing this network of regulations and by-laws. This colonial legacy still obtains in independent Zimbabwe as Mupedziswa

(1991) observes that all enterprises are required to register with a statutory or a government authority. However, to circumvent these problems most operators just operate illegally. Despite the efforts to stifle its growth, the informal sector emerged to become a 'major employer' by the late 1970s.

At independence, the potential role of the informal sector in job creation and poverty alleviation was also noticed by the Riddell Commission (1981) which recommended that the new Zimbabwe needed to recognise and promote this sector in order to raise the standard of living of the majority of the people. It was evident that urban poverty was on the increase and the formal sector would not be able to provide jobs to all. The rapid growth in the number of increasingly educated people unable to penetrate the formal sector inevitably means that they must and will have to fend for themselves. Out of 300,000 school leavers churned out by the country's education system, the formal sector only has room for 70,000. The remaining 230,000 thus have to find their own means of earning a living. In a study of the urban informal sector carried out in Harare, Bulawayo and Gweru, it was found that the decline in real household incomes and retrenchment provided new entrants to the sector. The safety net function of the informal sector is very evident from this study.

The most serious problems are the lack of capital and restrictive by-laws and legislation. Mupedziswa (1991)'s study found that the operations of 41% of the respondents had been negatively affected by lack of capital. This is mainly because financial institutions view the informal sector with contempt. Their lack of collateral security has often been cited for denying them access to credit. Very often informal sector operators have to be based at premises sanctioned by the relevant authorities. Such places are not necessarily strategic (in terms of customer traffic) for the operators and this affects their enterprises negatively. The process of obtaining a workplace is also frustrating and often cumbersome for regulations require that they be registered and that their proposed ventures be approved. In adopting the informal sector strategy in urban poverty alleviation, it is imperative that these constraints be recognised and addressed. It is also important to note that urban poverty alleviation cannot be achieved solely through informal sector initiatives, and other complementary strategies have to be formulated and implemented. For the informal sector to play an effective urban poverty alleviation role, there is need for a review of policies and regulations and other constraints facing the operators. It is also through the organised efforts of the informal sector operators themselves that lasting improvements to their situation can be realised. In view of the discussion above, the following suggestions for the way forward are made.

### *2.7.3 Compositional Changes of the Urban Informal Economic Enterprises*

Informal activities have complex compositional structures (Guha-Khasnobis et al., 2006). The composition or structure refers to the different parts of objects and their organisation. In this study, the focus will be on the components of the IES in Zimbabwean cities and their relationships to those of their FES counterparts. In particular, the focus is on structural changes that have taken place within the two economic sectors and how these have influenced linkages between the FES and the IES (Thiele & Böhme, 2011). Zimbabwean IEEs have been changing their ways of doing business over the years (Mupedziswa & Gumbo, 2001). Informal enterprises that have been operating mostly without licences have started to operate on designated sites after getting official approval to occupy the city council spaces. Informal economic entrepreneurs have also increasingly been employing people in their businesses to assist in the activities of their enterprises.

## 2.8 Causes of Second Economy in Zimbabwe

Literature on the subject matter has advanced multiple reasons as the major causes behind the existence and growth of the informal sector. Below are some of these reasons which caused the growth of the second economy in the case of Zimbabwe over the years.

### *2.8.1 Tax Burden (High Tax)*

The greater the tax burden, the greater will be the incentive for individuals to remain in the informal sector. In the case of Zimbabwe, the income tax has been above 30% for nearly 3 decades and this contributed to some economic activities to continue remaining in the informal economy.

### *2.8.2 Foreign Exchange Controls*

The presence of foreign exchange controls or shortages provides an avenue for illegal transfer, foreign exchange contrabandist and development of fake statements for import–export activities and these are all better done in second economy. For Zimbabwe, foreign currency shortages and accompanying black market of foreign currency have been part of the economy since the early 1980s. In sum, the financial system of Zimbabwe experienced foreign currency shortages around 1987 and later on from 2000 through 2009.

### 2.8.3 High Unemployment

The greater the number of unemployed, the more will be individuals willing to find a job in the second economy.

### 2.8.4 High Level of Poverty

If individuals have low disposable income, they are mostly likely to be willing to do various jobs, some of them in the informal sector. Zimbabwe's poverty rates have been rising over years.

### 2.8.5 High Inflation

High inflation implies increased seigniorage or inflation tax and this accentuates the effect of taxes upon individuals, thus increasing the effective tax burden on tax payers. This forces some individuals to go into informal sector. Although the country's annual inflation rate in the first decade of independence (1980–1990) was below 20%, by July 2008 the month-on-month rate was estimated at 2600% or 231.2 million per cent year on year (Siyakiya, 2014).

### 2.8.6 High Rate of Return

High rate of return on informal sector (illegal and underground) operations provides an incentive for individuals to enter this type of economy (Bagachwa & Naho, 1995). The fact that informal sector activities are largely not taxed in Zimbabwe means that there is relatively a high rate of return as the owners of such businesses retain all the profits.

### 2.8.7 Limited Pursuit by Tax Collectors

The fact that revenue agencies do not understand fully the immense revenue potential of the sector or have limited resources causes them not to vigorously pursue tax collection in this sector, thus acting as an incentive to operate in informal sector (Bagachwa & Naho, 1995; Chipeta, 2002). According to Mbiriri (2010), the Zimbabwe Revenue Authority (ZIMRA) does not pursue the activities of the informal sector as far as tax collection is concerned. This might be, among other things, due to minimal if not negative rate of return, whereby the potential revenue to be collected from informal sector activities will be lower than the costs expanded by ZIMRA to collect the same tax revenue.

### 2.8.8 *Easy Entry and Exit*

The fact that moving in and out of the informal sector is relatively easy is an incentive for individuals to quickly consider this sector. In the case of Zimbabwe, any individual can start his or her own informal economic activity and in most cases without any regulations required to be undertaken (Mbiriri, 2010).

## 2.9 Urbanisation: Post-Independent Urban Development: Planning and Policy Developments

Like in most sub-Saharan African countries, urbanisation in Zimbabwe was a result of colonialism which brought in new socio-political and economic dispensation. Before colonialism, human settlements were entirely scattered and sparsely populated rural with no cities and towns except the long disserted pre-colonial city states of Great Zimbabwe, Khami and Dhlodhlo to mention but only the largest. This is explained by two fundamental features of society then: population was still very meagre relative to today; and also, the disposition of economic activities was mainly primarily farming, small-scale mining and limited trade.

The British colonial regime set up administrative structures and centres. They also developed supportive infrastructure such as urban centres and communication linkages in the form of railway lines, roads and telegram lines. The new administration also reorganised spatial land use by expropriating prime land from the indigenous people and forcibly moving them in to marginal areas, where the soils were not only sandy and very poor, but also received very low and unreliable rainfall. The same system of land expropriation was used for all urban and mining centres. This spatial reorganisation was enabled by a number of statutes, such as the Land Apportionment Act of 1930, the Land Husbandry Act of 1950 and the Land Tenure Act of 1969.

Munzwa and Wellington (2010) observed that while policy may easily be changed or even reversed, it is a near impossibility to do the same with the spatial physical developments such as buildings and infrastructure. These include roads, water reticulation, sewerage reticulation, treatment works, railway lines, telecommunication lines and power lines. As a result of these realities, the form and structure of our cities have remained to a large extent as originally conceived, designed and developed with cosmetic changes in the form of redevelopments and densification of certain sectors or areas and sprawling expansion. This has also led to the many challenges of urban poverty, inadequate housing, inadequate provision of serves and environmental quality.

Since independence in 1980, the Zimbabwean government embarked on an ambitious programme of decentralisation and local government reform. Thus, the post-independence era has been marked by vigorous non-racial systems including the urban and rural settlement systems. The one city concept was one kind of a move to non-racialised cities so that the barrier concomitant with the separate development was sterilised. With the lifting of controls at independence, urban populations grew by leaps and bounds. This was due to the rural–urban drift that characterised the times. Urban areas were very attractive as they offered better job opportunities as well as social facilities relative to the rural.

## 2.10 Policy Developments

The colonial policies as already been alluded to were restrictive, in terms of population movements, especially on the part of the black populations. Such measures allowed control of the growth of urban populations. But one thrust also in the colonial policy was to try and bring 'development' into the rural areas. The colonial growth point policy was one policy to this effect. This was supposed to enhance the policy of separate development. The practice was adopted at independence but now with a different underlying principle and focus. At independence, the Department of Physical Planning (DPP) was tasked to locate focal points of urban development by making provision for infrastructure development and treating the whole matter as a matter of urgency. In principle, the plan was to identify potential areas for economic growth, which would curb rural–urban drift and facilitate decentralisation of economic activities in pursuance of the growth with equity policy. The implementation of the Growth Point/Rural Service Centre Strategy was geared towards the translating the Growth with Equity (GWE) Policy into a spatial reality. We will revisit GPs in detail in Chap. 6.

**Urban Physical Planning and Development**

The physical expansion of urban settlements is the outcome of economic, institutional and social forces. As urban areas harboured industrial and services actors so they acted as magnets for labour. This development translated into physical development of these centres. Institutionally, legislation like the Land Husbandry Act of 1951 acted as prime movers of the landless Africans into urban centres. In direct conflict to this development were other legislation like the 1931 Land Apportionment Act and the Native (Urban Areas) Act, the 1969 Land Tenure Act, the African (Urban Areas) Accommodation Act, the Africans (Registration and Identification Act) and the Vagrancy Act. These made it very difficult for the African to move to towns. In urban areas, Africans were restricted to certain designated areas called locations. Housing demand grew and increasing urban labour saw cities expanding outwards and upwards.

## References


Agere, S. (1990). Issues of equity in and access to health care in Zimbabwe.

Bagachwa, M. S., & Naho, A. (1995). Estimating the second economy in Tanzania. *World Development, 23*(8), 1387–1399. https://doi.org/10.1016/0305-750x(95)00055-h

Bate, R., Tren, R., Urbach, J., & Ncube, A. P. (2007). *Tyranny and Disease-The Destruction of Health Care in Zimbabwe.* https://coilink.org/20.500.12592/sbt33w on 13 Sep 2024. COI: 20.500.12592/sbt33w.

Chipeta, C. (2002). The second economy and tax yield in Malawi. *African Economic Research Consortium.*

Chiripanhura, B. M., & Makwavarara, T. (2000). The Labour Market and Economic Development 1980–2000,' in Zimbabwe Congress of Trade Unions (ZCTU).

Chirisa, I. (2009). The geography of informal sector operations (ISOs): A perspective of urban Zimbabwe. *Journal of Geography and Regional Planning, 2*(4), 66–79.

Colclough, C. (1990). Education in Zimbabwe: Issues of quantity and quality. *A Joint Swedish/Zimbabwe Education Sector Study, SIDA.*

Dzvimbo, K. P. (1991). The transition state and the dialectics of educational transformation in the third world: The case of Zimbabwe. *International Studies in Sociology of Education, 1*(1–2), 43–58. https://doi.org/10.1080/0962021910010104

Food and Agriculture Organisation of the United Nations. (2001). *Global Watch Report.*

Gaidzanwa, R. B. (1999). *Voting with Their Feet: Migrant Zimbabwean Nurses and Doctors in the Era of Structural Adjustment.* Nordic Africa Institute.

Government of Zimbabwe. (1995). *Zimbabwe's Agricultural Policy Framework 1995–2020.*

Guha-Khasnobis, B., Kanbur, R., & Ostrom, E. (2006). *Beyond Formality and Informality* (Vol. 4). Oxford University Press.

Gundani, P. (1988). *The Catholic Church and National Development in Independent Zimbabwe. Church and State in Zimbabwe.* Mambo Press.

Hammer, J. S., & Berman, P. (1995). Ends and means in public health policy in developing countries. *Health Policy, 32*(1–3), 29–45. https://doi.org/10.1016/0168-8510(95)00727-a

Johnston, T. (1999). Meeting the health care challenge in Zimbabwe. *The World Bank Economic Review.*

Kreuter, U. P., & Workman, J. P. (1996). Cattle and wildlife ranching in Zimbabwe. *Rangelands Archives, 18*(2), 44–47.

Makochekanwa, A. (2012). The impact of economic performance on health in Zimbabwe.

Mandaza, I. (1986). Southern Africa: US policy and the struggle for national independence. *African Journal of Political Economy/Revue Africaine D'economie Politique, 1*(1), 120–141.

Mangoyana, S., & Meda, T. (2001). *Food security and sustainability in Zimbabwe.* University of Zimbabwe Publications.

Mbiriri, R. P. (2010). *Can Zimbabwe use its informal economy as a means for sustainable development in the current reconstruction process* [University of the Witwatersrand].

Mhike, I., & Makombe, E. K. (2018). Mission and state health institutions: "Invisible" public-private partnerships in Zimbabwe, 1980–1999. *Studia Historiae Ecclesiasticae, 44*(1), 1–12. https://doi.org/10.25159/2412-4265/3330

Mubika, A. K., & Bukaliya, R. (2011). Education for all: issues and challenges: The case for Zimbabwe. *International Journal of Social Sciences & Education, 1*(4).

Munzwa, K., & Wellington, J. (2010). Urban development in Zimbabwe: A human settlement perspective. *Theoretical and Empirical Researches in Urban Management, 5*(14), 120–146.

Mupedziswa, R. (1991). *A Decade of Development: Zimbabwe 1980–1991.* Mambo Press.

Mupedziswa, R., & Gumbo, P. (2001). *Women informal traders in Harare and the struggle for survival in an environment of economic reforms.* Nordic Africa Institute.

Nhundu, T. J. (1992). A decade of educational expansion in Zimbabwe: Causes, consequences, and policy contradictions. *The Journal of Negro Education, 61*(1), 78–98. https://doi.org/10.2307/2295630

Pedersen, P. O. (2004). Zimbabwe's changing freight transport and logistical system: Structural adjustment and political change. *Journal of Southern African Studies, 30*(3), 577–602. https://doi.org/10.1080/0305707042000254119

Siyakiya, P. (2014). *An analysis of the effects of hyperinflation on manufacturing sector output. A case of Zimbabwe's manufacturing firms 2000–2013* International Institute of Social Sciences of the Erasmus University of Rotterdam. The Hague. https://thesis.eur.nl/pub/17462/done-PURUWETI-SIYAKIYA.pdf

Tekere, M., & Kuda, N. (1999). *Study on the impact of the WTO and other international trade agreements on Zimbabwe's agricultural sector: Key issues for WTO 2000* Harare.

Thiele, R., & Böhme, M. (2011). Is the informal sector constrained from the demand side? Evidence for six West African Capitals.

World Bank. (2019). *Zimbabwe public expenditure review with a focus on agriculture.* World Bank.

Yoshino, N., & Nakahigashi, M. (2000). The role of infrastructure in economic development (Preliminary Version). *Unpublished manuscript.*

# Chapter 3
# Achievements Over the Four Decades and Looking Ahead

## 3.1 Introduction

This chapter will explore selected notable accomplishments that have shaped Zimbabwe's growth, analysing the country's achievements in sectors such as education, health care and human development. Some of these milestones have been important in aiding visibility of Zimbabweans in the region and beyond. Zimbabweans are often lauded for skills competence in different occupations and have often excelled in strategic positions.

Tracing the four decades of Zimbabwe's existence as an independent state, there are a number of encouraging achievements which the country has managed despite the difficult journey. It is crucial for us to examine the achievements of Zimbabwe because the milestones are in a way related to most parts of the early post-independent Zimbabwe in Chap. 2. For instance, the remarkable literacy levels to be articulated later has a close connection to the developments in the education sector. The achievements supported by early independent Zimbabwe known then as the jewel of Africa were supposed to act as a tide upon which the country was supposed to ride on. The milestones would give traction for the country to *look ahead*. When a country is developing sustainably, it should not only be moving forward but it is important for it to look ahead. For us looking ahead is all about anticipating the future. For instance, conjecturing the future problems an economy is likely to encounter as it travels the vast expanse of its development journey. Not only should problems be anticipated but also proffering appropriate solutions as well. For instance, when an economy is grappling with massive unemployment of labour, real jobs will only help to change the lives of people to the point of turning around the fortunes of the economy. Thus, the most significant thing is the quality of the jobs the economy will deliver to its expectant masses.

One thing which Zimbabwe has been trying to do is to move along the development trajectory just like other states. Sustaining respective development path is key for posterity. The disturbing thing however with respect to Zimbabwe is that

 
K. Mahuni et al., *Zimbabwe's Economy*, Advances in African Economic, Social and Political Development, https://doi.org/10.1007/978-3-031-81588-1_3

despite moving forward, not much was done to plan also about the future in the process. The country did not anticipate much about what the future would have in store for the economy. The outcome of this then was the mounting of challenges. Trying to address the problems through firefighting means has been unsustainable. For example, remarkable literacy levels meant at least an enlightened population. However, with few entrepreneurial skills against the backdrop of deteriorating economic conditions at the disposal of scores of graduates, employment is thus becoming elusive. Therefore, the main issues of this chapter deal with significant milestones in the four decades of Zimbabwe. Achievements attained cannot be exhausted; however, we flag out some we considered to be key.

## 3.2 Increased Participation of Women in the Mainstream Economy

In general, the roles women play in societies are often overlooked. For instance, the gender pay gap which is of concern even in most developed countries is one such problem. For most developing countries, roles women play are often not valued much at times due to cultural and traditional norms in different societies. In the African context, the issue of women taking a role in leadership positions has always been contested for the sole reason that their place lies in running domestic chores. These gender stereotypes and roles have hindered women's role as potential leaders.

Over the years, many institutions and central governments have established mechanisms to ensure there is parity in terms of the roles of both men and women, thereby discouraging the general disparities in spaces such as work and sports. Zimbabwe over the years has managed to show some efforts in trying to ensure that women are also enhanced in society. This is laudable. The country is signatory to international and regional instruments for gender equality and the empowerment of women and girls. Some of gender-related challenges the country faces include coordination of the national gender management system, inadequate implementation of the National Gender Policy, partial domestication of international and regional instruments, low participation of women in politics and decision-making positions, limited access to productive resources and gender-based violence.

To show compliance with global standards regarding gender, the government has signed and ratified several international conventions and instruments and embracing international human rights framework and has gone further to come up with a National Gender Policy Framework. However, there is so much activity in the civil society as compared to the government itself when it comes to the implementation of gender empowerment programmes, especially in rural communities, a gap which still needs to be addressed.

Soon after the 1995 Beijing Conference, the Zimbabwean government came up with its own National Plan of Action for gender empowerment. This indicated the government's total commitment for ensuring the full and equal participation of women in all spheres of life. The National Plan of action followed the Gender and Development approach which seeks to mainstream gender into all spheres of life and development, unlike the women in development approach. The National Plan of Action was developed by and for all stakeholders involved in the advancement of women including government ministries and non-governmental boards. Critical areas of concern included women in politics and decision making, education and training of women, institutionalisation mechanisms for the advancement of women and the economy. The Government of Zimbabwe recognised the need for full participation of men and women in development processes at all levels in order to ensure sustainable development and attainment for equality between both sexes. The Government of Zimbabwe has enacted legal frameworks, policies and strategies in education, women in decision making, reproductive health, HIV/AIDS, gender equality and equity, children and youth, including women rights in order to achieve social development. Economic empowerment has also been the government's thrust to enable the empowerment of women. The country has also ratified most of the fundamental conventions designed to achieve gender justice across all sectors. The government crafted the National Gender Policy which was designed to translate and deliver on the provisions of an array of international, regional and national provisions.

We will look at some of the policies adopted by the government in the National Gender Policy. At international level, Zimbabwe is part to a number of international conventions that include the Convention on the Elimination of all Forms of Discrimination against Women (CEDAW) (1991), the Beijing Declaration on the Platform for Action (1995), the Convention on Civil and Political Rights (CCPR), the Equal Remuneration Convention among many others. At regional level, Zimbabwe has endorsed the protocol to the African Charter on Human and People's Rights on the Rights of Women, the 2004 Solemn Declaration on Gender and Equality in Africa, and the Southern African Development Community's (SADC) Gender and Development Protocol. Zimbabwe has also endorsed the COMESA Gender Policy which fosters gender equality and equity at all levels of regional incorporation and cooperation.

On the other hand, nationally, Zimbabwe has made significant developments in amending and enacting legislations to advance the gender equality and equity objective. These include the Maintenance Act (1999), Administration of Estate Act (1997), Education Act (2004), Labour Act (Chapter 28.01), Domestic Violence Act (2007) among some others. Moreover, the new Zimbabwean Constitution adopted in 2013 is also widely acknowledged for its commitment to gender equality. These policies and legislative framework and the prevailing social, economic and political developments provide a firm basis to pursue gender equality and equity defined in the National Gender Policy. The introduction of the Ministry of Women Affairs, Gender and Community Development has been welcomed as a positive development towards the empowerment of rural women. This ministry works closely with the Victim Friendly Unit (VFU) department, a section that was formed within the Zimbabwe Republic Police to assist victims of gender-based violence. The department of social services has also been known for complementing the efforts by the Ministry of Women Affairs, Gender and Community Development to promote gender-related programmes.

The National Gender Policy and other actions which were taken by the government and other programmes mainly from the non-governmental organisations have empowered women in Zimbabwe to the extent of having them participating in the economic mainstreams. Non-governmental organisations conduct some training and workshops in order to impart to women leadership skills in order for them to be more confident and influential so that they can be leaders in organisations and also in the society. The efforts from the government and the NGOs have seen women taking part in politics; for example, there are a lot of women who are members of parliament and some are ministers. Women are also participating in the critical sections of the economy for example in mining and a lot of women have managed to be in top and influential positions in many companies. Besides the above overview of efforts at trying to enhance the role of women by the government in the country will briefly look at some of the achievements spearheaded by government in detail in post-independent Zimbabwe.

### *3.2.1 Administration of Estates Act (1997)*

Amendment made surviving spouse heir and not the eldest son as was before, which discriminated against women. This is an act to consolidate and amend the law relating to the administration of the estates of deceased persons, minors, mentally disordered or defective persons and persons absent from Zimbabwe, and to provide for the control of monies belonging to persons whose whereabouts are unknown. One of the problems solved by this act was the unfair distribution of wealth after the husband dies. Before, there was discrimination against serving women (spouse) who would end up losing some of the basic properties after the death of the husband.

### *3.2.2 National Gender Policy (from 2004)*

Through the Ministry of Women Affairs, Community, Small and Medium Enterprise Development, the Government of Zimbabwe supports the promotion of gender equality across all government programmes, using the National Gender Policy (NGP). The NGP which was launched in 2004 places strong emphasis on gender equality and equity and envisions a gender-just society in which men and women enjoy equity, and benefit as equal partners in the development of the country. Establishment of the Ministry of Women Affairs, Gender and Community Development (MWAGCD) in 2005, from initially being a Department in the Ministry of National Affairs at independence in 1980, is a notable achievement. The Ministry is dedicated to elevating the status of women, youth, children, disadvantaged men and other gender groups. The NGP is an overarching instrument to guide the implementation of all gender-sensitive legislation and socio-economic policies and programmes. The policy is designed to redress the imbalances in decision making and political positions by increasing women's representation to 52%.

The National Gender Policy from 2004 outlined strategies for addressing the main problem of violence against women and gender-based violence.

The main objectives of this policy mainly are to:

- Mainstream gender issues into all sectors in order to eliminate all negative economic, social and cultural practices that impede equality and equity of the sexes.
- Strengthen links between government, non-governmental organisations and the private sector in mainstreaming of gender in the respective sectors.
- Develop, maintain and provide gender-sensitive information and gender-disaggregated data for use in planning and project implementation at all levels and in all sectors.
- Promote equal and equitable access, control and ownership of resources in order to address gender inequalities.
- Promote equal advancement of women and men in all sectors.
- Create equal opportunities for women and men in decision making in all areas and at all levels.
- Promote the projection of both women and men's efforts and contributions in national development.
- Establish the institutional framework to ensure implementation of the gender policy as well as the monitoring and evaluation of its impact.
- Strengthen the institutional and legal capacity to deal with gender violence, inheritance and land property rights.

From this came the Domestic Violence Act stated below. This was a specific act addressing the problem of domestic violence. The rising domestic violence cases in the society prompted to the crafting of the act.

### *3.2.3 Domestic Violence Act (2007)*

Under this act, abuse derived from any cultural or customary rites or practices that discriminate against or degrade women, such as forced virginity testing, female genital mutilation, pledging of women and girls for purposes of appeasing spirits, abduction, child marriages, forced marriages and forced wife inheritance, and other such practices are prohibited. Prior to enactment of the DVA, violence in the home was treated as common assault or dismissed as domestic affairs and not criminalised. Women were thus vulnerable to abuse.

### 3.2.4 *Constitution of Zimbabwe (2013)*

Zimbabwe's Constitution provides a strong legal framework for the promotion and attainment of gender equality and women's empowerment. Chapter 4 of the Bill of Rights states that all customs, traditions and cultural practices that infringe on the rights of women are to that extent void. Section 17 notably compels the state to ensure gender balance and fair representation of disadvantaged groups, and promotion of women's participation in all spheres of society on the basis of equality with men. Section 56 provides a strong framework for the protection and promotion of the rights of women and men, girls and boys in Zimbabwe. It recognises the equality of all persons and goes further to explicitly outlaw discrimination on the grounds of sex or gender.

### 3.2.5 *Zimbabwe Gender Commission (2015)*

Section 245 of the Constitution of Zimbabwe provides for the establishment of the Gender Commission, the main function of which is to monitor gender equality issues; to investigate possible violations of rights relating to gender discrimination; to advise public and private institutions on steps to ensure gender equality; to secure appropriate redress where rights relating to gender have been violated; and to do everything necessary to promote gender equality. The Gender Commission commenced operations in 2015.

### 3.2.6 *Regional and International Protocols on Gender Equality*

Zimbabwe is part of key regional and international human rights instruments protecting and promoting gender equality in general, and the empowerment of women and girls in particular. These include 1965 Convention on the Elimination of all Forms of Racial Discrimination (CERD); 1979 Convention on the Elimination of all Forms of Discrimination Against Women—CEDAW; Protocol to the African Charter on the Rights of Women in Africa; Southern Africa Development Community (SADC) Gender and Development Protocol (including its Addendum on Prevention and Eradication of Violence Against Women and Children); Beijing Platform for Action; Universal Declaration of Human Rights; International Convention on Economic, Social and Cultural Rights; (vii) Convention on Civil and Political Rights (CCPR); Equal Remuneration Convention (ERC); Protocol to the African Charter on Human and People's Rights on the Rights of Women 2005 (the Maputo Protocol); Millennium Declaration of 2000; and United Nations Sustainable Development Goals (SDGs).

### 3.2.7 Gender Focal Persons

The establishment of Gender Focal Persons (GFPs) in all line ministries, departments and agencies, supported by the MWAGCD through capacity building programmes, has been another positive impact of the gender policy on mainstreaming gender in the country. GFPs are at director levels in the ministries and are responsible for mainstreaming gender in all policies, programmes and projects in their various sectors.

### 3.2.8 Quota System (Women's Proportional Representation in Parliament)

Under the Millennium Development Goals (MDG 3), now the Sustainable Development Goals (SDG 5), one target is to increase the proportion of seats held by women in national parliaments. Section 124 (b) of the Constitution of Zimbabwe provides for the women quota system of 60 seats in parliament which are given to each political party based on their tally of votes in the House of Assembly elections for each province. The goal is to increase numbers of women in parliament thus empowering women and moving towards gender equality. This has been hailed as an achievement and most are calling for extension of the quota system post its expiration in 2023.

### 3.2.9 Financial Inclusion of Women

United Nations (2007) defines financial inclusion as access to credit saving and payment services to everyone for all bankable people and firms and that inclusive finance does not require that everyone is eligible to use each of the services but should be able to choose them if desired. The female population in the sub-Saharan Africa stood at 50.01% for the year 2011. According to the Zimbabwe National Statistics Agency (Zimstat) in its recent national population census of 2012, a female population stood at around 6.74 million against a male population of about 6.23 million. These statistics clearly indicate the population of female is more than that of males in Zimbabwe and in the global context. However, in Africa when it comes to the involvement of women in financial transactions reverse is true. According to the Centre for Financial Inclusion reports, less than 30% of women in the sub-Saharan Africa hold an account with formal financial institution while only a 15% of the female population have saved with a financial institution in 2012. Access to financial services has remained limited especially to the rural compared to urban populace. The RBZ's Monetary Policy (2013) states that access to financial services remains a challenge for the marginalised Zimbabwean communities, particularly in remote parts of the country.

Despite the above limitation of women being not financially included, Zimbabwe has strived to put in place the structures and institutions that promote women's participation in the financial sector. The Zimbabwe's traceable effort to improve woman's financial inclusion started in 2007 when the RBZ introduced a Financial Inclusion Framework. This was followed by the launching of the National Financial Inclusion Strategy in 2016. This has provided a significant stride in improving the low financial inclusion level in the economy. To increase the financial inclusion for women, the National Financial Inclusion Strategy is focusing among others on the following interferences:

(a) The establishment of dedicated Woman Entrepreneur Desks at banking institutions,
(b) Increasing women's awareness of their legal rights regarding property ownership,
(c) Raising awareness of financial products and financial services for women through the National Financial Literacy Framework/strategy and
(d) Building the capacity of financial institutions to better serve women entrepreneurs.

RBZ has established a Credit Registry and Collateral Registry to strengthen the country's credit and collateral infrastructure to improve the availability of credit information and increase formal financial intermediation. These registries are particularly useful for women and micro, medium and small enterprises (MSMEs) because they promote them to keep track of their operations and to access more loans with the types of collateral instruments and assets they possess, such as movable properties. The RBZ has also licensed the country's first women-centred bank. Besides the Women's Bank, the Empower Bank was formed which basically caters for the empowerment of youth and women by financing different business enterprises. The bank was formed with the main purpose of providing social and financial solutions to the financially excluded population with greater focus on youth.

Through the Women Finance and Development Thematic Working Group of the National Financial Inclusion Strategy, various financial literacy programmes for women are being rolled out that leverage financial technology and innovation, as well as social media platforms. These have enabled banks and other institutions to reach out to many women, girls, MSMEs and other disadvantaged groups. The MSME Thematic Group of the NFIS is also dedicated to addressing the specific needs and challenges of MSMEs, including women-owned enterprises. Other financial inclusion strategies include low-cost bank accounts, the establishment of a Credit Guarantee Scheme and the licensing and support for Savings and Credit Cooperative Societies (SACCOs), which primarily serve women (Tarinda, 2019).

SACCOs are crucial in meeting the financial inclusion objectives. According to Tarinda (2019), the number of licensed SACCOs in Zimbabwe, of which women, MSMEs and youth are among the largest beneficiaries, increased to 436 by the end of December 2017. At the same time, savings deposits mobilised through SACCOs increased by 3.81% from $13.27 million in 2016 to $13.62 million in 2017. Total loans issued to SACCO clients also increased, from $11.10 million in 2016 to $11.19

million in 2017 (Tarinda, 2019). This shows the improvement in improving the financial inclusion for woman in Zimbabwe.

## 3.3 Management of HIV/AIDS Prevalence

The ravaging impact of HIV/AIDS on weak economies of most developing countries has been profound. Women in particular those of SSA where Zimbabwe is located are the hardest hit by HIV/AIDS as summarised by Ramjee and Daniels (2013) in Mahuni (2020):

> Thirty years since the discovery of HIV, the HIV pandemic in sub-Saharan Africa accounts for more than two thirds of the world's HIV infections. Southern Africa remains the region most severely affected by the epidemic. Women continue to bear the brunt of the epidemic with young women infected almost ten years earlier compared to their male counterparts.

Between independence and the mid-1990s, Zimbabwe had one of the strongest economies and health systems in southern Africa. Lately, the country's health sector has been facing numerous challenges including a shortage of skilled professionals and healthcare staff; poor infrastructure—ill equipped hospitals with many lacking functional laundry machines, kitchen equipment, boilers and a lack of essential medicines and commodities. The system breakdown has seen outbreaks such as exacerbated by cholera around 2008 difficult to manage.

The deterioration in Zimbabwe's healthcare services coincided with a fall in demand for services, following the introduction of user fees. These fees, which are often applied in an ad hoc way and so vary from provider to provider, act as a barrier to basic health services for many of the most vulnerable people in Zimbabwe. Government policy is to provide free-of-charge health services for pregnant and lactating mothers, children under five and those aged 60 years and over, but the policy has proved to be difficult to implement. Currently, in the absence of substantial government financial support, user fees provide the main income for many healthcare facilities, enabling them to provide at least the minimum service.

In spite of the turmoil of the years, the healthcare system has scored significantly in the management of HIV/AIDS prevalence. Government in partnership with various stakeholders has made milestones in the fight against HIV/AIDS over the years. Despite a harsh economic climate, Zimbabwe reduced HIV prevalence from 29% in 1997 to 16% in 2007, largely due to community awareness and behaviour change.

Zimbabwe offers free HIV testing services through the New Start Centre; this encourages a lot of citizens to get tested and be aware of their HIV status. The New Start Centre also offers a lot of counselling and education to both the positive and negative people so that they can take precautions which will help to lower the prevalence rate. There are also a lot of awareness campaigns which are funded by both the government and the non-governmental organisations; these campaigns cover both the towns and the rural areas and their aim is to influence the behaviour change to the Zimbabwean citizens so as to curb the spread of HIV/AIDS. These awareness campaigns also aim at fighting stigmatisation of people living with HIV; it ensures that the societies accept each other and live together without stigma. Sex education was introduced to the primary and secondary education curriculum; these faced a lot of criticism but it has yielded a lot of benefits towards fighting the HIV as children grow up aware of the disease and they are taught how to behave. Zimbabwean government also offers free antiretroviral drugs (ARVs) to all the HIV-positive citizens. This has saved a lot of lives as people are now able to live a long life with HIV/AIDS.

In the decade following independence in 1980, Zimbabwe experienced some of the most rapid improvements in HNP indicators in all of sub-Saharan Africa. Infant mortality declined from 90 per thousand in 1980 to 53 per thousand in 1988. Household incomes increased only modestly during this period, however, suggesting that the government's strong emphasis on basic health and family planning services, health education and community outreach, bolstered by a strong focus on prevention, was responsible for the improvements. In the 1990s, health and health service indicators stagnated or declined under the combined burdens of AIDS, economic crisis and drought, although fertility continued to decline. After a decade of decline, both infant and adult mortalities are increasing, as are opportunistic infections such as tuberculosis. Although economic crisis may have a role in weakening the health system, these increases in mortality are primarily attributable to AIDS. Despite HIV/AIDS is best addressed through prevention and behaviour change, declining per capita health spending and growing demands for curative care have weakened the preventive focus that characterised the successful programmes of the 1980s.

In Zimbabwe in 2018:

- 1,300,000 people were living with HIV.
- HIV incidence per 1000 uninfected which is the number of new HIV infections among the uninfected population over one year among all people of all ages was 2.79.
- HIV prevalence, the percentage of people living with HIV among adults (15–49 years), was 12.7%.
- 38,000 people were newly infected with HIV.
- 22,000 people died from an AIDS-related illness.

There has been progress in the number of AIDS-related deaths since 2010, with a 60% decrease, from 54,000 deaths to 22,000 deaths. The number of new HIV infections has also decreased by 40%, from 62,000 to 38,000 in the same period.

The 90–90–90 targets had a vision that, by end of 2020, 90% of people living with HIV should be knowing their HIV status, 90% of people who know their HIV-positive status should be accessing treatment and 90% of people on treatment will have suppressed viral loads. Zimbabwe's health system is working tirelessly to ensure that it reaches the 90–90–90 target. In terms of all people living with HIV, reaching the 90–90–90 targets means that 81% of all people living with HIV are on treatment and 73% of all people living with HIV are virally suppressed.

Currently 90% of people living with HIV know their status while 88% of people living with HIV were on treatment. Of all adults aged 15 years and over living with

HIV, 89% are on treatment, while 76% of children aged 0–14 years living with HIV are on treatment.

Ninety-four per cent of pregnant women living with HIV have access to antiretroviral medicine to prevent transmission of the virus to their baby, preventing 11,000 new HIV infections among newborns. Early infant diagnosis which is the percentage of HIV-exposed infants tested for HIV before eight weeks of age stood at 63% in 2018.

Zimbabwe introduced self-HIV testing as another way to increase testing, particularly among hard-to-reach groups. In 2015, Population Services International and UNITAID began HIV Self-Testing Africa (STAR), a four-year project to scale up self-testing in Zimbabwe, Malawi and Zambia.

Through STAR, close to 1 million self-testing kits were distributed in Zimbabwe by 2019. Interim results published in 2017 suggest STAR is working; 20% of those using self-testing kits were first-time testers, 39% were aged between 16 and 24 and 35% were adult men. This implies that the number of men testing for HIV was improved through this programme. Moreover, there are other programmes which were used by Zimbabwe in order to manage the HIV prevalence; this includes the voluntary male medical circumcision and the door-to-door HIV testing.

The government has strengthened the institutions towards the management of HIV/AIDS. For instance, the establishment of the National AIDS Council (NAC) with the support of local and international organisations is providing effective leadership and responsive stewardship for the national HIV and AIDS response. For example, the gender policy for the NAC gives a framework within which institutional policies, strategies and programmes mainstream gender and women's empowerment into the national response to the HIV and AIDS epidemic. The NAC also engage the youth in Zimbabwe in implementing sexuality education programmes. This includes discussions between NAC and hundreds of young people in Zimbabwe to build up momentum towards the implementation of sexuality education programmes in schools.

The government through the National Aids Council also introduced the trust fund, also known as the AIDS Levy which was effectively introduced in 2000. The trust fund is pool of resources collected through a parliament special tax act, and all formal employers and their employees in Zimbabwe contribute 3% of their income towards it. For instance, in 2011, the government collected US $26 million through the trust fund. This has made a very significant and substantive results especially in the provision of antiretroviral drugs. The AIDS Levy is considered a resourceful method to ensure sustainability and reducing aid dependency in the national response to the disease.

The Government of Zimbabwe is promoting the fighting against HIV/AIDS through many other initiatives. Another initiative was through the establishment of wellness programmes in the private sector. The government launched the Zimbabwe Private Sector HIV/AIDS and Wellness Coordination Board (ZIPSHAW). This board oversees the implementations of HIV and wellness programmes in the working environments in the private sector in a bid to reduce the spread of non-communicable diseases and HIV in the working environments. This initiative in the private sector is one of the strategies the government started to close the gap between the private and public sectors in fighting the disease.

Zimbabwe also commemorates the World AIDS day on the first day of December of each year. It is an international day dedicated to raising awareness of the AIDS pandemic caused by the spread of HIV infection and mourning those who have died of the disease worldwide. Zimbabwe is one country that commemorates this day together with non-governmental organisations, and individuals around the world, often with education on AIDS prevention and control.

In summary, Zimbabwe has done much progress in controlling and managing the spread of HIV/AIDS. The government has through NAC initiated many strategies and programmes to effectively manage the pandemic.

## 3.4 Milestones in Human Development: Remarkable Literacy Levels

Soon after independence, the new government committed itself to democratising the education system such that education was treated as a basic human right. The first major reform was the merging of the separate education systems to remove anomalies and inequalities in the education system. The thrust was to put emphasis on human development which would in turn foster economic development. At independence, the government adopted a socialist principle: 'Growth with equity' to redress the inequalities in access to education and other basic needs such as health services. The government's socialist principle was perceived through Karl Marx's concept of 'polytechnic education' whose main objective was to link mental and manual work and produce totally developed individuals. It had been observed that the inherited colonial education system placed undue emphasis and value on paid employment and white-collar jobs. It failed to instil good work habits and ethics and did not prepare school leavers for the demanding world of work. The new government was thus preoccupied with trying to address this anomaly, as much has been explored in this chapter leading to remarkable literacy levels.

The current education system in Zimbabwe has four stages, namely early education; primary education; secondary education; and tertiary education. In the early education, pre-schools are directed by the Early Childhood Development (ECD) system under the Ministry of Primary and Secondary Education. Early childhood education is offered for children from the ages of three to five through the ECD. Zimbabwe's education system mandates seven years of primary school, encompassing Grades 1 to 7.

Secondary education is made up of two cycles, the General Certificate of Education, or Ordinary Level, for four years and the General Certificate of Education Advanced Level, or Advanced Level, for two years. The tertiary sector of education is operated by the Ministry of Higher and Tertiary Education which includes universities, technical, polytechnic and teacher training colleges and various vocational

**Table 3.1** Literacy rate by age group and sex: 2017

| Age group | Male | Female | Total |
|---|---|---|---|
| 15–19 | 98 | 98 | 98 |
| 20–24 | 97 | 98 | 98 |
| 25–29 | 98 | 98 | 98 |
| 30–34 | 98 | 98 | 98 |
| 35–39 | 98 | 96 | 97 |
| 40–44 | 98 | 97 | 97 |
| 45–49 | 98 | 93 | 95 |
| 50–54 | 96 | 89 | 92 |
| 55–59 | 93 | 80 | 85 |
| 60–64 | 91 | 79 | 84 |
| 65 + | 82 | 66 | 73 |

*Source* ZIMSTAT (2018)

training centres. Zimbabwe had only one university when it attained its independence which is the University of Zimbabwe (formerly University of Rhodesia).

The National Council for Higher Education was established in 1990 as a measure of quality assurance of higher education in Zimbabwe. Increasing access to education in recent decades has increased the number of learning institutions in the country as we pointed earlier. For example, eight more universities were established between 1999 and 2005. The Zimbabwe Council for Higher Education (ZIMCHE) was formed in 2006 as another measure to guarantee quality and accreditation for university education. As of 2019, there were twenty registered universities (fourteen public and six private).

Comparatively, Zimbabwe has performed well among other states in Africa due to policies around education resulting in remarkable literacy levels.

Table 3.1 presents disaggregated statistics along age and gender parameters. Over 95% literacy rate are the youths aged between fifteen and twenty-four years. The adult literacy rate which is fifty years and above is 88.7% and the elderly literacy rate which is sixty-five years and above is 81.1%.

In terms of the physical increase in the number of schools across the country, Fig. 3.1 gives an overview. Thus, the number of both primary and secondary schools has been increasing in Zimbabwe over the years. This is done to improve education availability to ensure coverage of remote areas.

### *3.4.1 Tertiary Education*

Zimbabwe's tertiary education comprises of colleges, polytechnics and universities. Before 1980, there were nine teacher training colleges, two polytechnic colleges and one state university. After independence, the country now has fourteen state

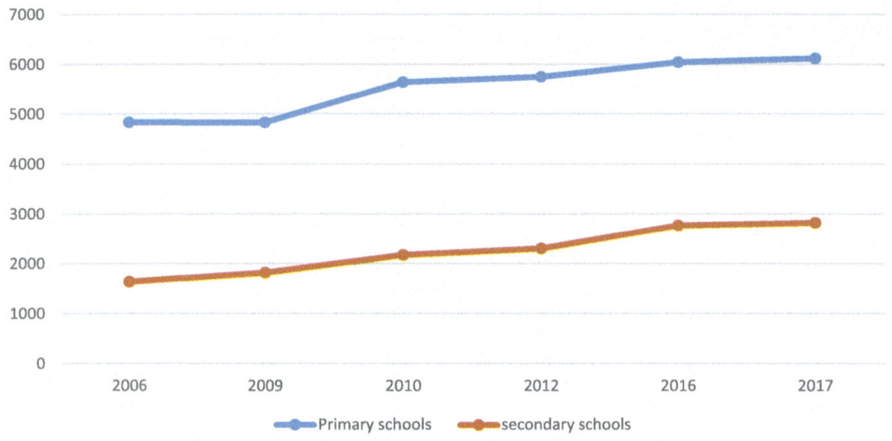


**Fig. 3.1** Primary and secondary education schools in Zimbabwe. *Source* ZIMSTAT (2018)

universities, seven private. Two major cities of the country Bulawayo and Harare now have institutions for industrial training, a very encouraging development. For instance, the increase in universities has itself resulted in increase in the enrolment in tertiary education as shown in Fig. 3.2.

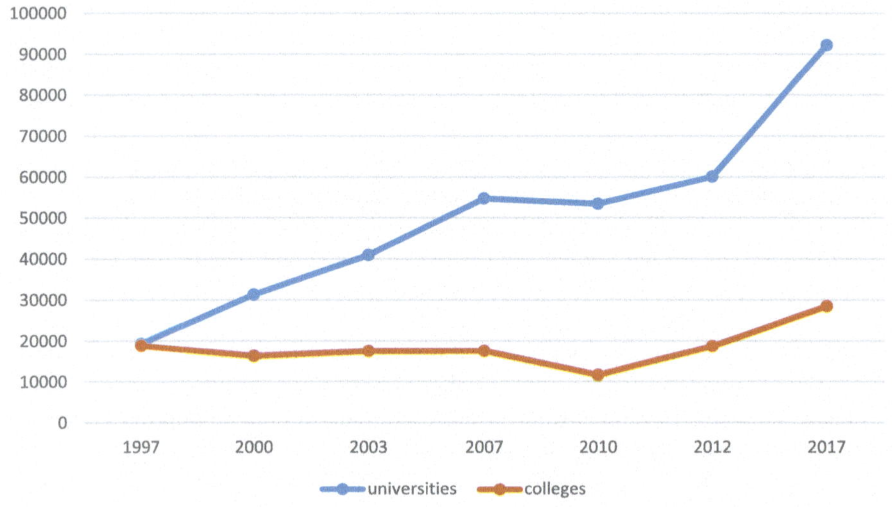


**Fig. 3.2** Enrolment in universities and colleges. *Source* ZIMSTAT (2018)

### 3.4.2 *Vocational Education*

After the National Manpower Survey (Zimbabwe, 1981) which was carried out after independence, the government realised a shortage of skills in technical fields in the economy which was mainly due to limited training infrastructure. Scarcity of semi-skilled labour was one of the major problems which needed to be addressed. As a way of addressing this problem, the government established the technical and vocational education and training (TVET) colleges. Between 1980 and 1990, the Government of Zimbabwe had already established additional five technical colleges which were later upgraded to polytechnics in 2001. As a way of facilitating the process of upgrading semi-skilled personnel through trade testing, two vocational training centres were created at independence and these were Msasa in Harare and Westgate in Bulawayo. Trade testing done by the government paved a way for the recognition of skills obtained via on the job training, non-formal programmes and through the youth skills training centres and vocational training centres.

To conclude the discourse on remarkable literacy levels, it is also important to note that English is the major medium of instruction in the education system of Zimbabwe from as early as ECD through tertiary. Major local languages as well as other minor languages are taught also in institutions. The strength in English language has made it easier for Zimbabweans to be able to be absorbed in job markets beyond our borders due to better language skills.

## 3.5 Zimbabwe—The People and the Environment

Over 40 years one other thing we celebrate as Zimbabwe is our identity as a people as well as the rich environment bestowed upon us by God. Identity of people is significant as well as the environment from which they come from. Through identity, a nation becomes unique in its own way(s). In turn, this says a lot about different facets of their day-to-day life experiences—be it social, political or economic. Briefly we explain how this is worthy celebrating despite the economic turmoil of the past decades.

Through our identity, there are a number of virtues about us as Zimbabweans which we always treasure. They have contributed to also carving the journey we are still travelling. Zimbabwe's population is estimated to be over 17 million and it is characterised by a lot of different people with diverse cultures and backgrounds which makes a lot of tourists to enjoy interacting with those people. Furthermore, Zimbabwe has generally been a peaceful country due to our peace-loving nature as a people making it a destination of choice for tourists across the globe. Zimbabwe has been in general a peace-loving country especially when comparing to other countries around the continent. In the global state of peace, Zimbabwe was ranked 124 in the world (Global Peace Index, 2018). Despite being ranked low in the world, in the region the country is relatively peaceful, for instance in 2018, it was ranked a peaceful country better than the region's economic giant South Africa.

Besides the hospitable people, Zimbabwe has a lot of beautiful environs resulting in the flocking in of tourists over the years. Tourism industry is the major contributor to the Zimbabwean gross domestic product (GDP) accounting for an annual average of around 7.2% in 2018. A number of natural phenomena and wildlife contribute to the tourism profile of the country. For instance, the Victoria Falls is classified as the Natural Heritage under UNESCO world heritage site is known to be among the five natural wonders of the world attracting thousands of tourists annually.

In Manicaland, a province on the eastern side of the country, there are also the Eastern Highlands which are a series of mountainous areas near the border with Mozambique. These highlands stretch from Nyanga in the north with the highest peak in Zimbabwe, Mount Nyangani at 2593 m is located there as well with the Bvumba Mountains further south and the magnificent quartzite Chimanimani range is the southernmost slope. Mt. Binga is the highest of the Chimanimani peaks but situated on the Mozambican side. It straddles both Mozambique and Zimbabwe. The endemic species of this trans-frontier park attract scientists and hikers from all over the world. Views from all of the Nyanga Mountains are famed that places as far away as 70 km are visible.

Zimbabwe is unique in Africa for its large number of medieval era city ruins built in a unique dry-stone style. The most famous of these are the Great Zimbabwe ruins in Masvingo which survive from the Kingdom of Zimbabwe and that's where the country got its name from. Great Zimbabwe ruins attract a lot of tourists from both local and abroad; everyone wants to have a glimpse of the rock structures which were built with no mortar. Other ruins include Khami Ruins in Bulawayo, Dhlodhlo and Naletale.

There are also Matobo Hills. It is an area of granite kopjes and wooded valleys located some 35 km south of Bulawayo, southern Zimbabwe. The Hills were formed over 2000 million years ago with granite being forced to the surface; this has eroded to produce smooth rocks and broken kopjes, strewn with boulders and interspersed with thickets of vegetation. Mzilikazi, founder of the Ndebele nation, gave the area its name, meaning 'Bald Heads'. They have become famous and a tourist attraction because Cecil John Rhodes, famous for his vision that led to foundation of Rhodesia, and other early white pioneers like Leander Starr Jameson, Major Allan Wilson, and most of the members of the Shangani Patrol are buried in these hills at another site named World's View. The famous three balancing rocks which are used as the face of the Reserve Bank of Zimbabwe (RBZ) are also found in this area.

There are a lot of natural environments and monuments in Zimbabwe which are majestic tourist attractions and the Government of Zimbabwe through the Zimbabwe Tourism Authority (ZTA) is working hard to ensure that this environment is more hospitable. Tourism was among the fastest growing sectors of the Zimbabwean economy contributing significantly to the country's Gross Domestic Product (GDP) during the period 1980–1998. The number of tourists arrival dropped after the land reform but the tourism industry in Zimbabwe has got the potential for growth and

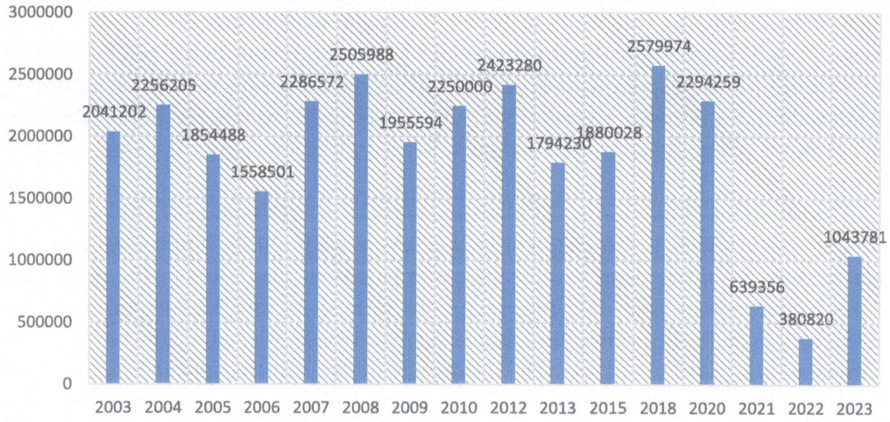


**Fig. 3.3** Tourist arrivals in Zimbabwe. *Source* Zimbabwe Tourism Authority (2023)

the industry currently employs approximately 300,000 people directly and indirectly. The Government of Zimbabwe through its Short-Term Emergency Recovery Programme (STERP) identified as an economic recovery platform with tourism being one of the key economic drivers with potential to contribute towards the country's turn around. The government of national unity (GNU) that was formed in 2009 also brought about confidence in destination Zimbabwe.

Zimbabwe often receives an average of two million tourists annually. Economic conditions and the political environment sometimes affect the visits. There was a decline on the visits to below two million in 2012, 2013 and 2014 but the visits started increasing again as from 2015. Zimbabwe has a potential of attracting a lot of tourists because of its natural aesthetic environments. Figure 3.3 gives us a glimpse of tourist arrivals to Zimbabwe from 2003 to 2023 showing the potential the sector has. Despite the tourism sector affected by the Covid-19 pandemic, Fig. 3.3 generally shows a relatively uptrend in tourist arrivals in the country. Zimbabwe's tourism is still in the recovery stage since the Covid-19 pandemic.

Zimbabweans also value family life. Does this matter? The reader will understand why as we shall explain. While in some countries and cultures the nuclear family is more important in Zimbabwe the extended family is also valued so much. You do not look after your immediate family members alone, instead you also extend help to even not so close relatives; this is our way of life.

As result of value we attach to family life, as a people we are also benevolent. Zimbabweans enjoy sharing and we mostly show compassion to the weaker members of the family/society. Moreover, even if you venture into the diaspora and strike even minimum fortune barely enough to just keep your head above the water you always look back and chip in to those members back home. This has mattered a lot for us. Our ship at times has been on the brink of sinking due to violent and often turbulent economic storms threatening to eject almost everyone out. In addition, the turbulence has often stripped people of basic decency. At the eleventh hour, the strong diasporian community due to the way we have been nurtured as Zimbabweans has always stepped in to restore dignity for people. Many locals continue to be clothed and fed by millions of diaspora friends and relatives. The numerous turbulence episodes which sadly have become a *normal* way of life have been weathered in part through interventions of the diaspora due to the value we place on family life anchored on benevolence.

In line with the above virtue, Zimbabweans also are a resilient and patient people. As indicated in Chap. 1, Zimbabwe is special. As a result of this, it provides a unique environment requiring dexterity for special adaptation, that's where the resilience of the people comes from. Despite numerous turbulence episodes experienced by the country even to the point of breaking, the majority of Zimbabweans have shown stamina, courage and big hearts. The turbulence of the years has pushed many under the deep waters of humiliation and deprivation as raw poverty pounced on the majority of hapless ordinary people. No matter how many times this has happened, they always come out smiling. It is very common sight to find Zimbabweans laughing off problems the turbulence has brought to them. This has seen for instance comedy industry slowly becoming popular. Subjects such as politics, poverty in the ghettos and general suffering are often tackled in a satirical way. The themes being explored are in many cases easy to relate to most people. It is unfortunate however that some people often misconstrue the resilience of the people to be a sign of cowardice. Whether this is true or false, it is a debate for another platform, Zimbabweans are nevertheless a resilient and patient people.

Zimbabweans are also hard workers who have achieved a lot and gaining international recognition besides academics. Fields such as arts, sports and athletics have seen a number of Zimbabweans excelling. For instance, Peter Ndlovu is among one of the players from Africa to make waves in Europe. On the other hand, Kirsty Coventry has been successful at Olympics scooping a number of medals for the country. The late musician Dr. Oliver Mtukudzi was one of the greatest musicians to grace the land which saw him touring the globe and earning him ambassadorial role with UN. His music helped to hoist our flag high as it spoke a lot about our values and culture as Zimbabweans. His music tackled subjects such as polygamy, child marriages, leadership, hard work, hardship and general relevant social commentary. The musician also made numerous collaborations with various artists nationally and internationally to show the versatility Zimbabweans have. Sculptors also such as Dominic Benhura have achieved global fame through stone curving in the process lifting high the profile of the country.

## 3.6 Conclusion

This chapter presented a thorough examination of Zimbabwe's progress over the last forty years. While there are a lot of these achievements, for the purposes of this book we focused on only four, including milestones in managing HIV/AIDS, participation of women among others. For example, participation of women helped to increase their participation in the mainstream economy. The chapter explored also the important traits of Zimbabweans including value placed on the importance of family hood and also extending help to those in need beyond one's family members. All this has shaped our being as a people. In addition, it has also helped as a coping strategy among people in the midst of challenges faced. The next chapter presents the policy execution dilemmas over the years.

## References


Global Peace Index. (2018). Measuring Peace in a complex World.

Mahuni, K. (2020). Climate change 'proofing' Sub Saharan African women, a step towards sustainable development. *International Economic Association (IEA).*

Ramjee, G., & Daniels, B. (2013). Women and HIV in sub-Saharan Africa. *AIDS Research and Therapy, 10*, 1–9. https://doi.org/10.1186/1742-6405-10-30

Tarinda, S. (2019). Gender, women's economic empowerment and financial inclusion in Zimbabwe. *Alliance Financ Inclusion*, 1–22.

United Nations. (2007). Press conference on best practices for financial inclusion.

Zimbabwe National Statistics Agency. (2018). *Education Report 2017*. https://www.zimstat.co.zw/

Zimbabwe Tourism Authority. (2023). *Tourism trends and statistics*. Zimbabwe Tourism Authority.

# Chapter 4
# Policy Execution Dilemmas Over the Years

## 4.1 Introduction

The desire to see lives of people improving by government of Zimbabwe has been witnessed through various policies and programmes which have been coined over the past four decades. Beautiful policies have been crafted intending to spur growth and development just like other economies worldwide. However, fully succeeding on whatever policy or programme in the wake of turbulence has proven not easy. In this chapter we discuss a number of policies and programmes which have been crafted to try to improve the economy. A brief analysis of the policies will conclude the discussions of this chapter.

## 4.2 Early Post-independence Policies of the 1980s Growth with Equity (1981)

The new Government faced the pressing challenge of reconstituting and realigning the inherited national policymaking structures in line with the new socio-politico-economic dispensation that had set in. The most notable government policy after independence was the Growth with Equity of 1981 whose aim was to achieve a sustained high rate of economic growth and speedy development in order to raise incomes and standards of living of all Zimbabwean citizens. The inherited economy was fraught with embedded inequalities in income and wealth distribution, with the agricultural, education, industrial and banking sectors among the most visibly affected. Against this background, the need to address inequalities and injustices wrought by yesteryear policies underpinned policymaking during the first decade. It also underlined the state-centric nature of policymaking in parastatal, agricultural, health, education, labour and social welfare sectors. The new government viewed itself first and foremost as the central instrument through which past imbalances were



K. Mahuni et al., *Zimbabwe's Economy*, Advances in African Economic, Social and Political Development, https://doi.org/10.1007/978-3-031-81588-1_4

redressed (Zhou & Zvoushe, 2012). Growth with equity sought to expand productive employment of rural peasants and urban workers.

The policy mainly focused on redistribution of wealth, expansion of rural infrastructure and redressing social and economic inequality including land reform. The economy recovered significantly in the early years of independence averaging 10% growth during 1980–82. This was mainly because the country had inherited one of the most structurally developed economies and effective state systems in Africa. At the time there were favourable domestic and external conditions, including the lifting of economic sanctions, motivation of overall demand in the economy with redistributive economic policies as well as the opening up of external markets. The Growth with Equity policy was also characterised by land resettlement on a willing-buyer willing-seller basis. Zhou and Masunungure (2006) observed that the first decade of redistributive policies witnessed marked improvements in access to health and education by the previously marginalised black majority as well as marked improvement in resource allocation. Health indicators such as life expectancy and infant mortality improved. The free for all basic education policy saw a rapid growth in schools and enrolment, in both primary and secondary schools by 1990.

**Problems with Growth with Equity**

One underlying assumption of Growth with Equity was that the economy would grow at a fast rate enough to generate sufficient revenue to fund national projects. This optimism was a result of the boom that was experienced from 1980 to 1982 due to excellent weather, lifting of sanctions, easy access to foreign aid and a decrease in defence expenditure. The economy experienced 11% growth in 1980 (Zhou & Masunungure, 2006). However, during the period from 1980 to 1990 the growth in social sectors was not matched with the growth in productive sectors. Reduced demand of Zimbabwean exports due to an overvalued currency, a decline in investment and capital formation as well as severe shortages of foreign currency combined to bring in recession towards the end of the decade. The arguments above show that the main assumptions, on which Growth with Equity was premised were unrealistic. The policies adopted were not sustainable as they drained the fiscus. Zhou and Masunungure (2006) pointed out that the socio-economic development goals could only be achieved through a subsidy policy that enabled parastatals to undertake and provide affordable services to the public. This removed the motivation to perform as poorly performing parastatals could be bailed out from treasury creating a government dependency culture in public enterprises.

The government also controlled the price of goods and services often setting them below the market levels and in the process making it difficult for public enterprises to cover their operating costs. This led to these public enterprises to be loss making entities all in the name of focusing on social issues even if they were not economical viable. By the late 1980s, the control regime was inhibiting the dynamism of the domestic economy and generating structural problems that were systematically undermining its economic and political sustainability. The rapid growth in civil service employment and spending on social services, drought relief and parastatals generated a chronic budget deficit, a high tax regime and a rapid increase in public debt.

## 4.3 Transitional National Development Plan (TNDP) (1981–83)

The TNDP policy was anchored on post-war reconstruction. The reconstruction agenda was generally achieved because at that time Zimbabwe was successfully recapitalised and integrated into the world economy (Nyoni, 2018). This plan focused on achieving social justice and equity. It called for a greater role by the state through creation of state enterprises (SEs) to implement government programmes, worker participation and social cooperation. At the core of this plan was the desire to accelerate economic growth through promotion of productive sectors. Government had a leading role to provide services and redistribution of resources to redress inherited inequities and imbalances and access to basic needs. Black people had limited capacity to meet these needs themselves. Employment and business opportunities were restricted; few people could develop the skills needed to prosper through own enterprise hence the state felt compelled to actively assist in the allocation of resources. Major successes of this era were on social services where primary education, for instance, was provided for free while secondary schooling was heavily subsidised with many schools being constructed.

**Problems with Transitional National Development Plan**

During the period of the TNDP, economic growth rates remained subdued, falling short of the target of 8%, largely due to low investment levels in the productive sectors, world recession and severe drought in the 1983–1984 agricultural seasons. The plan failed to address issues like equitable land redistribution and black empowerment, product beneficiation, fiscal restraint among other measures. The TNDP was largely a failure but to its credit it created over 150,000 jobs and enhanced agricultural production of small-scale communal land farmers (Mapuva, 2015). Due to the failure of the TNDP the government embarked on another policy to try and remedy the TNDP failures.

## 4.4 The First Five-Year National Development Plan (FFYNDP) (1986–1990)

The First Five-Year National Development Plan (FFYNDP) was formulated after comprehensive and detailed review of economic performance during the first five years of independence. During the period 1980–1985, the economy registered an average growth rate of around 5% compared to the target of 8% largely due to low levels of investment in the productive sectors. Inflation remained high during the period, averaging 13%, coupled with rising budget deficits. The overall domestic and external debt positions escalated concomitantly with budget deficits.

It is against this background that Government unveiled the First Five-Year National Development Plan targeting an average GDP growth of 5.1% per annum during the life span of the plan. The government experienced another severe drought during the 1986/1987 agricultural season that adversely reduced output for both rural and commercial farmers. Erratic economic performance coupled with the channelling of substantial amounts of resources in redressing social inequalities, which were characteristics of the Plan period, resulted in limited resources being available for productive public investment. Public investment expenditure as a proportion of GDP stagnated at less than 1% and was thus largely recurrent, with salaries and wages, interest on debt and transfer payments accounting for over 90% of total government expenditure. During the same period capital expenditure only accounted for 5% of total government expenditure. The manufacturing sector was the chief economic growth driver, followed by agriculture and the retail and hotel industry. During the period 1986–1990, the budget deficit remained high against a backdrop of substantial foreign financing. The economy was faced by internal and external imbalances reflected in relatively high inflation, high unemployment levels (around 30%) and high budget deficits.

The FFYNDP which aimed at 5.1% growth failed to achieve its goals as the average economic growth from 1980 to 1987 was 4.93 which prompted Nyoni (2018) to conclude that the first decade after independence was a failure in terms of policy. However, despite the challenges of the 1980s, Mumbengegwi and Mabugu (2002) were of the view that Zimbabwe stood out as one of the few African countries that registered growth rates comparable to those of other developing countries regardless of the controlled macroeconomic environment which prevailed a decade following its independence. Much of the economic policies adopted for the period 1980–1990 had origins in the preceding Rhodesian government which had adopted inward looking, import substituting policies in response to international economic sanctions and isolation.

### *4.4.1 Health Policy*

Zimbabwe's health policy was informed by two main factors. First, the health sector was characterised by inadequate health infrastructure, and provision of such consumed a considerable part of the available resources to the extent that government, by the mid to late 1980s, was financially hamstrung to effect a paradigm shift from curative to preventive health. Second, the rhetoric of socialism and the euphoria of independence had a bearing on health policy. Government considered healthcare provision as one avenue through which it could alleviate poverty and, therefore, decisions on health became entangled in the political cycle. Hammer and Berman (1995) argue that governments, trapped in five-year electoral cycles, are increasingly driven by short-term pressure and considerations.

The first health policy intervention is the Plan for equity in health which was implemented in 1980. The major drivers of this intervention were the dictates of the Alma Ata declaration of 1978, which emphasise the need for primary health care and that health care is a fundamental human right that needs to be prioritised as a social worldwide goal and the unacceptability of inequality in health care on both grounds. Additionally, the International Conference on Primary Health Care calls for urgent and effective national and international action to develop and implement primary health care throughout the world and particularly in developing countries.

The government of Zimbabwe implemented various programmes to deal with the aspects of equality, mortality human workforce, finance and service delivery among others. First, free health care was implemented in September 1980 especially to those earning less than Z$150, hospitals and healthcare building programmes. By June 1987, 224 rural health care has been completed as well as the number of provincial health care upgraded. Further, immunisation programmes against six killer diseases, and by 1984, percentage of children between 12 and 23 months fully immunised rose from 25 to 42 in rural areas and in urban areas rose from 56 to 80. National Nutrition programmes, Diarrhoea disease control programmes, National village health worker programmes and child spacing programmes were also implemented in the first decade under the Plan for equity in health. Under this policy, positive changes were noted particularly to mortality rate which reduced from estimated 120–220 per 1000 in 1980 to 83 per 1000 by 1983, with an estimate of 23%. Morbidity and Malnutrition were also reduced from 1980 to 1983. However, despite having positive outcomes, these programmes had implications particularly on budget. Health budget rose to 5.1% and doubled by 1982, preventive services risen from 7.9 in 1980 to 14% by 1986, the reason being that, the Plan required donor funding which contributed towards increase in foreign debt. Having realised this, another intervention had to be put in place as a remedy of the Plan for equity for by it the government fails short to realise equity as programmed.

### *4.4.2 Policy Implications of Health Policy*

Makochekanwa (2012) drew policy implications as, firstly, although the health policies are, on paper sound, the state need to intensify their implementation. The other policy implication is that the complexity of health delivery system in Zimbabwe, coupled with limited government resources to adequately intervene calls for collaborative work between government and all stakeholders working in this sector. Makochekanwa (2012) further recommended that the government should put in place strategies to lure back health professionals who left the country to come and work in the health facilities in the country. Government should also ask the help of well-wishers, friends and donors in addressing some of the challenges in the health sector including shortage of health personnel, drugs and problem of old or dysfunction medical equipment. In this instance, through liaising and soliciting for help from such organisations and/or donors as UNCEF and WHO.

In conclusion, in the decade following independence in 1980, Zimbabwe experienced some of the most rapid improvements in HNP indicators in all of Sub-Saharan Africa. Infant mortality declined from 90 per thousand in 1980 to 53 per thousand in 1988. Household incomes increased only modestly during this period, however, suggesting that the government's strong emphasis on basic health and family planning services, health education and community outreach, bolstered by a strong focus on prevention, was responsible for the improvements. Yet the government's failure to control the budget deficit and its financing of that debt by borrowing domestically at high-interest rates led to escalating interest payments. This mounting debt threatens to lead Zimbabwe into deeper economic crisis, and without a concerted effort at deficit reduction, it will further undermine the health sector (Johnston, 1999).

## 4.5 Economic Policies of the 1990s

### *4.5.1 Economic Structural Adjustment Programme [ESAP] (1991–1995)*

When it became apparent that the economy of Zimbabwe was not generating the much-awaited jobs, especially in the context of depressed investment, the government decided to adopt the World Bank and IMF prescribed ESAP in the year 1991 (Nyoni, 2018). The primary theme of ESAP was to transform the economy from being heavily regulated to liberalisation. ESAP's primary targets were to: achieve GDP growth of 5% during 1991–95; raise savings to 25% of GDP; raise investment to 25% of GDP; achieve export growth of 9% per annum; reduce the budget deficit from over 10% of GDP to 5% by 1995 and reduce inflation from 17.7 to 10% by 1995. The World Bank and IMF advised the government to liberalise all markets in order to achieve the targets set out in the ESAP policy framework.

### *4.5.2 Problems with ESAP*

Unfortunately, the performance of the economy under ESAP was not as expected and the results were far less than the planned targets. Due to the failure of ESAP, socio-economic ills such as poverty, unemployment and social unrests continued to exacerbate in Zimbabwe. There are a number of reasons why ESAP failed. The most important reason why ESAP had to fail was the absence of fiscal discipline on the part of the Zimbabwean government. Mumvuma et al. (2006) argued that the failure to consult with stakeholders was a mistake since there was no awareness about the policy reforms and therefore resulted in ignorance and lack of ownership on the part of many relevant interest groups.

### *4.5.3 Zimbabwe Programme for Economic and Social Transformation (ZIMPREST) (1996–2000)*

Most Zimbabweans were not satisfied with ESAP. In April 1998, ZIMPREST was launched and yet the policy was actually supposed to cover the period 1996–2000. This apparently means that when ZIMPREST was launched, it was already two years behind schedule. Basically, ZIMPREST sought to achieve a target average annual growth rate of GDP of 6%, create 42,200 new jobs in the formal sector per annum, per capita income growth of 3.4% and consumption growth of 4.4%. To surpass the minimum target growth, government was supposed to reduce the budget deficit from 10% to at most 5% of GDP, reduce inflation from over 20% to a single-digit level by the year 2000, achieve higher levels of savings and investment (an average of at least 23% of GDP), export growth of at least 9% per year and raise the health budget from the average allocation of 2% of GDP to at least 2.5%. Just like ESAP, ZIMPREST was not successful. While there are a number of reasons why ZIMPREST failed, lack of fiscal discipline, slowdown in global economic performance in 1998 as well as a sharp depreciation of the Zimbabwean dollar in 1998 greatly contributed to ZIMPREST's failure. Both ESAP and ZIMPREST lacked local ownership and were thus viewed as IMF and World Bank imposed.

## 4.6 Policies and Programmes (2000–2008)

### *4.6.1 Millennium Economic Recovery Programme (2000–2003) and National Economic Recovery Programme (2003–2006)*

When it became clear that both ESAP and ZIMPREST were useless economic blueprints, the government decided to unpack, the Millennium Economic Recovery Programme (MERP) early in 2000. MERP was basically hinged on the fiscal policy adjustment targets under ESAP, ZIMPREST and the Millennium Budget announced on 21 October 1999. At this juncture, it is imperative to remember that MERP was just a continuation of the commitments and targets of ESAP and ZIMPREST. The target of MERP, in line with the 2000 budget, was to reduce the budget deficit to 3.8% of GDP. MERP aimed at allocating at least 25% of total expenditures to capital projects. In apparent contrast, in the 2000 budget, the capital budget was only allocated 8% of total expenditures, down from 11% in 1999. Statistics indicate that the capital budget amounted to 4%, 8.1% and 11.7% in the years 2001, 2002 and 2003, respectively. After the government realised that MERP was not a good policy, in February 2003 the National Economic Revival Programme (NERP) was launched. The main objective of NERP was to provide humanitarian support in the face of a long-term drought that had already ensued in the year 2000. Both NERP and MERP failed largely due to loss of macroeconomic balance as a result of a highly constrained budget.

### 4.6.2 *Emergency Recovery Programme (STERP I)*

In February 2009, after the formation of the inclusive government in the context of an economy that had a myriad of socio-economic problems, the Short-Term Emergency Recovery Programme (STERP I) was launched. STERP I's goal was to stabilise the economy. It involved measures to reduce inflation, encourage savings and investment and laying the foundation for solid economic growth. It was during this period that the Zimbabwean dollar was demonetised and a basket of major trading currencies such as the USD, the SA Rand and the Batswana Pula became legal tender. The key objective of the STERP I was to resuscitate manufacturing activity and increase capacity utilisation levels from the low levels of approximately 5% in 2008. The economy has been facing severe challenges, with the annual real GDP growth suffering declines averaging 5.9% since 2004. Cumulatively, output declined by more than 40% during that period. The deepening economic crisis was reflected in sectoral performance, which followed the same trend. Since 2006, virtually all sectors recorded declines in output with agriculture, manufacturing and mining estimated to have declined by 7.3%, 73.3% and 53.3%, respectively in 2008. In 2012, average capacity utilisation in most industries is between 30 and 60% (Nyoni, 2018).

The major achievement of STERP I was the rapid reduction of inflation due to the adoption of multicurrency which helped ease inflationary pressures from an estimated rate of more than 1 billion per cent in December 2008 to -7% by December 2009. The other notable milestone of STERP I was the introduction of cash budget for Government to operate within available resources restrained expenditure overruns.

The short-term nature of STERP meant that some programmes and projects would not be fully implemented within the time frame of nine months and little support on donor funds to implement the programmes, hence the launch of STERP II to consolidate gains from the initial recovery efforts under STERP.

### 4.6.3 *Sterp II (2010–2012)*

This was launched on 23 December 2009 with a three-year macroeconomic policy and budget framework by the Ministry of Finance. After STERP I successfully stabilised the macroeconomy, STERP II was to facilitate sustainable rapid growth and further development of the economy. More broadly, STERP II sought to put a price tag on the 'critical financial investment' needed to restore the economy to 1997 levels, emerging with a grand total of US$45 billion of which $20 to $30 billion of this amount was needed over the three years to 2012. The objectives of STERP II were to:

- Stabilise and consolidate STERP I;
- Support for rapid growth and employment creation;
- Increase capacity utilisation in manufacturing: from 10% to above 60%;
- Encourage public and private investment; and
- Promote regional integration.

The impact of political will in fostering economic growth is well demonstrated in STERP II because its first 3 years were very successful as politicians worked together coherently to operationalise it. After embracing STERP II, inflation dramatically fell to single-digit levels and stabilised at below 5% by the end of the year of 2010. Capacity utilisation in the manufacturing sector increased from about 10% to 40% and GDP per capita increased from US $403.1 in 2007 to USD $499 in 2010. There was improved macroeconomic stabilisation. Although the economic sector improved a bit, international donors shunned the policy hence the introduction of the Medium-Term Plan (MTP).

While there were major gains achieved by STERP, however the programme faced the following challenges as discussed below. At the time of its implementation electricity generation by the power utility Zimbabwe Electricity Supply Authority (ZESA) could not power the local industry while the National Railways of Zimbabwe (NRZ) could not move inputs and goods. Local authorities could not supply adequate treated water to industry. The coal miner, Hwange Colliery Company (HCC) had no capacity to provide enough coal to power ZESA's thermal power stations or to the agricultural entities and heavy industries. Sable Chemical Industries and Zimphos Limited could not supply fertiliser for the agricultural sector and Seed-Co, Pannar and other seed breeders had no capacity to meet the seed needs of the local farming sector.

The absence of an overarching developmental vision to anchor STERP II was one of its major limiting factors. The development strategy should have provided a guiding framework of where the country was going. STERP was only a short-term economic revival document and it did not address the structural development challenges inherent in the economy. STERP contained no specific measures to deal with the structural distortions and rigidities arising out of the dual and enclave economic structure. The demise of the formal sector coupled with the likely adverse impacts of the global financial crisis and anti-inflation measures, implies the decent work deficits that characterise the economy and entrenches poverty and its feminisation will abound. More importantly, STERP failed to provide stimuli for a new paradigm that is pro-poor and inclusive, failed to promote the integrability of marginalised groups (women, youths, people with disabilities and people living with HIV/AIDS) and sectors, especially the informal and rural economy, and unleash a more employment-intensive pathway out of poverty.

Revenue generation constraint had an immediate impact on expenditure, thus aggravating social and humanitarian problems for the government. The inclusive government also received inadequate support from the international community visible improvement in day-to-day conditions for most Zimbabweans. The government also did not make meaningful progress on property rights and the rule of law, and the rehabilitation of physical infrastructure and therefore investor confidence remained low.

### 4.6.4 Medium-Term Plan (MTP) (2010–2015)

MTP was launched in July 2011 with a view to guide all Government plans and programmes beyond short-term stabilisation and build foreign exchange reserves sufficient to cover at least three months imports by 2015. Its theme was restoration and transformation of capacities for sustainable economic growth and development. Its objectives were among other things; infrastructure development with emphasis on rehabilitation and completion of outstanding projects, employment creation, human centred development, entrepreneurship development, macroeconomic stability, ICT and science and technology development, good governance, investment regulation, coordination and promotion, resource utilisation and poverty reduction, gender mainstreaming into economic activities all focusing on promotion of programs that endure gender parity in access to education, health and other social services (Government of Zimbabwe, 2010). MTP specific targets:

- Average annual GDP growth rate of 7.1%;
- Single-digit annual inflation;
- Interest rates that promotes savings and investment;
- Current Account Deficit of $\leq$ 5% of GDP by 2015;
- Average annual jobs creation rate of 6%;
- Sustained Poverty Reduction in line with MDGs targets;
- Foreign Exchange Reserves of at least 3 months import cover by 2015;
- Double-digit savings and investment ratios of around 20% of GDP by 2015;
- Budget deficit of less than 5% of GDP by 2015;
- Reduce sovereign debt to at least 60% of GDP by 2015.

MTP suffered a still birth as it was abandoned after the 2013 harmonised elections in favour of the Zimbabwe Agenda for Sustainable Socio-Economic Transformation.

### 4.6.5 *Zimbabwe Agenda for Sustainable Socio-economic Transformation (ZIMASSET) (2013–2018)*

The Zimbabwe Agenda for Sustainable Socio-Economic Transformation (Zim-Asset) was a policy document that was pertinent to industrial production. Zim-Asset was anchored on four clusters, namely food security and nutrition; social services and poverty eradication; infrastructure and utility; and value addition. Zim-Asset was envisaged to create an empowered society and grow the economy providing an enabling environment for sustainable economic empowerment and social transformation. It was meant to guide Zimbabwe from October 2013 to December 2018.

While crafted to achieve sustainable development and social equity anchored on indigenisation, empowerment and employment creation, Zim-Asset was hinged on four strategic clusters that were believed to enable Zimbabwe to achieve economic growth and also reposition the country as one of the strongest economies in the region and Africa. However, Matutu (2014) says that Zim-Asset does not in any way provide reference to Vision 2020 nor link its development aspirations to the country's vision.

The implementation of Zim-Asset was being constrained by the volatile political situation in the country and the power struggles that have been taking place within the ruling party according to Sibanda and Makwata (2017). Moreover, economic performance has not been to expectations and to potential capacity, with most of the Medium-Term Plan and the Zim-Asset (2013–18) targets not being realised (Government of Zimbabwe, 2018).

### 4.6.6 *Challenges*

Zim-Asset being the socio-economic development plan did not in any way provide reference to Vision 2020 nor link its development aspirations to the country's vision (Matutu, 2014). It is the contention of the analysis that Zim-Asset's capacity to turnaround the economy was highly impaired due to its short-sightedness and unclear link to the country's vision. The Government has since independence, reduced development to five-year blocks defined by various economic blue prints at different epochs. Zim-Asset remains trapped in the development planning shortcomings of the country, thus limiting its capacity to attain its defined goals.

Zim-Asset lands itself in a country with serious challenges on transparency, accountability and corruption which are one of the country's challenges (Sibanda & Makwata, 2017). The prevalence of corruption in Zimbabwe has increased over the last two decades. According to the Transparency International Corruption Perception Index (CPI), Zimbabwe's score declined from 3.0 out of 10 in 2000 to 2.2 in 2011 (Matutu, 2014). Over the same period, Zimbabwe's CPI ranking has fallen from 65th out of 90 countries to 154th out of 183 countries. Similarly, the World Bank's Control of Corruption Index ranks Zimbabwe in the 5.2 percentile, down from 15.1

in 2000 (Matutu, 2014). While the CPI is a contested indicator due to the fact that it's a perception-based indicator which is also value-laden. However, what cannot be disputed in Zimbabwe is the fact that corruption is at its worst levels in both the public and private sectors. Weak public accountability systems sustained low civic engagements have added to governance challenges facing the country. In addition, institutions for public service delivery are weak with serious capacity challenges thus a weak engine for Zim-Asset. The government cannot deliver the public goods which are the base for total economic and social development. The current governance crisis prevailing in the country whose redress requires a time period which is beyond the Zim-Asset implementation time frame, the capacity of the government to deliver the Zim-Asset goals remains blurred. A new value system was required to address the governance crisis and this is a mammoth task which was beyond frameworks and policies.

The performance of the public sector which was at its worst at during the Zim-Asset era remained critical to the turnaround of the country. The quality and performance of the public sector combined with its effects and impact were pervasive to both the public and private sectors thus ultimately determining the country's socio-economic development (Matutu, 2014). The public sector determines the country's capacity to meet its goals with respect to poverty reduction, economic growth and unemployment. The success of Zim-Asset is also determined by the quality and performance of the public sector. The current efforts to institutionalise Result Based Management (RBM) in the public sector had little impact due to limited resources to fully fund the public sector and more so the same efforts were being duplicated in the private sector. Efforts by the Government to institutionalise RBM and the corporate governance framework only provided a framework for good governance and performance management with little positive change during the life span of Zim-Asset. As argued above, the implementation time frame for Zim-Asset despite its well-intended cause remained too short to transform the economy due to complexity of the challenges bedevilling the country.

### *4.6.7 Industrial Developmental Policy (2012–2016)*

Giving a preface to the Industrial Development Policy in 2012, the President of the Republic of Zimbabwe, the late Robert Gabriel said:

> Our country's economy has historically been anchored on four pillars, namely, agriculture, mining, manufacturing and tourism. The industrial pillar not only adds value to products from the agricultural and mining sectors but, more importantly, contributes to the reduction of poverty since industrialization is a critical driver of economic growth and development.

From this statement it can be deduced that manufacturing is a key driver to economic prosperity and poverty eradication in Zimbabwe. The government launched the Industrial Development Policy 2012–2016 to address the challenges which weigh down on industrial sector in order to enhance its performance and give it the competitive edge it needs in the challenging global environment. Value addition or beneficiation is one of the cornerstones of this policy. Zimbabwe is abundantly endowed with natural resources, which include many industrial minerals and agricultural resources.

The Industrial Development Policy itself envisages transforming Zimbabwe from a producer of primary goods into a producer of processed value-added goods for both the domestic and export market through the promotion of viable industrial and commercial sectors. The overall objectives of the policy were to restore the manufacturing sector's contribution to GDP of Zimbabwe from 15 to 30% and its contribution to exports from 26 to 50% by 2016 consistent with the Medium-Term Plan. An average real GDP growth of 7% was targeted under this Policy Framework of 2012–2016.

The other objectives of the policy were to create additional employment in the manufacturing sector on an incremental basis and reduce unemployment levels and increase capacity utilisation from around 57% to 80% by the end of the planning period. In addition, the policy aimed to equip and replace obsolete machinery and new technologies for import substitution and enhance value addition.

### *4.6.8 National Trade Policy (2012–2016)*

Zimbabwe had not developed a National Trade Policy (NTP) document to guide the country's trade with the rest of the world and inferences had to be made from a number of trade-related laws and regulations administered by various Government Ministries and Departments. In this regard, the country's trade issues have been guided over the years by policies such as the Industrial Development Policies (1999–2003 and 2004–2010), the National Export Strategy (2006–2010), Economic Structural Adjustment Programme (ESAP) (1991–1995), Zimbabwe Programme for Economic and Social Transformation (ZIMPREST) (1996–1999), Millennium Economic Recovery Programme (MERP) (2000), National Economic Development Priority Programme (NEDPP) (2006) and the Short-Term Emergency Recovery Programmes (STERP I & II) (2009–2011).

Trade plays an important role in economic growth and development in the face of globalisation. With the development of the Industrial Development Policy (2012–2016), it became increasingly important to spell out how trade policy will complement and leverage Zimbabwe's industrial development, as well as support the broad-based economic growth objectives of the Medium-Term Plan. The National Trade Policy specifies measures and strategies that enable trade to be the engine for sustainable economic growth and development. The policy sets out the key principles and strategies to drive the economy towards export-orientation and international competitiveness, in order to transform Zimbabwe from being an exporter of primary commodities to an exporter of value-added high-quality processed goods and services. The policy was supposed to be implemented through strategic trade policy instruments, based on regional and multilateral trading arrangements, supported by an export development and promotion package.

Further, the policy sought to diversify the country's exports, expand and explore new markets, as well as promote the consumption of locally produced goods and services. Human skills and institutional capacity development in both the public and private sectors were also an important guiding principle for the effective and efficient implementation of the National Trade Policy. The achievement of the objectives of the National Trade Policy hinges on policy consistency and coordination within Government, and participation of all stakeholders in a strategic and focused manner.

### 4.6.9 National Industrial Developmental Policy (2019–2023)

The Zimbabwe National Industrial Development Policy (2019–2023) was expected to leverage on the positive momentum gained during the implementation of the IDP (2012–2016). The policy was a blueprint for industrialisation which derived from Vision 2030 meant to transform Zimbabwe into an upper middle-income economy by 2030. It was premised upon the decision by the Government to open the country for business, modernise, industrialise and promote investment, with the ultimate goal attaining broad-based economic empowerment, inclusive economic growth and employment creation. To achieve real economic transformation, the implementation of this policy was centred on developing linkages across key sectors of the economy namely agriculture, mining, manufacturing and services. Value addition and beneficiation were the main anchors of the industrialisation strategy.

### 4.6.10 Rationale for the ZNIDP

The industrial sector performance had been subdued and thus, provides the rationale and context for new policy interventions to stimulate industrial growth and development The ZNIDP recognised the strengths, weaknesses, opportunities and threats that characterise the Zimbabwean economy. The economy's major strengths include, rich mineral resources, agricultural and horticultural potential, highly skilled human resources, a vibrant and highly marketable tourism sector as well as a central and land linked location in the region. Challenges of antiquated machinery and equipment, lack of affordable and long-term funding for industry, foreign exchange shortages, high utility costs and competitiveness require robust policies and strategies to grow and sustain the manufacturing sector.

Vast opportunities are however, available for the country to exploit, and these include, a highly skilled diaspora, the ongoing global trend away from combustion engines towards battery-powered vehicles which will increase the demand for the battery input, lithium, which is abundant in Zimbabwe. The growth in online services and e-commerce is also an opportunity for the country to harness its skills and tap into this global phenomenon.

The most prominent threats were macroeconomic challenges in the form of current account deficits and high public debt. In addition, evolutions in technology are eliminating traditional industries such as paper milling and the use of robots in the manufacturing in more industrialised countries will result in efficiency gains and stiffer competition for the local industry, should it fail to adapt. Also, tobacco which has been a mainstay of the local economy is an increasingly shunned industry globally, due to public health concerns.

This policy was aligned to the SADC Industrialisation Strategy and Roadmap (2015–2063). The SADC industrialisation strategy envisions the region to 'progressively move from being factor-driven to investment-driven, then to efficiency-driven; and ultimately to the high growth trajectory-driven by knowledge, innovation and business sophistication'. The industrialisation strategy was also linked to the national strategies of Member States and to the African Union's Accelerated Industrial Development of Africa and Agenda 2063.

The objectives of the Zimbabwe National Industrial Development Policy sought to facilitate the sustainable growth of industry, the development of new industries and the transformation and diversification of the Zimbabwean industry. Some of the policy objectives were to attain:

- Manufacturing sector growth rate of at least 2% per annum;
- Contributing towards attainment of a gross domestic savings rate of at least 30% of GDP;
- Merchandise export growth rate of (10)% per annum to orient the manufacturing sector towards exports and generate capital for a high savings rate; and;
- Increasing the manufacturing sector share of employment to 20% in 2023.

The thrust of the policy will be two-pronged, anchoring on Investment-led and Innovation-led Industrialisation.

### 4.6.11 Policy Implementation

Once the various laws and policies related to industrialisation and manufacturing have been developed, they need to be fully implemented. Although the existing laws and policies are inadequate, they are a solid foundation as regards developing the economy as an industrial hub. If these policies and laws were fully implemented, manufacturing which is vital in industrialisation of the economy, could have been fairly advanced in Zimbabwe. While the development of specific laws, regulations and policies governing manufacturing will be a welcome development, their success is wholly dependent of the speed and depth of implementation.

### 4.6.12 Incentives

There is need for incentives to promote production and exports of value-added goods by business. Such incentives could be in form of tax rebates or export bonuses.

### 4.6.13 Funding

There is need for the creation and establishment of an Industrial Manufacturing Fund to assist manufacturing firms with investment and working capital. The fund should assist both SMEs and large firms in need of capital and working capital.

### 4.6.14 Instruments vs Targets: Synopsis of the Policies and Programmes and Why Most of Them Are Failing to Achieve Desired Targets?

Policy execution is a problem not only for the developing world, but also for advanced economies. Since independence in 1980, Zimbabwe came up with policies and programmes that aimed at promoting economic growth and development so as to improve the living standards of its citizens. However, most of these policies and programmes did not yield the desired results. During the first decade of independence, while the government managed to stabilise and open up the economy, the policies were not sustainable as government expenditure outstripped its revenue. In 1992, Zimbabwe including countries in Southern Africa were hit by a serious drought that significantly contributed to the poor performance of the economy as evidenced by a growth rate of approximately − 9%. Many workers lost their jobs during this period and this gave birth to a great deal of social unrest. When it became clear that ESAP was not a good policy, the government adopted ZIMPREST which also failed. By 2003, economic growth had already fallen down to − 17%. The new millennium was met with negative economic growth rates as economic programmes such as MERP and NERP did not prove to be useful as indicated by staggering economic growth right on the onset of the early 2000s. This was the period that was characterised by extreme formal unemployment and very high levels of inflation that culminated in the hyperinflation of 2008, with economic growth as low as -17.7%. The 2008 hyperinflation marked the demise of Zimbabwean dollar which was unceremoniously dumped in 2009 in favour of the US dollar.

When the government of national unity was formed in 2009, the economy stabilised and started to grow. The economy continued on a progressive growth trajectory until the year 2011 when economic growth was approximately 12%. However, when the government of national unity ended in 2013, the economy has not been doing well, and the reason could be that from 2013, the USD was appreciating against major trading partners, thus making Zimbabwean goods uncompetitive on the international market. In 2016 the government introduced a surrogate currency, the bond note, as a way to solve the liquidity crisis and as an incentive to exporters. These measures however did not materialise as the liquidity crisis continued. In fact, the introduction of bond notes actually gave birth to get another problem of parallel foreign currency market which has been havocking the economy to this day.

## References

Government of Zimbabwe. (2010). *Medium-term plan, 2011–2015.*

Government of Zimbabwe. (2018). *Towards an upper-middle income economy by 2030.*

Hammer, J. S., & Berman, P. (1995). Ends and means in public health policy in developing countries. *Health Policy, 32*(1–3), 29–45. https://doi.org/10.1016/0168-8510(95)00727-a

Johnston, T. (1999). Meeting the health care challenge in Zimbabwe. *The World Bank Economic Review.*

Makochekanwa, A. (2012). *The impact of economic performance on health in Zimbabwe.*

Mapuva, J. (2015). Skewed rural development policies and economic malaise in Zimbabwe. *African Journal of History and Culture, 7*(7), 142–151. https://doi.org/10.5897/ajhc2015.0269

Matutu, V. (2014). Zimbabwe agenda for sustainable socio-economic transformation (ZIM ASSET 2013–2018). A pipeline dream or reality. A reflective analysis of the prospects of the economic blue print. *Research Journal of Public Policy, 1*(1), 1–10. https://doi.org/10.2139/ssrn.2505008

Mumbengegwi, C., & Mabugu, R. (2002). Macroeconomic and adjustment policies in Zimbabwe (1980–2000): An introduction and overview. In C. Mumbengegwi (Ed.), *Macroeconomic and structural adjustment policies in Zimbabwe* (pp. 3–20). Palgrave.

Mumvuma, T., Mujajati, C., & Mufute, B. (2006). Reforms: The case of Zimbabwe. In J. Mensah (Ed.), *Understanding economic reforms in Africa: A tale of seven nations.* Palgrave Publishers.

Nyoni, T. (2018). A critical diagnosis of the success/failure of economic policies in Zimbabwe during the Banana (1980–1987) and the Mugabe (1988–2017) administrations: Learning the hard way. *Dynamic Research Journals Journal of Business and Management (DRJ-JBM), 1*(2), 27–33. https://doi.org/10.2139/ssrn.3133565

Sibanda, V., & Makwata, R. (2017). *Zimbabwe post independence economic policies: A critical review.* Lambert Academic Publishing (LAP).

Zhou, G., & Masunungure, E. (2006). *An analysis of the objectives and effects of privatisation on the public sector and the role of the state in Zimbabwe.* Zimbabwe Coalition on Debt and Development & the Southern Africa Peoples.

Zhou, G., & Zvoushe, H. (2012). Public policy making in Zimbabwe: A three decade perspective. *International Journal of Humanities and Social Science, 2*(8), 212–222.

# Part III
# Writing on the Wall…Stoking the Fires of Economic Turbulence

# Chapter 5
# Making or Breaking Zimbabwe: 1987–2020 Issues

## 5.1 Introduction

Focus of this chapter is on exploring issues spanning from 1987 up to 2020 in the history of Zimbabwe. Any episode which an economy experiences has an impact on its overall well-being. For instance, a country frequently facing droughts can have serious food security challenges.

From 1987 to 2020 in the economic history of Zimbabwe, there are key developments over this period which in one way or the other positively shaped or impacted negatively on Zimbabwe. Most of the issues stoked fires of economic turbulence. Turmoil and more turmoil was to come. Thus, the reader will observe that most factors which will be articulated in this chapter point to more problems to haunt the economy even later on. For example, it is during this period when the monetary sector started to take a knock due to the imploding economy. There are a lot of issues during this period, we however cannot cover all of them. In spite of this, those which we will examine provide a solid background in illuminating issues playing out during this period.

Deftly analysing Zimbabwe's development path since independence offers a classic case of how a developing country can start well and miss a golden opportunity to curve a steady development path. According to Jones (2011, p. 6) when Zimbabwe attained her independence in 1980, she also inherited an unjust and high-interest debt amounting to approximately US $700 million from the Rhodesian government led by Ian Smith which borrowed excessively to buy arms during war and as sanction-busting measures imposed by the United Nations. Despite all these, the country was not deterred from developing and it started on a fairly good trajectory.

Thus, those factors that exacerbated turbulence turning the country into one of the fastest shrinking economies in the continent and the world will be examined in this chapter. The reader should note that generally, the economy started well during the first decade, especially in its first five years after independence. However, during the end of the second decade things reached a turning point characterised



K. Mahuni et al., *Zimbabwe's Economy*, Advances in African Economic, Social and Political Development, https://doi.org/10.1007/978-3-031-81588-1_5

by waves of protests against rising costs of living, deteriorating public services and escalating corruption. The worsening performance of the Zimbabwean economy was exacerbated in the third decade when problems kept on piling alongside a lot of other non-economic factors feeding into the humungous problem set. At the end of the chapter the multi-million-dollar concern which comes to any inquisitive reader is *will Zimbabwe ever catch up with other progressive nations as long as it continues being stuck in cycles of challenges?*

## 5.2 Issues

### *5.2.1 Drought Cycles*

Droughts are a particular form of natural hazard which are gradually coming in as significant arguments into Zimbabwe's developmental journey and the majority of struggling countries in Sub-Saharan Africa. They frequently threaten to tear the country apart by bringing unprecedented suffering to the majority often exposed to these weather vagaries. Since independence, Zimbabwe experienced a lot of droughts namely extreme droughts in 1983 and 1992, severe drought in 1982 and 2004, then mild droughts in 1984, 1987, 1991, 1995, 2002–03, 2005, 2007–10, 2012 (Nangombe, 2015) and in 2015 and 2019. However, the 1992 drought was the worst in the country's history and living memories of most Zimbabweans as it resulted in the death of over one million head of cattle and almost no harvest in the country with the Grain Marketing Board (GMB) managing to receive a mere 13, 000 tonnes of maize (Maphosa, 1994; Nangombe, 2015). Also, the 1992 drought occurred at a time when the country was implementing economic structural adjustment programme (ESAP) which in turn had severe impact on domestic savings further exacerbating the economic woes of the country (Benson, 1998).

Drought problems are not only limited to inadequate surface water, but water tables are also affected. About 50–60% of family or shallow wells that are the common sources of water in Zimbabwe's natural regions 1, 2 and 3 and deep wells in regions 4 and 5 dry up during droughts. In urban areas dam water levels fall resulting in water rationing for domestic and industrial activities.

Well-documented studies by Benson (1998); Diersen et al. (2002); Edwards et al., (2009, 2019) and Horridge et al. (2005) reveal that droughts have negative impacts on an economy. According to Benson (1998), the impacts of droughts are more severe in developing countries than developed ones. This is because developing countries depend mainly on the primary sector, particularly agriculture while developed countries produce more of manufactured commodities than agricultural commodities. In the case of Zimbabwe, close to 80% of the population's livelihoods including those in urban areas depend on farming (Madzwamuse, 2010, p. 57).

Drought can have a considerable undesirable direct economic, social and health impact on people whose income and livelihood depend on the agricultural sector like farmers and those employed in that sector. Also, those whose services depend on the agricultural sector are affected indirectly when there is a drought. As a result, policymakers need to take both the direct and indirect impacts into account when wanting to design effective responsive strategies towards mitigating the effects of drought. The extent of the impact of drought on the economy depends on the economy's productive structure, levels of existing stocks, price elasticities of both demand and supply for intermediate and final consumer goods and the degree of openness of the economy to the rest of the world as well as its composition of trade by reducing drought-related exports and increasing drought-related imports thereby worsening the balance of payment (Benson, 1998).

Generally, droughts reduce the amount of water in water bodies thereby affecting wildlife and water-related tourism and recreation activities. Besides the above, droughts also disrupt the ecological system; they also affect timber industry, threaten food security, increase fire risks and impoverish people. Those in the rural areas are the worst affected as their livelihoods depend on agriculture and during droughts crop production falls and livestock die. Consequently, deforestation also increases due to veld fires, water deprivation on plants and trees and cutting down of trees for sale of fuel wood as a source of livelihood. Rural communities also rely on natural resources for food, fuel, craft production, medicinal use and shelter and such impacts of droughts can cause significant negative consequences to the nation as a whole.

In addition to the above, droughts mostly affect community's lives through reducing their sources of income since activities that generate income depend on agriculture or availability of water also diminish. This has the potential effect of reducing consumption, investment and savings in the formal economy. As a result, increased cases and engagements in illegal activities like gold panning and felling down trees for charcoal production as people try to seek alternative means of earning a living can be rampant. The generation of electricity is also affected negatively since most of the country's electric power is from hydro. These further impact development and industrialisation in the country. In addition, it marked the beginning of a cycle of poverty for most vulnerable sections of the Zimbabwean population.

For Zimbabwe, during the 1991–92 drought generation of electricity in the country declined by nearly 50% even though the decline was not related to drought, but mismanagement (Benson, 1998, p. 244). Also, national output and income, employment, especially in the informal sector where there are no laws to protect workers, and export earnings were negatively affected by droughts. As an example, according to CEDRISA et al. (2009), the 1991–92 drought that happened in Zimbabwe induced a 25% and 6% decline in the volume of manufacturing sector output and foreign currency earnings respectively. Benson (1998) also stresses that during the 1991–92 drought gross domestic product (GDP) at factor cost, agricultural GDP, industrial GDP and manufacturing GDP declined correspondingly by 5.8%, 18.4%, 8.5% and 9.5% while according to World Bank [WB] (1993, p. 106) GDP growth rate was −8.2% in 1992.

For Zimbabwe, agriculture is closely linked to the manufacturing sector. Following prolonged droughts, the manufacturing sector took more time to recover compared to the agricultural sector. Firstly, the reason may be attributed to low income and high demand for agricultural commodities and low demand for manufactured commodities as suggested by Engel's Law. Secondly, it is because the manufacturing sector depends on the agricultural sector as we indicated and once agriculture is strained the impact of constrained supply hits harder on the manufacturing sector. In the face of the above, having in place policies that support the recovery of the manufacturing sector is pertinent. Because of the linkage that agriculture has with other sectors of the economy, policies to shock proof the economy from recurrent droughts have not been very convincing adding to turbulence build-up in the process.

### *5.2.2 Economic Structural Adjustment Programme (ESAP) 1990*

Between 1980 and 1990, Zimbabwe continued with the stance of excessive government intervention by way of controlling and regulating macroeconomic policies (Mumbengegwi, 2002). However, these regulations were incompatible with the open economy mantra of the early 1980s. As a result, the country's competitiveness and efficiency slowed down in the face of international markets. As time passed it later became increasingly evident that operating in a heavily regulated and protected economy was the reason for lack of economic progress in the country.

Resultantly, in 1990 Zimbabwe adopted an economic reform programme from the International Monetary Fund (IMF) and WB which was commonly known as ESAP from 1991 to 1995. For many developing countries the programme was mainly aimed at addressing balance of payments and budget deficit problems. ESAP programme remains one of the most terrible prescriptions by powerful institutions to poor countries, and Zimbabwe was no exception. For most people who were old enough to understand and observe things as they unfolded on the already weakening economy, the programme largely stirred turbulence. In Chap. 4 we looked at policy execution dilemmas experienced by Zimbabwe, we featured ESAP also in the analysis. We in part revisit the ESAP episode in this chapter because to us a not-so-good prescription was made to an economy which was gradually disintegrating. ESAP ripped through the country as we shall discuss briefly.

During the initial stages of ESAP, Zimbabwe's external debt was US $2 billion in 1991 and by 1992 and at the beginning of 1995 it had risen to US $4 billion and US $5 billion respectively, and the 1995 figure represented close to 91% of the GDP of the country which was twice bigger than the 1989 debt to GDP ratio (Mlambo, 1997).

According to the African Development Bank [AfDB] (1997), in the case of Zimbabwe the programme was predominantly meant to decontrol the maze of regulations which had been imposed by the Rhodesian Government in the wake of international sanctions which arose from the Unilateral Declaration of Independence (UDI) and the establishment of white minority rule government. A 1997 report by AfDB which meant to evaluate the performance of the country under the programme confirmed that Zimbabwe's economic performance continued to be uncertain after the implementation of ESAP. Furthermore, Bond (2007) highlights that ESAP failed to correct and address the inherent economic imbalances and inequalities that existed before independence. Also, the increase in interest rates and inflation which were accompanied by the drought in 1991/1992 compounded the slow implementation of ESAP. Soon after attaining independence, the country invested heavily in order to improve human development of the black Zimbabweans who were generally at the hands of marginalisation and discrimination during the Rhodesian government. The Zimbabwean government under the leadership of President Robert G. Mugabe devised numerous innovative programmes that were meant to accelerate the provision of basic primary education, health care, housing and water and sanitation. As the United Nations Development Programme [UNDP] (1996, p. 83) stresses Zimbabwe had a remarkable improvement in terms of her human development index which rose from 0.386 to 0.576 between 1980 and 1987. However, by the late 1980s it fell back to 0.398 due partly to lack of government to create economic opportunities and insufficient investment from IMF and WB which were pressurising the government to adopt adjustment programmes. By 1995 the gains from free primary education and health care as well as subsidised basic consumer goods like mealie-meal and other foodstuffs which were meant to benefit the Zimbabwean poor population slowly vanished.

With ESAP, the turbulence grip had a tight grip on the Zimbabwean economy just like other struggling countries also. Effects of ESAP on the economy and its people were devastating. For instance, besides what we covered above, later in the mid-1990s the expansion of informal sector and mushrooming of illegal housing structures were rapid as people who were once employed in the formal sector lost their jobs when the formal economy was shrinking because of ESAP (Musoni, 2010; Zimbabwe Human Rights NGO Forum, 2005). Both the central and local government were struggling to cope with the rising demand for formal employment and decent housing by citizens who were living in towns.

### 5.2.3 *War Gratuities 1997*

In 1997, that is 17 years after Zimbabwe attained independence, the war veterans felt neglected and they protested to the government requesting to be given land and immediate payment of the claims made under the War Victims Compensation Fund. The war veterans' association, the Zimbabwe National Liberation War Veterans Association (ZNLWVA) which was formed in 1989 was now very influential and had reorganised under the leadership of Dr. Chenjerai Hunzvi. The protests occurred after revelations that some able-bodied party and government officials fraudulently classified themselves as up to 80% disabilities during the war of liberation and got huge sums of money in what was called the War Victims Compensation Scandal of 1994. Several prominent politicians and senior government officials fraudulently benefited from the scheme most are captured by AMANI Trust (1998, p. 11). After several months of protests by war veterans, a once-off payment of 50,000 Zimbabwean dollars, that was an equivalent of 4300 US dollars[1] was made. Furthermore, a monthly 2000 Zimbabwean dollars (174 US dollars) to every bona fide war veteran and free health care and education to members of their families were also unveiled (Nyathi, 2004, p. 71).

However, the war veterans were still unimpressed and felt the amount was not enough and they further protested demanding a redress on land distribution. As such plans for the compulsory acquisition of white-owned commercial farms were made, and again this was hurriedly announced without first putting a clear financing mechanism (Kairiza, 2009). The payment packages on war veterans and compulsory land acquisition from white commercial farmers were not included in the national budget of 1997. These created a huge budget deficit which caused panic to investors resulting in capital flight out of the country. This further led to the immediate crash of the Zimbabwean dollar against the US dollar by 75% according to Dashwood (2000, p. 83); Raftopoulos (2008) or by 74% in four hours according to Bond (1999, 2007, p. 149) in what is known as the *Black Friday* on 14 November 1997 marking another wave of turbulence.

Initially, the government had planned to finance war veterans' packages and land reform by increasing tax rates in the budget of 1998. This however received a backlash as the nation plunged into widespread protests in January 1998, organised by the Zimbabwe Congress of Trade Unions (ZCTU) and subsequently the government monetised the debt after reversing its initial policy stance (AMANI Trust, 1998). By the end of 1997, Zimbabwe had started to experience a deep economic crisis that was emanating from corruption, mismanagement and politics of patronage. According to Bond (1999); Kairiza (2009, p. 5); Makina (2010, p. 99) and Makochekanwa (2008, p. 6), the Black Friday of 14 November 1997 was when the dark side of the economic predicament in Zimbabwe began to seriously unravel. The rest was history.

### *5.2.4 Labour Unrest and Food Riots 1998*

As turbulence took charge of the economy, labour began to be restive. For example, in Chap. 1, when we reviewed some headlines which gave us a glimpse into the turbulence journey, we also encountered the headline *Struggling Zim workers vow massive strikes in 2016* (Financial Gazette). This implied that the workers had been badly bruised by the turbulence also. Not spared also are the ordinary people as turbulence was also visiting kitchens of the masses living a trail of starvation culminating into food riots as prices shot through the roofs.

[1] http://www.aparchive.com/metadata/ZIMBABWE-GOVERNMENT-OFFER-COMPENSATION-TO-WAR-VETERANS/3e478af6d00c84c174e833d78ca29a2e?query=rhodesia&current=2&orderBy=Relevance&hits=33&referrer=search&search=%2Fsearch%3Fquery%3Drhodesia%26allFilters%3DZIMBABWE%3AKeyword%2CGuerrilla%2520warfare%3ASubject&allFilters=ZIMBABWE%3AKeyword%2CGuerrilla+warfare%3ASubject&productType=IncludedProducts&page=1&b=a29a2e.

The background to food riots and labour unrests of 1998 is that economically Zimbabwe had had a bad performance in the second half of 1997 as economic growth dropped from 9.7% in 1996 to 1.4% in 1997 (Makina, 2010, p. 106). The 1997 growth rate was not bad considering that in 1995 it was 0.2%, but it was due to drought which negatively impacted the agricultural sector and ultimately the economy as a whole. However, as for the 1997 economic growth rate it was mainly due to government budget indiscipline and high appetite for spending on war veterans' gratuities. These events proved the year 1998 growth fragile as there had been an increase in interest rates, taxes and inflation and a depreciating currency the preceding year. Despite the government having made numerous initiatives and missions in Europe, the Far East and the USA to lure foreign capital, investors remained sceptical about Zimbabwe as no actual investment came forth.

During the end of 1997, the government took a stance to raise funds for war veterans' gratuities and monthly pensions by introducing a 5% war veterans' levy and increasing tax. These were, however, overwhelmingly rejected by parliament and also sharply criticised by all sectors in the economy forcing the government to later drop the initiative. Nevertheless, government through finance ministry then still proposed to announce new measures to generate the much-needed funds to finance war veterans' gratuities and monthly pensions.

On top of economic challenges, by 1997 corruption in the country's public sector and parastatals had already reached alarming levels with war veterans seen protesting over the abuse of War Victims Compensation Fund. The Government Tender Board was also awarding contracts to non-deserving bidders. The economic hardships brought in by inflation, interest and tax rates induced poverty and deterioration of living standards for many Zimbabweans especially the working class. Life became unbearable and strikes gripped the nation and across various sectors and companies, hotels, construction, banking and postal services and other industries as many workers were demanding their employers to pay them a living wage. Workers were discontented and demanding an upward review of their salaries by at least 40% since their current incomes were not commensurate with the cost of living.

On 9 December 1997, workers in major cities responded to a call by ZCTU for a peaceful protest against general price and tax increases so as to engage the government. Commuters who were travelling to town were forced to go back by armed riot police who were blocking all roads. Citizens who were resisting were beaten up by the police, but some managed to sneak into the city and it is reported that they assembled at Africa Unity Square in the central business district (CBD) of Harare. However, armed riot police with teargas, dogs and button sticks descended on them and they ran towards different directions. The government was not prepared for a peaceful engagement with demonstrators, but instead silenced them with teargas and thorough beatings. People became tired of the teargas and chase from the police and they started to block roads with some hooligans squeezed in and joined the fracas and this resulted in stoning of many cars, buses and property, and breaking and looting of several shops. Prices of most basic goods rose by up to 50%, for instance maize meal prices rose by 45% in a space of one week, and the reason was the collapse of the Zimbabwean dollar. Government also introduced price controls and a variety of tariffs on imports as a way to get revenue to finance unplanned programmes.

The events above culminated to massive Food Riots that ensued in the country in January 1998. The 1998 riots started in the early morning hours of 19 January and crowds were seen marching from the southern part of the CBD of Harare. Police set up roadblocks and used teargas to stop traffic and keep crowds from entering the CBD. However, as the day progressed rioters became restive and started to barricade all traffic to the CBD. Motorists who resisted the call from rioters had their cars burnt or overturned and for some who were lucky had their cars' window screens smashed. Hooligans and criminals took advantage of the deplorable, riotous and troubled situation and began to loot, steal property from shops and commit other litany of crimes. Supermarkets in the suburbs of Chitungwiza, Glen View and Mabvuku were vandalised and looted. The following day riots remained tense in most parts of Harare and there was heavy presence of the police. By the end of the second day of rioting at least 500 rioters were arrested with more than 200 arrested in Chitungwiza alone. On the second day, incidents of rioting, looting and vandalism of shops were also reported in Chegutu and Gweru with calm in other cities and towns. On the evening of 20 January 1998, government announced the deployment of arm in all parts of Harare and Chitungwiza. On the third day, the atmosphere in Harare and Chitungwiza calmed and business, work and school slowly resumed. However, police and arm presence remained in suburbs until the situation fully normalised. In some towns like Beitbridge and Mutare riots were erupting. On the fourth and fifth day, things got back to normal.

According to AMANI Trust (1998) eight people were reported dead and numerous people sustained injuries due to excessive application of force by the police and the arm who were trying to contain the situation and maintain order in cities. Thousands were also arrested and detained during the three-day food riots that rocked the nation. On the commerce side, business persons and companies suffered financial losses due to riots and some who were unfortunate and did not have insurance or some form of compensation failed to re-establish themselves after riots. Police also managed to recover part of the goods looted.

During the same year in August, Zimbabwe took part in the DRC war so as to help the country counter insurgence, millions were spent in that participation. This had a serious knock on the local currency as foreign currency was being mopped out of the country. The following year the country ran out of foreign currency, thereby defaulting on most of its foreign liabilities.

### *5.2.5 Land Reform 2000*

Land has been the epicentre and source of political and economic confrontation in Zimbabwe backing date to colonial times. The reason is that during colonial times the white minority farmers owned vast acres of fertile and arable commercial land while the black majority were forced to live in overcrowded, less fertile and sometimes unproductive arid communal areas. This created a system which gave white people more opportunities to accumulate wealth while blacks would remain as labourers and weak financially, thereby perpetuating them in poverty.

The Land Apportionment Act of 1930 was the first legislation to establish land segregation legally, designating more than half (51%) of the country's land for whites while the blacks were assigned only 22% (Mutasa, 2015). The assigned land was the best part of the country's land, yet they (whites) constituted just five per cent of the population. The Act had also provisions to forcefully evict indigenous Zimbabweans to dry and unproductive regions of the country.

The signing of the Lancaster House Agreement[2] officially gave birth to land reform in 1980 in independent Zimbabwe. This marked the first effort by the Zimbabwean Government to correct land imbalances that were in place during the colonial era. Furthermore, the redistribution of land had to be done in a more equitable way while protecting those who occupied the land during colonisation as specified in the Land Apportionment Act of 1930. The aim was to address land access, ownership, and use imbalances that had been in existence prior to the country attaining independence. At that time as enshrined in the Lancaster House Agreement the law protected white minority commercial farmers' interests at the expense of those of the black majority who were landless.

According to Mutasa (2015), since independence Zimbabwe's land reform is divided into four phases namely: (a) during the first 10 years after independence a market-based system which involves willing seller-willing buyer approach was used, (b) then from 1992 to 2000 government made compulsory acquisition of the land, (c) however before 2000 violent and extrajudicial occupations of land took place with the war veterans on the frontline and finally (d) from 2000 there was the famous Fast Track Land Reform Program (FTLRP) where there was appropriation of land from whites without compensation.

The first phase of land reform in the new Zimbabwe was partly financed by the British Government and in that process approximately 70,000 people landless Zimbabweans were resettled on over 20,000 km$^2$ of land. According to Manby (2002, p. 6) government acquired around 40% of the eight million hectares which was targeted and over 50,000 families were resettled on more than three million hectares of land during the first 10 years from independence. However, with time the government seemed less concerned and the pace of redistributing land and resettling people slowed down as less than 20,000 families were resettled on less than one million hectares in the 1990s and by the end of 1997 a total of around 71,000 families against a target of 162,000 families had only been resettled on almost 3.5 million hectares of land (Manby, 2002, p. 6). A detailed explanation of the number of beneficiaries and hectares of land distributed over years is shown in Table 5.1.

As the population continued to grow the political landscape in the country also changed and this saw a number of such initiatives undertaken over the years and they were done through several amendments in the law. A lot of black people especially War Veterans felt sidelined as they were still waiting for the government to

[2] https://en.wikipedia.org/wiki/lancaster_house_agreement.

**Table 5.1** Distribution of land acquired to beneficiaries over time

| Period | Resettlement phase | Number of beneficiaries (families) | Size of land (ha) |
|---|---|---|---|
| 1980–1990 | Willing Buyer-Willing seller combined with compulsory government acquisitions | 71,000 | 3,498,444 |
| 1998–2000 | Inception of violent land occupations | 4,697 | 168,264 |
| 2000–2008 | FTLRP: A1 Module for smallholder schemes<br>FTLRP: A2 module for large commercial schemes | 145,775<br>16,386 | 4,137,085<br>2,681,642 |
| Total | | 237,858 | 10,485,435 |

*Source* Government of Zimbabwe (2009)

fulfil its promises to acquire more land for resettlement. This fuelled displeasure among villagers and war veterans as their patience with government's promise on land ran out and they invaded nearby commercial farmers owned by whites. In a bid to gain a huge following from disgruntled war veterans and villagers as well as to correct its waning popularity owing to hard economic conditions prevailing in the country, the ruling party. Later on, land reform followed in different phases so as to address colonial imbalances on land distribution. This coincided with the run-up to the 2000 parliamentary elections. The motto at the time was '*Land is the economy; economy is the land*'. Using Presidential Powers (Temporary Measures) Act of 1996, the government through parliament further amended the Land Acquisition Act in May and November 2000. As cited in the Human Rights Watch Report of 2000,[3] these changes in the Land Reform and Resettlement Programme: Revised Phase II, paragraph 2.5 were done with the aim to '*clarify and streamline various procedural aspects of the acquisition process and to prescribe new compensation rules in accordance with the Constitution*'.

The most famous programme was the FTLRP which was officially launched in 2002 although it was introduced in early 2000. Taking advantage of its majority in parliament and without delay, the government made several amendments regarding land. Since then, FTLRP has been inscribed with a lot of controversy on Zimbabwe's political and social-economic landscape. From its onset, at the global level it has attracted international attention with a lot of criticism especially from the erstwhile coloniser and her allies while at the same time locally it has empowered land beneficiaries as well as drastically transformed their lives and livelihoods (Matondi, 2012). Although there are significant benefits from land redistribution, it is a fact that Zimbabwe's economy is agro-based and in that regard the million-dollar question is about the welfare of those who were once working on the redistributed farms, and also FTLRP's consequential impact on downward and upward industries which used to depend on agriculture. In particular, the Zimbabwean manufacturing sector which is highly agro-dependent shrank considerably. Because of the contrasting

[3] https://www.hrw.org/reports/2002/zimbabwe/ZimLand0302-02.htm.

views and benefits of FTLRP, its effectiveness has been a subject of extreme debate both locally and internationally for more than a decade. According to Juana (2006), if it was well-planned and systematically and carefully implemented, land reform could have generated economy-wide benefits to Zimbabweans. Also, it could have led to more income distribution to the once marginalised population.

The main challenge until FTLRP was that from the outset since the willing seller-willing buyer phase, the government was willing to buy more land, yet on the other hand the whites were not prepared to sell part of their land to the government at reasonable price. FTLRP also disrupted farming activities due to its chaotic nature and as such maize production during that farming season decreased by three quarters which further threatened the country's exports, food security and income (Clemens & Moss, 2005).

The authors fully support government's stance on land reform exercise and the indigenisation economic empowerment policy as these were necessary in addressing inherent socio-economic inequalities created during the colonial era. Black Zimbabweans by owning land and shares in companies they would increase their source of wealth income base, rather than just relying on income from labour. Moreover, this would also go a long way in empowering people. Zimbabwe is one of those countries in Africa which has been implementing empowerment programmes to its people. However, like many other programmes done in Zimbabwe the land reform and indigenisation policy had many challenges and were marred by scandals and corruption as majority of the intended targets and beneficiaries did not benefit contributing to turbulence despite the good intentions. In addition, problems of multiple farm ownership has been rampant.

### *5.2.6 Cyclones—Eline and Japhet 2000, 2002*

For many years, Zimbabwe has not been a flood- and cyclone-prone country until around the year 2000 onwards. Frequent floods that used to occur were the ones caused by rivers overtopping their banks especially in the Muzarabani area of the Zambezi Valley. However, by the turn of the new millennium things took a different course. The month of February 2000 will for a long time be in people's memories for devastating floods induced by tropical cyclone Eline which affected and destroyed human and animal life, property, infrastructure and nature in Madagascar, Mozambique and parts of Malawi, South Africa, Zambia and Zimbabwe. As in CEDRISA et al. (2009), the Meteorology Services reported that Cyclone Eline originated in Sumatra on the 8th of February 2000 and it dragged westwards passing through Reunion Island. The cyclone weakened for a short while over Madagascar but it regained strength before touching down over Mozambique on 22 February 2000. Reason and Keibel (2004) reveal that tropical cyclone Eline stretched 2000 km starting from cool southeast Atlantic to the semi-arid southern Namibia.

However, destruction was more severe in Mozambique than in other countries. In the case of Zimbabwe, according to the Ministry of Agriculture Zimbabwe et al.

(2000, p. 5) and CEDRISA et al., (2009, p. 27), cyclone Eline hit the eastern and southern parts of the country from 23 to 25 February 2000 and the affected areas were Mutare, Manicaland Province (Chimanimani and Chipinge Districts), Masvingo Province (Chiredzi, Mwenezi and Zaka Districts), Matabeleland South Province (Beitbridge, Bulilimamangwe, Gwanda, Insiza, Plumtree and Umzingwane Districts) and in Midlands Province (Mberengwa, Mvuma, Shurugwi and Zvishavane). According to the Herald[4] of 12 February 2015, in Zimbabwe alone cyclone Eline is estimated to have killed 136 people, destroyed 59,184 houses and huts, 14,999 toilets, 538 schools, 54 clinics and a total of 20,000 head livestock were lost. In addition to that, about 230 dams burst. Furthermore, because of severe storms and floods falling trees affected telecommunications and electricity lines leading to loss of communication with other parts of the country and power to drive economic activities. However, studies show that the economy as a whole is very sensitive to low rainfall like during drought periods than to excessively high rainfall like floods and cyclones (Benson, 1998).

The tropical cyclone by the name Japhet which occurred three years down the line (that is in 2003), around the same month of February worsened the already deplorable situation in some places of the country. Cyclone Japhet caused unexpected heavy and continuous rainfall that ravaged crops and caused floods in parts of Mozambique, Zambia and Zimbabwe. In two provinces of Mozambique alone, the cyclone destroyed 25,000 houses and an estimated 23,000 people were left homeless while 17 deaths were recorded. In Zimbabwe, 8 people died and also a bridge, several houses and crops, particularly yields, were severely destroyed. However, in Zimbabwe compared to Cyclone Eline the damage by Cyclone Japhet was not more rampant. In Mozambique the damage from Cyclone Japhet could have been more than that from Cyclone Eline. However, because of effective disaster preparedness and good cooperation between government, communities and humanitarian organisation causalities and damages were kept to a minimum.[5]

The trail of destruction left by the cyclones over the years only piled misery to the struggling economy. In the process the turbulence has often scored more victory points, thereby breaking economy. In observing the devastating effects of weather vagaries such as the cyclones just discussed, of great concern is the level of disaster preparedness in Zimbabwe which seems to have more challenges/problems. Successful disaster preparedness would require support and implementation of sound and cost-effective national response measures and policies, collection and sharing of quality data and information about environment by all stakeholders. Like droughts, cyclones and floods are also natural hazards. Even though, crises are life and socio-economic threatening, they are not at all times bad as they can also facilitate change. During times of crisis policymakers can maximise on the crisis to craft and implement policies and polities that can shape economies in new directions. In times of hazards

---

[4] https://www.herald.co.zw/cyclone-eline-ghost-haunts-zim/

[5] https://reliefweb.int/report/mozambique/preparedness-pays-mozambique-0. https://reliefweb.int/report/mozambique/preparedness-pays-mozambique.

such as these robust social safety nets are key since they cushion weaker members of the society who often bear the brunt of natural disasters.

### 5.2.7 *Look East Policy 2003*

In 2003 the Zimbabwean government promulgated the 'Look East Policy', which was aimed at expanding bilateral investment, political and trade relations to Asian countries that include China, India, Indonesia, Japan, Malaysia, Singapore, South Korea, Vietnam, Russia and many others (Ojakorotu & Kamidza, 2018; Tukić & Tombindo, 2016b). The Look East Policy was described as the new policy direction as looking east where the sun rises, and giving the back to the west where it sets. Of all the Asian countries targeted in the policy, China has emerged as the biggest ally to Zimbabwe and as a result, China also stood to be the biggest beneficiary from the Look East Policy with a lot of mega deals done favouring China. For example, around 128 Chinese official development finance projects were established between 2000 and 2012 and with all these investments in the country has been Mickey Mouse in translating to meaningful social and economic development (Zindiye, 2015). According to Moyo and Mdlongwa (2014) and Ojakorotu and Kamidza (2018), the policy was necessitated by or was in response to economic sanctions that were imposed on the country by the USA, Britain and their allies due to Zimbabwe's condemnation on grounds of human rights abuse, lack of democracy and governance as well as the land reform. The move was also meant to empower Zimbabweans by learning from the growth strategies of countries like China, Indonesia and Malaysia which took deliberate initiatives to instil small and medium-led economic growth in contrast to Western policies of funding projects.

Many analysts have raised many varying opinions and questions about China's relationship with African countries. Mahuni et al. (2020) in the book *Africa's Incomplete Cycles of Development* make interesting observations about China's relationship with Africa. Specifically, the authors pose the following eight key questions;

For some the relationship is premised on China's need for resources and raw materials to sustain her fast-growing economy (Goldstein et al., 2006; Youde, 2007). Today China is Africa's largest trading partner after having surpassed the USA in 2009 (Ighobor, 2013, p. 7). Also, many African countries' exports are destined to China with the bulk of them being agricultural products, mineral ores and crude oil. At the same time, cheap Chinese products are flooding many African markets, thereby negatively affecting both their agricultural and manufacturing sectors and locals' livelihoods in the long run because local industries are shutting down. Giovannetti and Sanfilippo (2016) also reveal that Chinese low value-added manufacturing exports are displacing African exports to main trading partners.

In the case of Zimbabwe, there are concerns that the Look East Policy has been giving investment preferences to Chinese companies and investors despite the promulgation of the indigenisation and economic empowerment programme into law (Ramani, 2016). This is most evident in the retailing and mining sectors where preferential treatment is accorded to Chinese-owned companies. In Chiadzwa for example, local diamond miners were forcefully removed to pave way for Chinese companies. The conditions of work and remunerations in some companies owned by Chinese are very deplorable and in some cases incidences of human abuse are cited. According to Moyo and Mdlongwa (2014, p. 9), in the construction industry Chinese workforce is seen using protective clothing while Zimbabweans work in their regular clothes, which is a gross violation of labour laws. On top of that, Chinese firms are seen employing Chinese workers instead of local employees even in areas which do not require technical expertise.

In the agricultural sector and construction industry, Chinese companies have managed to fill the void left by Western companies despite the level leaves a lot to be desired. The entry of Tian Ze in the tobacco auction floor in 2005 saw the price of the golden leaf rising by 100% from a paltry US $1.61 to US $3.32 per kilogram (Tukić & Tombindo, 2016a). This was a welcomed move since it meant a lot to tobacco farmers' livelihoods. However, the time of Tian Ze's entry was controversial since it did not provide support to farmers during the time of growing. In return, China also supplies agricultural equipment and this has helped in resuscitating, mechanising, modernising and revolutionising Zimbabwe's agricultural system. In the construction industry, Chinese companies have built or face lifted hospitals, schools and contribute to the country's power generation at Hwange Thermal and Kariba Hydro power stations. They also built the National Defense College and currently the construction of the new parliament building is among the recent projects the Chinese are doing in the country. However, the quality of work in majority of these Chinese-built infrastructural projects leaves a lot to be desired as they lack durability (Moyo & Mdlongwa, 2014, p. 11).

The fact that Zimbabwe was forced to look east makes her with little choice or bargaining power when dealing with China. And this lack of bargaining power and the circumstances that Zimbabwe is finding herself at the hands of China has been framed look least instead of look east by Moyo and Mdlongwa (2014). Additionally according to Ojakorotu and Kamidza (2018) compared to China, Zimbabwe is weak both economically and politically hence its failure to garner satisfactory results from the bilateral arrangement. On a general note, Chinese's support in the development of Zimbabwe is good especially during this time when the country is under sanctions imposed by the West. However, it has failed to match that of the traditional Western partners.

As recommendations, in areas where Zimbabweans can engage, they should be reserved for Zimbabweans and if possible, a partnership with Chinese firms can be arranged so that the locals can benefit in terms of expertise and technology. Look East Policy is based on few elite politicians benefiting while the general populace of Zimbabwe is suffering. Even though China plays an important role in the economy of Zimbabwe, her activities in all spheres of the economy should be closely monitored and regulated in cases where economic sabotaging and gross violation of labour laws and human rights occur. Control mechanisms at the country's border posts and in cities should be initiated so that cheap substandard Chinese products with no value to the country do not easily find their way and flood the domestic market. This had a detrimental effect on local industries as they could not compete with influx cheap products thereby resulting in closing shops and laying off workers.

### *5.2.8 Currency Crisis 2006–2009 and the Subsequent 'Burial' of the Zimbabwean Dollar*

When the Zimbabwean dollar was introduced to replace the Rhodesian dollar after Zimbabwe attained independence in 1980, the Zimbabwean dollar at its inception was worth more than the American dollar. The official exchange rate stood at 1 Zimbabwean dollar (1 ZWD) = 1.47 American dollar (USD). Also, main notes of Z$2, Z$5, Z$10 and Z$20 denominations were circulation in 1980s. However, marking a reversal of fortunes from 1980, the Zimbabwean dollar lost its value very rapidly and by the end of July 2006 ZW$1,000,000[6] was equivalent to 1 British pound sterling. Appetite for printing of money continued until a Z$100 trillion note was issued out in 2008. At that time, it could not even cover a bus fare for a single trip to one of the nearest high-density suburbs in Harare, hence it never found its way in the circulation system. Zimbabwe continued in doldrums since institutions such as the IMF and WB stopped lending to the country in 1999 after it defaulted on her debt repayments. Additionally, in June 2002, IMF further suspended technical assistance to Zimbabwe when the arrears were amounting to US $132 million. Since then, the country has often relied on loans from the African Development Bank.

In an attempt to address the worsening and chronic daily cash shortages that were ravaging the economy, the government through the country's Central Bank (Reserve Bank of Zimbabwe) and Ministry of Industry and Commerce, introduced a raft of measures, among other things, include price controls and rationing of cash by putting daily maximum withdrawals. Despite all these measures structural and economic headwinds such as slow and rapid decline of growth rate, elevated policy uncertainty and a hyperinflationary environment continued to characterise, haunt and weigh on the outlook of the economy. These measures in turn also aggravated the cash crisis, excessive pricing and a bout of shortages of drugs, food, fuel and other basic commodities, thereby threatening the security in the country and survival of the ruling party as well as abating its popularity. Because of the severity of the crisis highly respected senior government officials were even duped by one Rotina Mavhunga and made into believing that diesel could ooze from rocks in Chinhoyi.

As Cagan (1956, p. 25) states:

> Hyperinflation as beginning in the month the rise in price exceeds 50 per cent and as ending in the month before the monthly rise in prices drops below that amount and stays below for at least a year.

[6] https://www.zimbabwesituation.com/old/jul28a_2006.html. Title: Zim dollar hits a million to the pound as Murerwa unveils 'scandalous' supplementary budget.

Dornbusch and Fischer (1993) also define hyperinflation as a period in which year-on-year inflation rate exceeds 100%. According to Watkins[7] it is a scenario when inflation rate is extremely high, out of control, imprecise and unpredictable. Using the above two definitions of hyperinflation Siyakiya (2014, p. 8) states that Zimbabwe's hyperinflation started in March 2007 when month-on-month inflation rate was 50.5% and in November 2002 when year-on-year was 103.8%. The second figure could be a true reflection of the outset of hyperinflation in Zimbabwe since the following year on 15 September bearer's cheques were introduced in a bid to contain the already deteriorating economy. Also prior to 2002, there had been a lot of economic damages ranging from Black Friday (November 1997—when the Zimbabwean dollar depreciated dismally against the US dollar), Zimbabwe's involvement in DRC war (1998) and land reform/invasion (February 2000).

The central bank had also tried without success several times printed money to fight inflation, but provided room for elites to loot as well. When things started to get out of hand in 2003, the central bank introduced what were called traveller's cheques, which were in denominations of $1000, $5000, $10,000, $20,000, $50,000 to $100,000, which were quickly phased out because of their unpopularity and consistently loss of value. Later in the same year, the bank introduced what were popularly known as bearer cheques in denominations of $5000, $10,000 and $20,000, and these were initially valid up to 31 January 2004.

Money printing escapades under the famous operation called *Sunrise* were also rampant during this period further weakening the economy. Under the operation the central bank also on several occasions devalued the Zimbabwean, but it could not keep pace with galloping inflation and the ballooning black market exchange rate. Despite all the policies and operations turning around the fortunes of the economy proved a difficult task resulting in the Zimbabwean dollar rendered useless.

Queues of people wanting to buy basic commodities were seen everywhere and sometimes customers would just join a queue and after waiting for hours only to find out what they were looking for had run out of stock or was not the one they needed at that moment. '*I vividly recall that in 2006, I once joined a queue in Harare at one of the TM Supermarkets and of the last around 100 people who were in the queue did not have any idea of what commodity were they queuing for*', said Puruweti Siyakiya. This is one example that showed the level of resilience and suffering that Zimbabweans experienced during hyperinflation. With inflation being the order of the day, it was not surprising to find empty shelves in supermarkets. If goods happened to be in store, their shelf prices normally differed from those actually billed at the counter since prices could change two, three-fold or more while a person was in the queue.

According to Chitando et al. (2015), people went up to the extent of coining Shona[8] phrases and proverbs such as *Kuita Madhiri Anoitisa Mari* (*to take part in unlawful transactions or deals that give a maximum return*), *Mbudzi inodya/inoguta payakasungirirwa* (*a goat feeds where it is tethered*), *Zviri Kufaya* (*things*

[7] http://www.sjsu.edu/faculty/watkins/hyper.htmz.

[8] Common local language spoken in Zimbabwe.

*are productive*) and *Wona Yokutamba/ Meka plani* (*find a way by making things possible your own way/ make a plan*) as ways of sanitising or legitimising their corrupt and bad habits during difficult times. These proverbs and sayings were very popular especially among those who occupied influential positions in society and workplaces. In some cases, if the formal way or channel of getting something could be unsuccessful, the person in control could tell you to make a plan in reference to paying a bribe. For others even if they could tell you that it was impossible to get something, however they could end up giving in after you insist to pay a token of appreciation.

Staying alive during hyperinflation was tormenting and a deadly concern on itself. Whether one was employed or not poverty and hunger among other things left a lot of people feeling hopeless and troubled. For those who were employed they had to cater for monthly expenses on accommodation, food, transport, electricity, water and many other expenses, yet their monthly salaries and wages could only take them for 2 weeks if not one week. Here we have just listed those expenses that we think are deemed very necessary, otherwise the list goes beyond that.

The Central Bank tried countless times in 2006, 2008 and 2009 to redenominate the Zimbabwean dollar so as to contain hyperinflation by knocking off the zeros, however throughout history the highest denomination in the country (100 trillion dollar note, which never saw the light of day as it was completely rejected because of hyperinflation) stood as the second currency with the most zeros after that of Hungary (Siyakiya, 2014, p. 15). Usually, when there is stability and predictability in the economy, the Central Bank would make public awareness about the features of the new note some days before it is introduced or would announce when it is going to be introduce, however during the peak of hyperinflation in the country such arrangements were deemed impractical and luxury as by the time the note was in circulation it was already worthless. The bank continued to give a blind eye to prevailing reality and maintained with its stance of using shotgun tactics against the market conditions and public who had lost confidence in the government's ill-conceived monetary policies by making sure that the Zimbabwean dollar would remain the sole currency to be used for local transaction purposes. However, on 10 September 2008[9] central bank submitted to the pragmatic realities that were obtaining on the ground by making a statement that allowed retail and wholesale shops, oil companies and fuel outlets to sell their wares in foreign currency on condition that they apply for licences. These licences were popularly known as Foreign Exchange Licensed Warehouses and Retail Shops (FOLIWARS), Foreign Exchange Licensed Oil Companies (FELOCS) and Foreign Exchange Licensed Outlets for Petrol and Diesel (FELOPADS). Despite all these pronouncements of allowing business sector to sell in foreign currency, surprisingly the ruling party through the Bank stuck to its

[9] https://allafrica.com/stories/200812221258.html.
https://www.newsday.co.zw/2020/02/forex-crisis-zim-comes-full-circl/.
https://www.iol.co.za/business-report/economy/zimbabwe-introduces-forex-licensed-shops-831101.

guns and kept on printing the local currency and expecting the general public to use it while retailers were accepting foreign currency.

The officially recorded hyperinflation figure soared to reach astronomic levels of around 230 million per cent in July (Siyakiya, 2014) while the unofficial one was estimated to be over 450 billion per cent (Bekaert & Hodrick, 2017, p. 201) by end of 2008. These alarming inflation figures would let one to wonder if Zimbabwe's hyperinflation scenario was still under the subject of economics or it had now shifted to astronomy. The cause of Zimbabwe's hyperinflation was by and large, from printing of money by the Central Bank which was too much involved and engaged in quasi-fiscal and less productive activities at the expense of productive and conventional government deficits. Hyperinflation was just a symptom or reflection of a deep-rooted structural problem whereby the ruling party was more concerned about political survival than economic revival. During hyperinflation, a lot of people lost their life time savings and assets, particularly those who had converted the assets into cash when things got out of hand.

The ruling party came to the realisation that using the local currency was moribund and later swallowed its pride and embraced the multicurrency which the people had already been illegally using for their transactions. On 12 April 2009, the government completely abandoned the use of the Zimbabwean dollar. Initially the US dollar and the South African rand were the main currencies used for trading and later in that basket of currency the Australian dollar, Botswana pula, Chinese yuan (renminbi), Euro, Indian rupee, Japanese yen and pound sterling were accepted as legal tenders.

For close two decades, Zimbabweans have had a nasty and painful relationship with their national currency. To this date, most people have lost confidence in the national currency. As a result, they don't want to hear anything to do with the local currency since it quickly reminds them of the painful relationship they had experienced and the loss in savings during hyperinflation as it could not hold any value or serve as a reliable medium of exchange.

### 5.2.9 *Diamond Rush, Chiadzwa (2006–2008)*

Zimbabwe is endowed with mineral resources with a massive potential to transform the economy. This section unravels the developments and illicit activities surrounding the mining and trading of diamonds, and how these events impacted on the livelihoods of people in Chiadzwa, Marange community, in particular, and Zimbabwe in general. The diamond fields are located in Chiadzwa, which is a small communal area in Marange under the district of Mutare, but Zimbabwe is about 60 km from the city of Mutare. A diamond mining rush started in 2006 following the expiry of De Beers' exclusive prospecting order to operate in Chiadzwa, Marange communal area. The company is an international corporation with vested interests in exploration, mining, retailing and trading of diamonds. It got the rights to operate in Chiadzwa since the early 1990s under an arrangement and it had to renew the prospecting licence after every four years. After De Beers' operation rights came to an end, African

Consolidated Resources (ACR) a British-registered company took up the operation in Chiadzwa. However, legal wrangles on who should mine and explore the area put operations on a temporary halt and during the same period illegal miners colloquially known by the moniker '*magweja or makorokoza*' found their way into the diamond fields. The illegal miners invaded the diamond fields in response to an invitation which had nullified ACR's claim (Saunders, 2014). This was in total violation of the general Mines and Minerals Act and the Precious Stones Trade Act as illegal miners were allowed to operate in the area only through a word of mouth without any permit. The Mines and Minerals Act regulates the general mining operations, health, management and safety while the Precious Stones Trade Act regulates the possession of and dealings in precious stones like diamond, emeralds, etc. The alluvial diamonds were easily accessible at surface level without the need for using heavy machinery. This presented opportunities for small-scale miners to venture at low cost through digging and panning.

Analysts wondered how De Beers operated in the area for such a long period without any declaration of diamonds, but for diamonds to only be discovered when they left. Some argued that politicians were behind this and were benefiting at the expense of the government. By the end of 2006, government through the Zimbabwe Mining Development Corporation forcefully took over the rights to operate in the area notwithstanding a court ruling that gave African Consolidated Resources the rights to continue operating (Thornycroft, 2006). However, in 2010 the High Court dismissed an application from ACR to stop the sale of diamonds from Marange and gave a ruling granting that government could do the selling instead.

The 2006 diamond rush simultaneously transpired when Zimbabwe's economic environment was already crippling with hyperinflation, poor working conditions, high unemployment rate and shortages of basic food stuffs and fuels. When the diamond rush occurred in the midst of the above economic ills people could not resist, but were forced to participate because of the deplorable economic situation they found themselves in.

Close to 10,000 illegal small-scale miners were working in very small plots under appalling conditions. At first, they were allowed to sell their proceeds direct to government as a way of empowering them. Some analysts claim that letting illegal artisanal miners operate under the guise of empowerment was just a cover up for big politicians who were benefiting big times from the diamonds. This huge number of small-scale miners presented a ticking time bomb that could explode into a health crisis due to lack of proper water, sanitation, toilet and accommodation facilities. Water was a precious commodity at that time and villagers in the area could go to the sites to buy diamonds with water. At first some illegal artisanal diamond miners would exchange their proceeds through barter in form of groceries including mealie-meal, cooking oil, bread, soap and sometimes furniture since the economy was already tumbling. Some of shop owners were even refusing to accept the stones insisting to exchange their wares only on cash not knowing the values in those stones. A black market offering better prices surfaced and the small-scale miners stopped selling to the cash-strapped government agency, the Minerals Marketing Corporation of Zimbabwe which could not compete with private buyers (Hawkins, 2009). Because of these better offers increased cases of illegal miners killing each other and gangs of armed robbers confiscating diamonds from illegal miners also surfaced. Also, smuggling of these diamonds became rampant as buyers from as far as South Africa travelled to Mutare with some camped in Mozambique to avoid confrontation with law enforcement.

By late November 2006 police launched its first operation against illegal miners dubbed '*Operation Chikorokoza Chapera*' (*end to illegal mining*) (Saunders, 2014). According to Human Rights Watch (2009), it is reported that close to 22,000 people were arrested countrywide with an estimated more than 9000 in Marange alone.

Since 2006 several police crackdowns against illegal miners and traders of diamonds were done with *Operation Restore Order* after 29 March 2008 elections. A decisive operation called '*Dzokera Kumusha*'—'*Go Back Home*' was carried out in January 2009 to flush out illegal artisanal miners at Chiadzwa. During that same month government made an announcement to resettle an estimated 4700 villagers from Chiadzwa to Arda Transau Farm on approximately 12,000 ha. However, the villagers protested against government's move since no proper accommodation and water system on the area.

Accountability and transparency in the mining and sale of diamonds by Zimbabwe got attention and criticisms due to some of the challenges discussed earlier. Government tried to address some of them through compliance with minimum Kimberly Process requirements in order to formerly sell the diamonds in the international market.

### *5.2.10 Global Political Agreement (2008–2013)*

First and foremost, it is important to give a synopsis or chronicle the events that led to the genesis of the GPA. The Zimbabwe general elections were held on 29 March 2008 to elect both the President and Members of Parliament. The main Presidential candidates were Robert Gabriel Mugabe of ZANU-PF, Morgan Tsvangirai—the other faction of the Movement for Democratic Change (MDC), former Finance Minister and ZANU-PF politburo member, Dr. Simba Makoni—Independent.

Since independence, these elections were arguably the most historic because for the first time both ZANU-PF lost its parliamentary majority and the President lost the first round of the Presidential election. SADC observer missions gave conflicting results on the credibility and fairness in which the elections were held. Also, there was lack of trust on the Zimbabwe Electoral Commission (ZEC) by the MDC and other opposition parties as they did not consider it independent.

Two weeks later after elections, that is on 13 April 2008, ZEC announced that there was going to be a recounting of both parliamentary and presidential votes in 23 constituencies on 19 April 2008. On 02 May 2008 from presidential results proclaimed, Tsvangirai had garnered 47.9%, Mugabe had received 43.2 and Makoni had received 8.3%. However, the MDC did not accept the outcome as they argued that Tsvangirai had garnered 50.3%. Since there was no clear winner with majority of vote as provided for in the amended Electoral Act of 2005 a second round of presidential elections had to be done. On 16 May 2008 ZEC made an announcement in the government gazette proclaiming that the run-off would be held on 27 June 2008.

In the run-up to the run-off elections, violence resulted in the main opposition withdrawing from the election race. On 24 June 2008, the MDC made a formal withdrawal of Tsvangirai's participation in the second round, but ZEC did not accept it since it was submitted late. The run-off election was held on 27 June and on 29 June the Electoral Commission announced Mugabe had won with 2,150,269 votes against 233,000 for Tsvangirai. Mugabe was quickly sworn in at State House for another term as the President of Zimbabwe. In his speech after being sworn in, Mugabe called in for dialogue among political parties as a way to promote peace, cooperation and unity in the country. Both the African Union and SADC as well as the international community slammed and condemned the way Mugabe won the elections. As a result, direct intervention from SADC through a designated mediator President Thabo Mbeki was arranged.

After several concerted efforts to bring the two parties, the two MDC formations and ZANU-PF, on the same page, a breakthrough was made and they agreed to join hands. On the one hand, ZANU-PF was forced into a temporary power sharing agreement because it lacked national legitimacy and also to avoid facing continued punitive measures from the international community which were hurting the economy. On the other hand, the MDC formations were pushed to accept the deal because they wanted to prevent political harassment, torture, violence and repression against its members, they had failed to translate electoral victory in 2008 election into state power due to resistance from ZANU-PF which controlled state apparatus (Raftopoulos, 2010).

Apart from the above, the crisis in Zimbabwe had reached unprecedented levels with astronomic levels of hyperinflation, increased unemployment rates, gruesome levels of poverty and erratic shortages of basic commodities being the order of the day. Additionally, the deplorable political and economic crisis in Zimbabwe had ripple effects to neighbouring countries as Zimbabweans flocked in numbers to countries like Botswana, Namibia and South Africa among others, to earn a living and for that reason Zimbabwe which was one of the most promising and prosperous nations in SADC was now being considered a sick man in the region (Gavin, 2007).

In a nutshell, the GPA was born out of political contestation and the disputed 2008 presidential election in Zimbabwe. The GPA was meant to provide a roadmap democratic transition and at the same time proffer solutions to address immediate demands for peace and economic stability (Connolly, 2011). The Agreement laid down solutions which were brokered through a power sharing pact among the three competing parties in the 2008 namely MDC-T, ZANU-PF and MDC-M led by Morgan Tsvangirai, Robert Mugabe and Professor Arthur Mutambara, respectively. The mediator to the deal was the former President of South Africa Mr. Mbeki and this deal was signed on 15 September 2008 in Harare, Zimbabwe (Mutisi, 2011). Years before his mediation role in the Zimbabwean political impasse Mbeki used to use a soft position on dealing with political situation in Zimbabwe. Mbeki's role was a difficult task as he had to balance between going against Pan-African ideology and the need for ensuring democracy as demanded by the West all for a broader African vision (Freeman, 2005). As cited in Mutisi (2011), Hoddie and Hartzell (2005) define power sharing agreement as a promissory contract that is premised on redistribution of political, territorial, military and economic power among belligerents.

In the pact Robert Mugabe was the Executive President, that is, Head of State and Government, commander-in-chief of the armed forces and chair of cabinet while Morgan Tsvangirai was the Prime Minister (Head of the Council of Ministers), and Prof Arthur Mutambara was the Deputy Prime Minister. The two MDC formations were awarded 16 Cabinet or Ministerial posts while ZANU-PF got 15 posts. The opposition were given less influential ministerial posts so that state operations and its illegal activities remain concealed from the public, but to continue under the watch of ZANU-PF. The Government of National Unity (GNU) was an attempt to address economic, democracy and governance issues and political polarisation in the country. On the economic side, inflation dropped from astronomic figures to single digits and the Zimbabwean dollar was also completely abandoned. Additionally, a Constitutional Parliamentary Select Committee (COPAC) from both parties was established in April 2009 to coordinate the consultative processes for constitutional reform. A new constitution was first approved in a referendum on 16 March 2013 and further approved by parliament on 9 May 2013. Everyone hoped the GNU would lead Zimbabwe into a new era of political tolerance among Zimbabweans, new ways of doing politics and new political leadership, but after the GNU Zimbabwe has found herself in the same old situation.

In sum the chapter covered major events which have unfolded in the history of Zimbabwe. Failure by the country to make use of opportunities have resulted in many challenges for the country. For instance, discovery of precious stones such as diamonds should have been a chance for the country to succeed in the mining sector. Not only diamonds, but gold is also plentiful in the country. Gold reserves available in the economy are estimated to be around 13 million tonnes, whereas at the end of 2016 only 586 tonnes have been extracted (Mangudya, 2016). Smuggling of the yellow metal alone is still rampant. The country lost about $200 million worth of gold on an annual basis, notwithstanding other leakages of the metal which may go completely undetected. Thus, the mining sector in conjunction with other sectors of comparative advantages like agriculture could have been used to frontload transformation of the country.

On the other hand, a modicum of peace and stability enjoyed by the economy during the GNU era was short-lived. Like morning dew, it quickly disappeared. The bigger lesson still lingering in the minds of most progressive Zimbabweans is that there are massive dividends to be enjoyed when people are united. Furthermore, political actors shoulder the greatest responsibility to cultivate this unity among the masses.

Hazards from droughts and cyclones the country began to experience long ago and will keep on experiencing into the future should have acted as tale signs of tougher times to come ahead. Shocks induced on economies by hazards such as these are unprecedented. All these hazards have heralded the grand arrival of climate change on the economic space of mankind. Whether we like it or not, climate change is slowly becoming a strong argument shaping economies. 'Climate change' proofing economies has thus become an imperative for modern economies, failure to ensure this results in a heavy price to be paid.

## References

African Development Bank. (1997). *Zimbabwe: Economic Structural Adjustment Programme Project Performance Evaluation Report (PPER).* A. D. Bank. https://www.afdb.org/fileadmin/uploads/afdb/Documents/Evaluation-Reports-_Shared-With-OPEV_/06050223-EN-ZIMBABWE-ECONOMIC-STRUCTURAL-ADJUSTMENT.PDF

AMANI Trust. (1998). A Consolidated Report on the Food Riots 19–23 January, 1998. 69. http://hrforumzim.org/wp-content/uploads/1998/01/consolidatedreportonfood.pdf

Bekaert, G., & Hodrick, R. J. (2017). *International financial management* (3rd ed.). Cambridge University Press.

Benson, C. (1998). Drought and the Zimbabwe economy, 1980–93. In T. J. O'Neill H. (Ed.), *A World without Famine?* (pp. 241–273). Palgrave Macmillan. https://doi.org/10.1007/978-1-349-26229-8_11

Bond, P. (1999). Political reawakening in Zimbabwe. *Monthly Review, 50*(11). https://doi.org/10.14452/MR-050-11-1999-04_1

Bond, P. (2007). Competing explanations of Zimbabwe's long economic crisis. *Safundi: The Journal of South African and American Studies, 8*(2), 149–181. https://doi.org/10.1080/17533170701370976

Cagan, P. (1956). The monetary dynamics of hyperinflation. In M. Friedman (Ed.), *Studies in the quantity theory of money* (pp. 25–117). University of Chicago Press.

CEDRISA, UNEP, & SARDC. (2009). Droughts and floods in Southern Africa: Environmental change and human vulnerability. In (pp. 49). Nairobi: Centre for Development Research and Information in Southern Africa (CEDRISA), United Nations Environment Programme (UNEP), Division of Early Warning and Assessment (DEWA), Southern African Research and Documentation Centre (SARDC).

Chitando, A., Chikowero, J., & Madongonda, A. M. (2015). *The art of survival: Depictions of Zimbabwe and the Zimbabwean in crisis.* Cambridge Scholars Publishing. https://books.google.com.tr/books?id=BrYPCwAAQBAJ

Clemens, M., & Moss, T. (2005). *Costs and causes of Zimbabwe's crisis.* Center for Global Development. Retrieved 26/04/2020 from https://www.cgdev.org/sites/default/files/2918_file_Zimbabwe_Crisis.pdf

Connolly, D. (2011). *The global political agreement and democratic transition in Zimbabwe* [Working Paper]. Oxford Transitional Justice Research. https://www.law.ox.ac.uk/sites/files/oxlaw/connollyfinal21.pdf

Dashwood, H. S. (2000). *Zimbabwe: The political economy of transformation.* University of Toronto Press.

Diersen, M. A., Taylor, G., & May, A. (2002). Direct and indirect effects of drought on South Dakota's economy. *Economics Commentator*, *432*(26).

Dornbusch, R., & Fischer, S. (1993). Moderate inflation. *The World Bank Economic Review, 7*(1), 1–44. https://doi.org/10.1093/wber/7.1.1

Edwards, B., Gray, M., & Hunter, B. (2009). A sunburnt country: The economic and financial impact of drought on rural and regional families in Australia in an era of climate change. *Australian Journal of Labour Economics, 12*(1), 108–131.

Edwards, B., Gray, M., & Hunter, B. (2019). The social and economic impacts of drought. *Australian Journal of Social Issues, 54*(1), 22–31. https://doi.org/10.1002/ajs4.52

Freeman, L. (2005). South Africa's Zimbabwe policy: Unravelling the contradictions. *Journal of Contemporary African Studies, 23*(2), 147–172. https://doi.org/10.1080/0258900042000229999

Gavin, M. D. (2007). Planning for post-Mugabe Zimbabwe. In (pp. 45). Council on Foreign Relations.

Giovannetti, G., & Sanfilippo, M. (2016). Do Chinese exports crowd-out African goods? An econometric analysis by country and sector. In S. Henson & O. F. Yap (Eds.), *The power of the Chinese Dragon: Implications for African development and economic growth* (pp. 10–41). Springer.

Goldstein, A., Pinaud, N., Reisen, H., & Chen, X. (2006). *China and India: What's in it for Africa?* Organization for Economic Co-operation and Development.

Government of Zimbabwe. (2009). *Memorandum to Cabinet by the Minister of Lands and Rural Resettlement, Hon. H. M. Murerwa on the Update on Land Reform and Resettlement Prograamme*. Harare

Hawkins, T. (2009). *The mining sector in Zimbabwe and its potential contribution to recovery* [Working Paper]. UNDP. https://cryptome.org/kimberly/kimberly-003.pdf

Hoddie, M., & Hartzell, C. (2005). Power sharing as an impediment to peace and democracy. In P. G. Roeder & D. S. Rothchild (Eds.), *Sustainable peace: Power and democracy after civil wars* (pp. 29–50). Cornell University Press. https://books.google.com.tr/books?id=FFGNRfzndl8C

Horridge, M., Madden, J., & Wittwer, G. (2005). The impact of the 2002–2003 drought on Australia. *Journal of Policy Modeling, 27*(3), 285–308. https://doi.org/10.1016/j.jpolmod.2005.01.008

Human Rights Watch. (2009). Diamonds in the rough: Human rights abuses in the Marange diamond fields of Zimbabwe. In (pp. 63). Human Rights Watch.

Ighobor, K. (2013). China in the heart of Africa. *Africa Renewal, 26*(3), 6–8. http://urban-africa-china.angonet.org/sites/default/files/resource_files/china_in_the_heart_of_africa_-_africa_renewal_jan_2013_0.pdf

Jones, T. (2011). *Uncovering Zimbabwe's debt: The case for a democratic solution to the unjust debt burden*. Jubilee Debt Campaign. https://eurodad.org/files/pdf/4733-uncovering-zimbabwe-rsquo-s-debt-the-case-for-a-democratic-solution-to-the-unjust-debt-burden.pdf

Juana, J. S. (2006). A quantitative analysis of Zimbabwe's land reform policy: An application of Zimbabwe SAM multipliers. *Agrekon, 45*(3), 294–318. https://doi.org/10.1080/03031853.2006.9523749

Kairiza, T. (2009). *Unbundling Zimbabwe's journey to hyperinflation and official dollarization* (09–12). National Graduate Institute for Policy Studies, Policy Information Center. https://www.grips.ac.jp/r-center/wp-content/uploads/09-12.pdf

Madzwamuse, M. (2010). *Climate Governments in Africa: adaptation strategies and institutions* (A synthesis report prepared for the Heinrich Boll Foundation, Issue.

Mahuni, K., Taru, J., & Bonga, W. G. (2020). *Africa's incomplete cycles of development*. Peter Lang Publishing.

Makina, D. (2010). Historical perspective on Zimbabwe's economic performance: A tale of five lost decades. *Journal of Developing Societies, 26*(1), 99–123. https://doi.org/10.1177/0169796X1002600105

Makochekanwa, A. (2008). *The impact of a budget deficit on inflation in Zimbabwe* (24227). Munich Personal RePEc Archive. http://mpra.ub.uni-muenchen.de/24227/

Manby, B. (2002). Fast track land reform in Zimbabwe. *Human Rights Watch, 14*(1(A)), 1–44.

Mangudya, J. P. (2016). *Walk the talk to restore trust and confidence*. Reserve Bank of Zimbabwe.

Maphosa, B. (1994). Lessons from the 1992 drought in Zimbabwe: The quest for alternative food policies. *Nordic Journal of African Studies, 3*(1), 53–58.

Matondi, P. B. (2012). *Zimbabwe's fast track land reform*. Zed Books.

Ministry of Agriculture Zimbabwe, USAID, WFP Zimbabwe, & Africa, F. S. a. E. (2000). *Assessment of the impact of cyclone Eline (February 2000) on the Food, Agriculture and Natural Resource Sector in Zimbabwe*. https://fews.net/sites/default/files/documents/reports/1000050.pdf

Mlambo, A. S. (1997). *The economic structural adjustment programme: The case of Zimbabwe, 1990–1995*. University of Zimbabwe Publications Office.

Moyo, T., & Mdlongwa, T. (2014). Look East or look least? The Zimbabwean experience of Chinese economic investment in selected texts and examples. *African Journal of Governance and Development*, *3*(2), 5–15. https://hdl.handle.net/10520/EJC191654

Mumbengegwi, C. (2002). *Macroeconomic and structural adjustment policies in Zimbabwe*. Palgrave Publishers.

Musoni, F. (2010). Operation Murambatsvina and the politics of street vendors in Zimbabwe. *Journal of Southern African Studies, 36*(2), 301–317. https://doi.org/10.1080/03057070.2010.485786

Mutasa, C. (2015). A brief history of land in Zimbabwe: 1890-Today. In *Brief* (p. 7): Focus on Land in Africa.

Mutisi, M. (2011). *Beyond the signature: Appraisal of the Zimbabwe global political agreement (GPA) and implications for intervention*. T. A. C. f. t. C. R. o. D. (ACCORD). https://www.africaportal.org/documents/5436/policy_practice41.pdf

Nangombe, S. S. (2015). Drought conditions and management strategies in Zimbabwe. Proceedings of the regional workshops on capacity development to support national drought management policies for eastern and Southern Africa and the near east and north Africa Regions, Harare.

Nyathi, P. T. (2004). Reintegration of ex-combatants into Zimbabwean society: A lost opportunity. In B. Raftopoulos & T. Savage (Eds.), *Zimbabwe: Injustice and political reconciliation* (pp. 63–78). Institute for Justice and Reconciliation.

Ojakorotu, V., & Kamidza, R. (2018). Look East Policy: The case of Zimbabwe-China political and economic relations since 2000. *India Quarterly, 74*(1), 17–41. https://doi.org/10.1177/0974928417749642

Raftopoulos, B. (2008). The crisis in Zimbabwe, 1998–2008. In B. Raftopoulos & A. S. Mlambo (Eds.), *Becoming Zimbabwe. A history from the pre-colonial period to 2008* (pp. 201–232). Weaver Press; Jacana Media.

Raftopoulos, B. (2010). The global political agreement as a 'passive revolution': Notes on contemporary politics in Zimbabwe. *The Round Table, 99*(411), 705–718. https://doi.org/10.1080/00358533.2010.530414

Ramani, S. (2016). Is China ready for a post-Mugabe Zimbabwe? *The Diplomat*. https://thediplomat.com/2016/08/is-china-ready-for-a-post-mugabe-zimbabwe/

Reason, C. J. C., & Keibel, A. (2004). Tropical cyclone Eline and its unusual penetration and impacts over the southern African mainland. *Weather and Forecasting, 19*(5), 789–805. https://doi.org/10.1175/1520-0434(2004)019%3c0789:TCEAIU%3e2.0.CO;2

Saunders, R. (2014). Geologies of power: Blood diamonds, security politics and Zimbabwe's troubled transition. *Journal of Contemporary African Studies, 32*(3), 378–394. https://doi.org/10.1080/02589001.2014.956501

Siyakiya, P. (2014). *An analysis of the effects of hyperinflation on manufacturing sector output. A case of Zimbabwe's manufacturing firms 2000–2013* International Institute of Social Sciences of the Erasmus University of Rotterdam]. The Hague. https://thesis.eur.nl/pub/17162/dono PURUWETI-SIYAKIYA.pdf

Thornycroft, P. (2006). Zimbabwe Government Seizes Diamond Mine. http://www.voanews.com/english/archive/2006-12/2006-12-15-voa18.cfm

Tukić, N., & Tombindo, F. (2016a). *Economic repercussions of the look east policy in Zimbabwe*. Centre for Chinese Studies, Stellenbosch University. http://146.232.129.77/bitstream/handle/10019.1/101548/tukic_economic_2016.pdf?sequence=3&isAllowed=y

Tukić, N., & Tombindo, F. (2016b). Economic repercussions of the Look East Policy in Zimbabwe (C. f. C. Studies, Trans.). In (pp. 4). Centre for Chinese Studies, Stellenbosch University.

United Nations Development Programme. (1996). Economic growth and human development. In (pp. 229). Oxford University Press.

World Bank. (1993). The World Bank Annual Report 1993. In (pp. 260). World Bank.
Youde, J. (2007). Why look east? Zimbabwean foreign policy and China. *Africa Today*, *53*(3), 3–19. https://www.jstor.org/stable/4187790
Zimbabwe Human Rights NGO Forum. (2005). Order Out of Chaos, Or Chaos Out of Order?: A Preliminary Report on Operation "Murambatsvina".
Zindiye, S. (2015). *Understanding China's activities in Zimbabwe: A review of literature*. Rhodes University.

# Part IV
# On the Edge of a Cliff…Crisis within a Crisis!!

# Chapter 6
# 'Jewel of Africa' Peeled: Four Blunders Over the Four Decades

## 6.1 Introduction

Contemporary Zimbabwe is quite different from Zimbabwe of yesteryear in many aspects. We saw in Chap. 2 how Zimbabwe was performing fairly well in terms of different indicators during early years of independence. The thought of life in early Zimbabwe often brings a sense of nostalgia to some elderly sections of the population. Time has since moved. It will continue. In a decade's time, Zimbabwe will be celebrating a golden jubilee as a sovereign state. What will she be having to show for that long and winding journey of sovereignty which she has failed to achieve over the past four decades? What then is a blunder?

## 6.2 Blunders—One After the Other

Although there might be slight variations in dictionary meanings of what a blunder is, many definitions point to a blunder as a mistake made especially through *ignorance or carelessness*. As the reader shall notice, this definition is quite compelling and befitting as we journey inside Zimbabwe's four decades of economic turbulence. There are a number of errors over the past four decades in the history of attempting to develop by our beautiful country in which sheer ignorance and carelessness marked the genesis of turbulence, which has become an albatross for our economy to this day.

Zimbabwe has not succeeded much in generating consistent, robust and self-sustaining growth and development over the past four decades due to a number of blunders committed in the journey. However, most literature on Zimbabwe's economic history is often mute on these. This chapter examines four blunders over the last four decades. Mathematically, it translates to one blunder per decade, however the math does not matter much as we unbundle the blunders. For the purpose of this

 
K. Mahuni et al., *Zimbabwe's Economy*, Advances in African Economic, Social and Political Development, https://doi.org/10.1007/978-3-031-81588-1_6

book, we will not match any particular decade with any specific blunder, instead we will try to examine the four in detail. Only four blunders over four decades? Yes. A question then comes to the reader, do these suffice as an explanation for the challenges the country has experienced? The answer again is yes as we shall explore.

While we have a plethora of factors explaining the challenges experienced by Zimbabwe, the discourse of blunders we examine is quite compelling. With respect to *peeling* of the jewel of Africa, we are therefore exploring those instances whereby the combined sum of ignorance and carelessness fuelled the escalation of challenges. The depth attached to each blunder we identified justifies this stand point. In this chapter we look at the demise of most growth points, the failure to embrace proper and modern industrial cluster models, over dependency on aid for development model, and weak social safety nets as some of the key blunders which contributed to the trashing of the jewel of Africa in the context of ignorance as well as carelessness. To conclude the chapter, we also try to explore how the blunders are connected.

### *6.2.1 Demise of Growth Points*

Zimbabwe had started well with the concept of growth points. This was going to help reduce rural urban migration. In the process, this was going to promote rural industrialisation. However, lack of attention led to the demise of most growth points (GPs) in Zimbabwe. One of the results of colonisation of Zimbabwe was the creation of a dual economy as discussed in Chap. 2. One related to the urban areas which were easily accessed by whites and were being supported with most amenities and all the requisite infrastructure resulting in an advanced economic set up catering mostly for the white minority whereas blacks were relegated to deplorable and backward rural economies. This made life enjoyable by the settler minority. The backward economy was starved of basic infrastructure with virtually no industries to talk about. Thus, white minority lived in comfort in urban areas whereas blacks lived in squalor in the rural areas. Consequently, life became unbearable for the majority of Zimbabweans.

After successfully executing the liberation struggle, one task faced by the first republic was to correct this imbalance. With almost no sustainable economies to talk about in the country side and devoid of opportunities, people from the rural areas flocked into urban areas in droves in search of opportunities such as employment causing a strain on social amenities in most towns.

So, to tame this tide of migration, there was thus a need by the government to intervene. One such way was to develop rural areas so that they also become sources of better standards of living like was being enjoyed in urban areas. Thus, the concept of GPs was born with the express purpose of transforming the rural areas so as to foster better living standards for rural dwellers also as we aptly explained in Chap. 1.

#### 6.2.1.1 Growth Point Strategy

Moyo (1991, p. 54) defines a growth point as 'a centre with an identifiable resource base capable of stimulating specific production and marketing activities'. Wekwete (1988), Wekwete (1994) indicates that *growth points* (GP) are of two types—rural and urban. Examples of urban growth points were Ruwa and Chitungwiza. Both are satellites of Harare, the Zimbabwean capital. Rapid and sustained growth should be the trademark of this spatial order, which in actuality, is the midpoint between the lower and the higher order centres. The economic base, substantial backward and forward linkages with the adjoining hinterland through processes of vertical and horizontal integration, plus provision of alternative but viable investment opportunities—all these give the growth point splendour and continuity (Government of Zimbabwe, 1991; Wekwete, 1988, 1994). Nonetheless, the above outlined GP features have remained in more theory than turned into a reality. Most of the GPs were 'created' with no resource base thrust aspect at all. Of such phenomenon are the typical GPs that have been stagnant in growth, unattractive and the kind. Wekwete (1988) identifies two types of rural district or growth centres, namely, the High Potential Centres (HPC) and Low Potential Centres (LPC). An HPC is a centre that has a wide range of low order and high order services, which include strong administrative infrastructure. Examples were Murewa, Mutoko, Gokwe, Gutu-Mupandawana, Chisumbanje and Sanyati.

On the other hand, an LPC is one that was elevated by the post-1980 designation. Wekwete (1988) foresaw that the future of the LPC depended on the 'continued public investment support'. LPCs have thus limited economic potential and, in essence, are the majority in numbers in the country. Rural service centres were meant to bring cheaper goods and services to rural people and reduce the need for them to travel to major rural centres for basic necessities such as groceries, household goods, agricultural inputs and banking services. A centre should at least be able to meet the basic requirements that place a settlement in harmonious congruency with its environment and give the inhabitants a 'hospitable' and less constraining milieu. The driving engine for the development of the rural service centres has been predominantly the government. It has been the sole provider of the infrastructure both social and physical. In terms of economic drive, again government has taken the lead through its state-operated corporations like the Grain Marketing Board, Cotton Marketing Board (now Cottco), Tobacco Marketing Board and a host of other parastatals. This is in terms of the agro-based settlements.

On the other hand, before independence the colonial government also conceived the idea of GPs, the key motive being to discriminate against blacks. A reporter in a local paper, The Herald indicates that the settler government first mooted this idea of growth points in 1969.We see this idea being pursued further later on when the reporter highlights that in 1978 the settler government came up with a policy framework through a document titled Integrated Plan for Rural Development. From this, rural and urban setup set aside for frontloading the growth point concept were designated. They included areas such as Mataga, Gutu, Chitungwiza, Murewa, among others dotted across the country, notes the reporter.

As alluded to earlier intervening to develop rural areas was also adopted by the first republic soon after independence. Post-independence, The Herald highlights that a huge resource envelope of $20 million was unveiled so as for creation of critical enablers as aptly captured in the following:

> Through the Public Sector Investment Programme, the then Ministry of Local Government and Housing spent about $20million providing piped water, access roads, sewer reticulation, bus terminuses, bus shelters and many other provisions around centres identified as potential growth points. The programme was initially carried at 11 growth points and 55 district service centres, all in communal lands.

#### 6.2.1.2 Growth Point Concept by the Settler Government Versus Growth Point Concept by the First Republic: Why There Has Been Limited Success?

To date a look around the country's ten provinces and their numerous districts, GPs are dotted across the country. Most services which dominate include residential, health centres, retail shops, police camps, banks, light industries, etc. This is a laudable achievement. However, what is worrying is that not all GPs do have the above mentioned, those that have for sure they do have but some are still severely lack and are also isolated. Most centres still have challenges of accessing critical services like telecommunications having little or minimal signal out of the three Mobile Networks Operators (MNOs), i.e. Econet, Netone and Telecel available in Zimbabwe, hospitals among other essentials. State-owned Telone provides fixed landline telephone services in few such centres, as it has suffered vandalism over the years coupled with old infrastructure among other challenges. This further makes these areas difficult to live in let alone develop as others. Sadly, there are those that have less of the above amenities. A majority of these centres still have poor and hard to access roads—the problem becomes worse during rainy seasons. A good example is an area such as Chirundu located to the north of Zimbabwe. People in the area for instance have to rely for hospital services from neighbouring Zambia. The nearest town in Zimbabwe for critical services such as mortuaries is Karoi, a town which is more than 100 kms away. Border centres such as Chirundu could have been modelled around growth point concept, in the process they would be further developed. For services such as mobile telephone, television and reception signal most border locations still depend heavily from neighbouring countries.

For most remote like areas in Zimbabwe which could have been used as starting points for growth points essentials such as electricity, clean running water, ICTs and other related amenities remain a luxury for people. Given that the country still subsists heavily on aid, even accessing these areas with humanitarian aid is a nightmare. However, peasant agriculture is still key for survival for most people in these places, with its sustainability being a challenge due to successive droughts fuelled by climate change.

These remote like places are preferred by polity for one purpose—votes. In Zimbabwe and a number of other African states, it is a common feature especially during electioneering period to find those hard to access areas being accessed with much ease by vociferous politicians and their convoys exhibiting much verve and gusto as they hunt for votes from the electorate. Occasionally you can come across aspiring parliamentarians or councillors sponsoring or 'influencing' public works such as rehabilitating gravel roads or in some cases a few bags of cement are availed by the candidate from his/her own pocket to do a few touch ups on the gravel roads. This can be by erecting water ways or just adding a slab on some substandard bridge which was built way back and has seen successive election seasons in that sorry state to connect the concerned people with other places. Once they are voted into office, they will be hardly visible in these places, only to resurface towards the next plebiscite peddling almost the same manifesto of 'working on that same gravel road'. If the community is very lucky, a borehole can be drilled for the people. The cycle continues one election after the other, the areas remain backward. This notion of trading projects with votes is common in African politics, Mahuni et al. (2020) prefer to call this phenomenon 'African transactional electioneering and politicking'. Much growth points around the country have thus not been fully stretched to their potential to be epicentres of development for the local economies, rather they have slowly declined over time.

So, the GPs concept by the settler government was used largely as a decoy to hoodwink disaffected black majority so that they remain in rural areas and never think of migrating to urban centres in search of better living conditions since the rural set were purported to provide the same. The end result was for the blacks to remain pacified and content. What was the outcome? The settler government did not succeed. The trick did not work much. Growing resentment towards oppression and intransigence of the settlers precipitated a war of liberation which eventually so the defeat of the settlers by the black majority.

Independence was won and the black majority became in charge. The first republic as we indicated above embarked on a plan of rural development using growth points as a special vehicle for this, partly to curb migration to urban areas. What was the outcome? Although temporary success was enjoyed by the government, challenges weighed down overall success of the concept of growth points.

One of the reasons for its failure by early Zimbabwe could be the issue of the motive which was not so well calculated just like in the settler government case. For the first republic, growth points were erroneously used as a first order condition of stemming migration of rural dwellers into towns and cities, hence later on they were easily forgotten in the development plan of the country. Thus, there was a lack of serious thought and commitment on the potential growth points could impact on the broader economy as reflected in the quality of infrastructure at these places to date as well as disconnection from other key centres of development such as big towns and cities. The steam which had gathered since their inception gradually cooled off. There was a significant disconnection between rural development and development policy of the country as a whole. The two were supposed to move together at the same time.

By now if the GPs concept had been fully supported the expectation was for the growth points to eventually mature into bigger centres run by say town boards and eventually migrate to full town status. At the same time standard infrastructure such as water, sewer reticulation, fire services, tarred roads as well as street lights will be in place 40 years since independence could have resulted in some of these centres becoming hubs of various economic activities fitting into the broader economy, consequently the with growth of GPs outwards and towards major centres they would then merge/gel together. Travelling across many parts of the country as you move out of major towns, further away differences are easy to pick between life in most rural areas compared to urban life-dualism we explored in Chap. 1 is still very evident. Moreover, the propensity for outward migration especially by the economically active as they scrounge for better opportunities remains high. There is still that divide between town and rural settings. Some growth points have few dilapidated and often defaced buildings, grocer shops here and there and substandard infrastructure being common features.

The main legislation for physical planning still in use in Zimbabwe is the Regional and Town Councils (RTCs) Act which has been in place since the 1960s. One of its features is that for every radius of 8 kms there has to be a major business centre. Reality on the ground however tells a different story. There are some places which are still devoid of basic infrastructure and all the supporting amenities. Success stories of the GPs relating to rural areas includes notable examples such as Mpandawana in Gutu. However partial successes are evident in places like Jerera, Nemanwa, Checheche, Murambinda, Chachacha, Sadza, Juru, Nyika to mention a few. In some of this where partial success is evident, a lot of work is still required to even out developments. For instance, residential areas are sprawling resulting in a surge in demand for services and goods by populations resident there. Supply of services has however been relatively inelastic so as to match buoyant demand. Industries, basic infrastructure etc. still fall short compared to demand from the burgeoning populations at these places. Migration is still evident as people look outwards for opportunities as we highlighted earlier. Four decades is a lengthy time period; remarkable milestones could have been leveraged from the GPs concept to create self-sustaining economies with propensity for contributing to the national GDP.

A better way was for GPs to be fused with the broader policy of economic growth of the country towards sustainable development. The idea of reviving GPs as means of developing rural areas is slowly gaining momentum with the second republic as evidenced in the Zimbabwe National Industrial Development Policy (ZNIDP) 2019–2023 policy document. Section 5.9.2 of the document on Rural Industry Development reads;

> The ZNIDP (2019–2023) recognizes that the majority of the populace in Zimbabwe is domiciled in the rural areas. In that regard, the policy prioritizes the need to empower and improve standards of living for people in these economically backward areas.

In conclusion, in both scenarios (colonial and first republic case) GPs did not succeed much, hence a gradual demise of growth points which we witness even until today which has prompted a revisit into the concept as espoused in the ZNIDP we highlighted. This is a serious blunder born out of inattentiveness on the power GPs could have on the economy. As long as not much is done in revamping the idea of growth points across the country, rural development will remain but a field of dreams. Moreover, the dual economy model no different from that of the colonial days will remain firmly in place. The only difference will be that of contexts, i.e. pre- versus post-independence but with identical outcomes.

#### 6.2.1.3 Why the Time for Reviving Rural Development Through Growth Points is Now?

Growth points were thus gradually forgotten in the first economy of the independent Zimbabwe. Rural development could have been pursued using GPs concept such that by now some of them could have merged with major towns and cities if the 40 years had been used so well to package growth points model resulting in self-sustaining 'little economies' producing significant GDPs. The results could have been amazing in terms of infrastructure, employment, empowerment, industrial linkages (both forward and backward) among other innumerable benefits. While we may lament about opportunities lost through failure to ride on the GPs model, Zimbabwe can still salvage some rural development via the growth points again. There is hope all the same. Plenty of hope. The second republic can foster this if we look at some two of the following important pre-existing conditions on the ground.

### *6.2.2 Devolution*

The concept of decentralisation of powers to provinces in Zimbabwe was mooted way back but serious efforts towards the actual implementation is evident in the tenure of the second republic, a giant step in the right direction. The national constitution provides for devolution. To date various resource envelopes (devolution funds have been availed to different provinces to stimulate development.

What is critical is continuous education among stakeholders on the demands of devolution to ensure that key deliverables such as employment, environmental sustainability in sync with national interests are pursued. Further, devolution should be centred on the ethos of ensuring that unity prevails among the people in the interest of nation building. Unity of purpose has achieved tremendous results for countries such as, Rwanda, Botswana to mention but a few.

Devolution funds should also be inclined towards creation of industries with a bias towards manufacturing besides provision of basic amenities like roads, clinics, schools, water (which in our opinion should have been provided way back—a journey of four decades punctuated with meticulous planning which began with a single step in 1980 should have ensured that all this is now in place!). These have a potential to create backward and forward linkages across different sectors. The resulting multiplier effects propel the local economies. Devolution planning should have at its core techniques such as Cost Benefit Analysis (CBA) in choosing optimal projects for communities. Going forward devolution funds thus should not focus too much on socially inclined projects for instance building schools as these are likely to have minimum multiplier effects compared to projects with potential to create fresh capital e.g. building factories.

### 6.2.3 Resource Endowments, Rich Sources for Comparative Advantages

Portuguese economist David Ricardo propounded the theory of comparative advantage in the eighteenth century which is anchored on specialisation when economies have varying resource endowments. The theory has powerful application to the Zimbabwean context even to this day. The gift of different resources across all the provinces in the country has potential to inspire respective provinces to utilise these differential endowments to also package the GPs concept. The different endowments also imply different capabilities across provinces of the country. Value Addition in numerous sectors. Nyanyadzi in Manicaland, Cairns would process tomatoes into semi processed sauce which was later completed final processing being done in Mutare. Karoi in Mashonaland West has plenty of tobacco growing activities, related activities such as processing could be done within Karoi. Manicaland province which lies on the eastern side of Zimbabwe has rich deposits of diamond in places such as Chiadzwa. The province has full potential to host diamond cutting and processing and associated activities. Growth points within Mutare could be centres for such diamond activities. These comparative advantages remain underutilised.

What is key to these endowments is to value add them. Policies which compel the companies extracting them to value add them at the source of extraction will be very necessary. For example, platinum is mined in Midlands Province. This could be exported after much value addition.

In conclusion a lot can be done to propel forward the issue of GPs using the numerous comparative advantages which are found throughout the country. Growth points in Zimbabwe can be useful in filling out gaps existing between urban and rural areas. Infrastructure, employment etc. can be developed by spreading the thin resource envelopes on respective GPs which will in turn will be upgraded. For devolution, while a lot needs to be done for it to be fully operational it however has immense potential to also compliment propagation of growth points in the country. Potential in most rural and related areas in Zimbabwe remain largely untapped.

### 6.2.4 Failure to Embrace Proper and Modern Industrial Cluster Models

Industrial clusters are easier said than done. So straight forward they may appear yet if they are not properly applied, desired results may not be achieved. Overall ignorance on a number of key aspects relating to industrial clusters by Zimbabwe led to *silent* industrial clusters. Best practices on clusters have resulted in high impacts in not only their home countries but beyond borders too. Their impacts have been phenomenal. On the other hand, poorly conceived industrial clusters have remained dormant with little impact and resulted in little noise globally. The beauty of industrial clusters in the development trajectory of Zimbabwe was not seriously considered. It was ignored. Ignorance is a serious blunder. We discovered that not only in Zimbabwe has the role of industrial clusters been overlooked, even a number of other countries in the continent. Moreover, where attempts towards clusters have been or are being made the results have not been so convincing resulting in silent clusters.

Do we have proper impactful industrial clusters in Zimbabwe? Are our clusters if any globally or regionally competitive? Can the clusters significantly contribute to overall GDP of our beloved country? Industrial clusters are time dependent; they do not simply appear or disappear but rather develop overtime (Ketels & Memedovic, 2008). When will ours 'mature' if at all they are growing? Can they be benchmarked against international best practices? Does Zimbabwe belong to international cluster organisations? Will Zimbabwe host any international industrial cluster forum at any given point in time?

Porter (1998) defines industrial cluster as a geographically proximate group of interconnected companies and associated institutions in a particular field linked by communalities and complementarities. On the other hand, OECD defines clusters as a network of closely related enterprises for production and added value and strategic alliance among main actors including universities, research organisations, knowledge service providers, brokers and consumers. While typology of clusters varies, Enright (2000) identifies five main. These are working, latent, potential, policy driven and wishful thinking. Over the four decades of swimming through difficult waters, Zimbabwe's clusters have largely been wishful thinking.

For success and efficacy of clusters models co-location of related firms, activities, supply chains are critical. In as much as they may be competition among these, they also complement each other. Competition is brought about by rivalry which exists among the numerous firms occurring in clusters. By competing against each other cluster firms are thus able to compete to the overall success of the cluster.

Economies can be transformed by proper clusters as experience with most developed countries and emerging economies has shown. Global examples of success stories of proper modelled industrial clusters are plenty. South Africa has a powerful textiles and apparels cluster which has had global impact. South Africa's Gelvenor Textiles is one such success story to come out of South Africa which commands 50% global market share for parachute fabrics. South Korea on the other hand has curved a niche in the semi-conductors market as well digital electronics. If you want to experience the 'heart of the floral world' (Todorova & Ilieva, 2011) then Netherlands' Western region will be the place to visit. Pakistan is well known for high precision surgical instruments clusters. For fashion enthusiasts, Italy is acclaimed for exquisite footwear. On the other hand, Austria's Vienna is well known for its biotechnology cluster. All these examples were born out of careful planning and appreciation of the beauty clusters can impact on an economy.

#### 6.2.4.1 Industrial Clusters Alone not Enough: Accompanying Cluster Initiatives an Imperative

For clusters to have an impact under the contexts in which they are formulated they need to be improved continuously, this way they remain relevant. They need constant rejuvenation and reactivation. This helps to promote dynamism which is also vital for competitiveness globally. Thus, for every clusters there is need for accompanying Cluster Initiatives (CIs) to be applied. Clusters thus lay the foundation upon which CIs will succeed.

Sölvell et al. (2003) define Cluster Initiatives as organised efforts to improve competitiveness and growth of clusters in a region involving cluster firms, government and research community. The authors further point to the importance of CIs by stating that they act as 'turbo chargers' and come at later stages after clusters have taken root. A turbo charger's purpose on an automobile is to add its power. Likewise, for clusters to make much more impact and relevance they require accompanying CIs.

Cluster Initiatives according to Sölvell et al. (2003) should build on three main policy areas which are regional & SMEs policy, Investment attraction policies and Science and Innovation policies. Properly organised and formalised Small to Medium Enterprises (SMEs) are important for driving research and innovation of an economy which aids success of clusters. Sadly, most players in this sector are largely the by-product of a turbulent economy in which the formal sector has been gradually shrinking.

Thus, through effective regional and SMEs policies CIs should allow improvement and development of weak and often marginalised regions/zones at the same time giving life to lifeless clusters. Directly linked to this, clusters can be a vehicle for local development leveraging on small and medium-sized firm competitive advantage.

In line with significance of regional policies in CIs, is the fact that there has to be strong links between regional and national policy frameworks. It is through this that vertical coordination of policies at all levels is enhanced. Due to the turbulence over the four decades in Zimbabwe, this has not been realised much. Regional and subsequent development of SMEs over the years has been and still remains weak in Zimbabwe. For instance, in the previous section we explained how most growth points are still to reach their full potential and with a number of them declining. So with most on the point of demise due to the heavy battering by the struggling economy, they remain weak to contribute meaningfully to development of the respective regions of the country. Having them at that state implies ignorance on how the power of clusters could be a significant game changer through leveraging on the presence of growth points, all which could come if proper regional and SMEs are fused together.

Furthermore, SMEs activity across the country remains haphazard, sporadic and heavily informalised for them to enable success of CIs. A survey by FinScope (2012) on the SMEs sector of Zimbabwe points to a number of issues bedevilling this sector. 71.6% of SMEs in Zimbabwe were found to be sole proprietors with no employees. In the medium category, 0.7% of respondents had employees ranging from 30 to 70. The survey also found that only 15% SMEs were registered/licensed. The remainder are still informal. The FinScope (2012) Survey further states that infrastructure remains a key impediment to SMEs with 39% operating at residential premises, due to the lack of access to infrastructure. SMEs activity which has largely obtained in the country is supporting hand to mouth as such with no proper efforts to change this status quo CIs will remain a big challenge to execute. Successful SMEs sector is easier to be fused with sound cluster initiatives. For Zimbabwe's SMEs sector which is mostly informal, its growth and propagation has not largely been a result of proper planning, but rather an outcome of a turbulent economy. For instance, most big companies over the years after taking enough clobbering from the doddering economy they collapsed plunging masses into the streets. With little or no alternatives for survival, the SMEs sector has provided some respite. Due to this even formalisation of this sector so as to salvage its meaningful contribution to the economy remains a mammoth task. An ideal situation was for the nurturing of robust and well-planned SMEs sector.

Cluster initiatives should also build on investment attraction policies. If correctly modelled, they act as magnets for attracting investment. Investment attraction should be targeting both domestic and foreign investors into the different but attractive sectors of the economy. Investment attraction efforts should look beyond attraction of individual firms but even other clusters from elsewhere into the identified sectors of the local economy. Investment attraction is a function of many factors including for instance how the domestic economy is perceived by potential suitors, economists often call this variable, 'perceptions. Remember we are journeying through four decades in which turmoil has reigned supreme. Zimbabwe has often been perceived as a difficult investment destination.

An onslaught from unfriendly media houses only saw Zimbabwe being perceived as a not so friendly investment destination. Deteriorating macroeconomic conditions later on only worsened the situation further battering the image of the embattled country. For instance, runaway inflation which ran to more than 10 digits—figures often experienced by war torn countries, depreciation of local currency, escalating production costs, shortages etc. only made it difficult for investment flows to come home but made it easier for them to seek refuge in other far away and safer havens. In Chap. 1, we showed how Zimbabwe has often experienced less FDI flows relative to other regional peers.

Cluster Initiatives however do not thrive where investment attraction is a laboured effort. Investment tends to follow stable environments in which planning horizons are easy to be mapped and general operating atmosphere favours business, so are cluster initiatives. However, for CIs to be executed, proper industrial clusters have to be in place.

Cluster initiatives should also enable attraction of not only investment alone from abroad, but should also strive for attraction of skilled talents from abroad. This has worked in most contexts e.g. the biotech cluster of Vienna, Austria. The third condition upon which CIs are contingent is local conditions/environments in which emphasis on Science and Innovation is promoted. Government policy which promotes innovation in an economy is instrumental. Due to innovation an economy obtains competitiveness when compared to other countries. For Zimbabwe while realisation on the need of science and innovation as evidenced by initiatives such as

Science Engineering Mathematics (STEM) came late, efforts for such have not been given special attention. STEM as a reorientation of policy is very laudable, however it should be accompanied by a process of institution building and all the supporting infrastructure.

For other countries inroads in embracing science and innovation were done and tremendous results continue being enjoyed to this day. Policies at national level should also be interwoven with regional policies for development of clusters. In particular, national policy level inclined towards innovation is crucial for fostering overall development of clusters and specific sectors of the economy. A good example of this includes the Austrian Genome Research Programme (GEN-AU). It was started in 2001 by the Ministry of Education, Science and Culture with a resource envelope of EUR 10.5 million per year until 2010. It strives to strengthen genome research in Austria through funding of various cross cutting disciplines by academic and/or industrial research teams to allow dynamic and formal knowledge flows among stakeholders.

There is a lot which comes with cluster initiatives which Zimbabwe ought to have experienced had it not been for the turbulence. Globally CIs have become a vital cog of microeconomic policy which acts as a conduit linking policies such as industrial policy, education policy, regional development policy, SMEs policy, FDI as well as research and innovation policies which can be adopted by an economy. Sölvell et al. (2003) support this when they submit that CIs have developed as a new policy agenda outgrowing traditional policies such as industrial, regional and innovation policy.

A survey on cluster initiatives revealed important aspects of CIs across the globe. The study showed that there were over 500 CIs across the globe with much of them being in Europe, North America, New Zealand, Australia etc. Much of these were in sectors oriented to science including IT, medical devices, communication equipment, production technologies among others.

Moreover, the study showed the importance of socio, political and economic environment on success of CIs in an economy. High performance CIs were anchored on a high level of trust and confidence on the socio, political and economic environment and also strong and influential local governments come into the picture. Owing to the four decades of turbulence, massive trust deficit ensued especially on the policy side between government and numerous stakeholders, expecting CIs to succeed will be a pipe dream.

#### 6.2.4.2 Strategies Zimbabwe Could Have Done to Nurture Proper Industrial Clusters

While the list of strategies Zimbabwe could have embraced to promote best practices in clusters can be limitless, the discussion below will only look at four. However, factors such as improving ease of doing business by Zimbabwe remain important. For instance, a stable environment helps also to attract good investments and talents from abroad. On the other hand, Zimbabwe has suffered massive decay of infrastructure over its four decades of turbulence. For instance, railway network which should anchor manufacturing industry is in a deplorable state. However, with pragmatic planning, transport and logistics cluster was very feasible in the country given the strategic nature of how the country is geographically positioned. We will look at only, investing in science and technology, joining global cluster networks and commitment to clusters as factors which should have been on the forefront of cluster programs.

### Investing in Science and Technology Sectors

Empirical evidence on successful, high performance and impactful clusters globally has shown that economies oriented towards science have high chances of success. Countries such as South Korea where investment in human capital oriented towards science have made remarkable progress in industrial clusters. Global brands of South Korea such as Samsung, Hyundai, LG the flagship of the Asian economy are born out of cutting edge technology, the bolts and nuts of what science and technology should bring to an economy. Clusters such as Silicon Valley of the USA, Motorsport valley of the UK, Paris optic valley, are citadels of science and technology hence among successful global clusters. Science and technology orientation opens a galaxy of opportunities for an economy in this global village.

Early post-independent Zimbabwe boasted of one of the best education systems in the continent as we explained in Chap. 2. This has been a remarkable feat. However, due to the turbulence which later unfolded as decades wore on, the country failed to ride on this 'tide'. Much was not done to invest in science and technology in the economy with respect to educational policies. Linkage of educational policies with other policies are key for successful cluster initiatives.

Education anchored on science and innovation helps to create problem solvers who are able to proffer relevant solutions to the modern world. Solutions to sectors such as medicine, engineering, financial, climate change, food security, artificial intelligence, among others require significant amount of innovation brought about by investment in science and technology.

Local institutions of higher learning have not done enough on the front of science and technology. Instead of producing better equipped twenty-first-century graduates who are capable of starting up their own ventures so as to also employ others, they have churned out wide eyed, half backed graduates who go job hunting as soon as they complete studies. With massive unemployment, an outcome of the turbulent four decades the job chase remains a mirage. Once a job is found there will be need for retraining again of the graduates to make up for the idle time wasted during the job hunt. The major explanation to this is the education we inherited from the bitter colonial past. Its emphasis was to train especially white-collar workers who will be quickly absorbed by industry as opposed to innovative entrepreneurs. The STEM initiative we explained earlier will in part help to change this narrative, although on its own it is not enough, it should be the final link in the puzzle when a sound industrial base has been laid. There is realisation of the need to produce mass graduates with science orientation with the hope that they will also give solutions to some of the problems we explained. The initiative is very noble. This initiative could have been handy in the early years when education system of the country was still top notch. It could have been easy to ride on the reputable education system. In Chap. 1 we borrowed a quote from the revered English writer Shakespeare about the tide which men should take advantage of in their affairs leading to fortune. Zimbabwe could have ridden on the reputable education system to also make strides in developing robust industrial cluster frameworks. Out of ignorance, this was not done. Real development even of regions still suffers still births yet clusters could be micro engines for this desired outcome. Realising the need for investment in science and technology now is it not akin to closing the stables when the horses have bolted?

A strong education framework anchored on investing in science and technology could have been formulated over the years. In addition to this, what was also key was for collaboration between government, industry and academia, a model known as the *'triple helix'* (Sölvell et al., 2003). This relationship will also be instrumental later on in driving CIs. As an example, the initiative 'Vienna Spots of Excellence' aims at promoting longer term university-industry partnerships.

Over the four decades of turbulence this government-industry-academia nexus has been weak, in fact very weak. Spin offs as a result of this direct relationship are not easy. A great gulf still exists between what government, industry and academic community are doing in Zimbabwe despite endless possibilities which can be explored towards a common goal-economic development. For instance, government can do a lot in sponsoring and commercialisation of researches in different sectors for development of the economy.

The triple helix synergy was feasible since government had made every effort to ensure that every province of the country has with it institutions of higher learning. What is then required is for them to then foster working relationships with empowered local governments. An empowered local government is able to influence decisions to grow the micro economy of the respective region with mutual cooperation with academia and industry in their respective purviews. This will then feed on to the national economy.

### Enhancing Closer Cooperation Among the 'Triple Helix'

Globally there is strong evidence to support importance close cooperation as given in the triple helix model. This gives an opportunity of bringing together top-notch institutions, government and industry to work on models of coproducing innovation and technology. These synergies help to create say start-ups and SMEs which will in turn drive innovation of the resulting clusters. Focus also should be promoting cooperative research centres between academic centres and companies. The government will also be crucial in availing funding and requisite infrastructure.

For example, in the USA the government has played a critical role in the Madison cluster. As a result of government there is sizeable government led funding for research and a number of funding programmes for technology spin-outs as a result of government efforts. Furthermore, promotion of a comprehensive strategy and investments in infrastructure and public services such as transport, housing, schools and personal services to meet new cluster requirements, all spearheaded by government to compliment the other stakeholders in the triple helix have been important in the Madison cluster.

Triple helix cooperation can also bring amazing results by producing spin offs originating from universities, research institutes etc. If successful, these should also give chance to second, third generation spin offs.

### Joining Global Cluster Networks

Having good clusters in an economy takes a lot of effort. Effort especially at learning from best practices is very important. Going it alone or applying incorrect formulas only create 'wishful thinking' type of clusters. Proper mentoring can only come from those that have succeeded in the journey of, clusters. The Cluster Initiative (TCI) formed in 1998 as importance of clusters grew in leaps and bounds is one such platform of cluster practitioners globally who regularly meet to share experiences on clusters. Its purpose is to 'support the effective use of cluster-based economic development approaches as tools to raise the competitiveness and innovative capacity of firms, regions and countries'. Countries which belong to this platform have been able to enjoy success. Other than benchmarking which a country can benefit from cluster platforms, according to Mahuni and Bonga (2016), TCI membership also helps in the following:

- Helps in expert advice on cluster mapping so as to identify workable networking in the economy;
- Study tours;
- Peer reviews;
- Hosting of TCI conferences so as to increase visibility of clusters, etc.;
- Mentoring of cluster practitioners;
- Matchmaking;
- Staff exchange programmes.

Zimbabwe just like most countries in the continent needs all the above seven important areas to at least formulate good clusters. Without getting requisite advice on the salient features of good clusters, basics such as cluster mapping will be difficult. Any meaningful networking in the economy will thus be very difficult to attain.

In the early paragraphs of this section, we gave a few examples of good clusters which have had a global impact. Zimbabwe needs fact finding excursions to study these and other successful clusters. This will help to inform decision making in the economy. This allows her to also copy best practices of course without having to paste everything copied. Remember clusters differ from country to country, it may not be easy replicating at home what may work elsewhere. To the reader I think we concur to the point that things such as promotion of research through funding, provision of infrastructure, human capital investment, etc. which other countries rode on are worth replicating in the home turf. Aspects such as how to fund etc. will then be a function of local conditions.

In addition, mentoring of cluster practitioners is also important for a country to be able to implement correctly. For instance, universities which are dotted across the country can be first mentored and capacitated on how proper cluster dynamics work. Around them university centric cluster can then be developed through the help of local government and industry. Wolfe (2009) gives an example of this by explaining how Waterloo, Canada ICT cluster developed around this idea. The cluster was formed around 1970s.

Wolfe opines that the cluster developed around Waterloo University mostly focusing on computing and software and later on robotics, biotech, automobiles and financial services. Wolfe (2009) further states that, Waterloo University, was key in developing plugging the gap between theory and practice in industry. This was enabled by massive collaboration between the university and the industrial community in the region through formation of the Waterloo Plan. This enabled creation of a robust cluster model ranking among the best in North America. A number of factors are attributable to this success.

The university served as an innovation hub which constantly churned a supply of professionals with hands on experience. Industry academia collaboration ensured a platform for networking. Business associations such as Canada Technical Triangle, Waterloo Regional Prosperity Council, etc. in offering support services (Wolfe, 2009). Of significance also was the role of SMEs. They partnered with large companies. Wolfe (2009) further states that general entrepreneurial culture of the region allowed focusing of efforts towards success.

In Zimbabwe, a good example is the National University of Science and Technology. Since its establishment it could have been crucial for leading in establishment of a lot of spin offs oriented towards science and innovation and creating a dense platform of these co-located in and around Bulawayo. This could have helped the transforming of Zimbabwe's second capital into a manufacturing hub supported by science and technology. The role in science and technology of this and other similar institutions are somehow diluted as they also venture into other disciplines instead of expending energies on science, a vital element of most successful clusters. To this cause the role of the government could also have been to help facilitate creation of an entrepreneurial culture with special focus on science and innovation. With less turbulence in the environment this would then be further enhanced by Weak entrepreneurial cultures. In Austria, the Best Biotech contest in the biotech cluster in Vienna is a good example of how academic related spin off can be encouraged. In the process business ideas are created.

### Commitment to Industrial Clusters

Half-hearted commitment towards clusters normally does not work any magic to an economy. In most countries where clusters have worked wonders, a strong commitment by the public sector has been the driving force of this success. Clusters have often led to a robust manufacturing sector which is a fulcrum for any progressive state.

But this commitment can only come if the public sector is aware of what others globally have done in this regard. As long as sheer ignorance and brilliant high sounding political ideas of no economic sense around healthy industrial clusters persist, then 'wishful thinking' type of clusters will only be achieved.

### 6.2.5 Aid Dependent Development Model

Zimbabwe was a potential economic powerhouse if the early post-independence economic growth momentum around the late 1980s to the early 1990s buoyed by performance of agriculture and manufacturing could have been maintained. From that achievement, a sustained momentum of prosperity was going to be at least easy to maintain. Building a simple economy anchored on the reasonable stability which was obtaining (a tide we failed to ride on) then was going to be a fairly reasonable task than trying to build a super economy when turbulence had taken root. This is not going to be easy at all. It is a herculean task. For example, the well-planned infrastructure of early Zimbabwe resulted in her making giant strides in manufacturing as well as agriculture as explored in the bulk of Chap. 2. Turbulence was to come later, hence this status quo could not last. For instance, infrastructure was left to decay with some subjected to vandalism, factories closing among other ills we explored in previous chapters, in the process setting perfect conditions for mild to moderate turbulence which became tell-tale signs of severe turbulence to be our companion to befriend us for the future decades to come.

High turbulence voltage was stirred as the country was to have substantial amounts of aid support to the imploding economy. Zimbabwe is a giant. No giant can be supported by mosquito limbs. It is impossible. This fact was ignored over the past four decades. Aid from various benefactors globally has of cause supported Zimbabwe all along. This is laudable. However, the issue of its sustainability so as to cause turning around of fortunes of the country needs interrogation.

Most developing countries have been hard done by aid. Instead for it to bring hope and a future, it has actually invited more problems to the journey of development on top of already existing mountains of challenges. Aid has thus become an encumbrance to development of most poor countries. Instead for it to be cherished as a panacea to development woes of most of these countries, it has further pushed most of these to the fringes of poverty. We highlighted earlier how Moyo (2009) explained how countries in Africa have been impoverished by overdependence on aid. Aid has also impacted on Zimbabwe in an adverse manner. However, this is not to say that the country has completely been failed by aid, but rather continued over reliance on it has in fact made solutions for real development difficult to sustain. In this section we will explain how Zimbabwe is continuously being burdened by aid as it gives false hope of 'aiding' her in her tumultuous journey.

While Moyo (2009) focuses much on developmental aid especially how it continues to hinder progress of African states largely due to misuse, we will look at how both developmental and humanitarian aid continue to pose more problems to Zimbabwe's fragile economy. We have concerns for each. Does continued aid to Zimbabwe make a difference with regards to development? But Zimbabwe has numerous resource endowments. Are these not enough comparative advantages to support a sustained growth path for our country? What has aid failed to do for Zimbabwe over the last four decades which it can now accomplish with respect to development? Zimbabwe's experience with aid (both developmental and humanitarian) is not very different from other countries pointed by numerous literature on the aid discourse. Like her other developing counterparts, Zimbabwe has been reluctant to come to terms with the sober reality that aid will only make her require more aid especially as turbulence continues. As the bulk of the economy implodes more aid will be required. For convenience we will call developmental aid, '*type A*' aid and humanitarian aid '*type B*' aid.

#### 6.2.5.1 Type A Aid

This type of aid is that form of assistance rendered to a country in order to support it in its quest to develop. It can be through loans which will then be repaid over a given time period. Developmental aid can also take the form of grants extended to a country. Zimbabwe continues to enjoy this kind of aid in sectors such as water and sanitation, health, education, food and nutrition among others.

Our Concern with 'Type A' Aid

*Aid Leads to Failure to Ownership of Development Programmes Especially in Marginalised Areas*

Development aid extended to countries remains significant as long as it is put to proper use. This we have no qualms about. Our main worry however is that once development is initiated and supported financially or through other means by benefactors there is a tendency for locals becoming reluctant to *own* these programmes. Ownership of these programmes has the main advantage of continuity once donors turn back their heads. A simple case for the reader to have a vivid picture of this point is to consider a situation whereby a donor drills a solar powered borehole in a village of 100 people after which a perimeter fence is erected around it. On top of that the donor constructs water troughs from which the villagers water their livestock using the borehole instead for water in a nearby polluted stream, as well as a nutrition garden. This is a noble development. Yes, we call this development by our standards. Recall that we pointed out earlier on that plenty of communities still exist in which basic items like water provision remains a big challenge. So having a village borehole is a timely intervention. There comes a challenge once the borehole breaks down. Days and weeks will pass without anyone attending to the problem. Normal life resumes for the village in which for their water needs they go back to their polluted stream, which will also be used by their livestock, the garden is will be left to wither.

After a few months you may pass through the same borehole site. A few surprises are likely to welcome you. The solar panels are usually the first target by thieves and vandals. Then comes the fence until everything is completely uprooted. These thieves are usually not a stone throw away from the borehole site. They also drink the water, water their livestock and subsist on the local nutrition garden. A number of donor driven 'type A' aid has suffered this predicament in a number of communities. Ownership of development programmes is key to which we believe that the sense of ownership should be an intrinsic value which a community should share and is not best taught but has to come from within rational beings.

For most projects the expectation among beneficiaries is spoon feeding throughout the inception and monitoring of the entire developmental project(s), a situation which is untenable. The end result of all this is that most projects despite being noble they suddenly collapse once donors withdraw. The mentality obtaining among most beneficiaries is that the donor should '*take care of his/her project*'.

This also happens even in donor funded projects within the education sector. Numerous communities across the country continue to benefit from educational programmes in which donors at times pay tuition, provide stationery, bicycles to pupils walking from faraway places, among other school needs. These and similar initiatives have resulted in even delay of child marriages for example in communities dotted along the Save River in districts such as Chiredzi in Masvingo Province, a very positive achievement. Once funding is exhausted and development partners withdraw there is usual ensuing chaos as school dropouts spike as most parents/guardians fail to afford school fees. In areas such as Gudo village located in Chiredzi there is a popular response among these parents and guardians as to why they fail to pay for their kids, the standard response is that '*vana ava ndeva Donny*', in the local Shona language. When translated it means 'these children belong to Donny'. 'Donny' is a corruption of the term donor. In other words, it implies that all the education responsibilities have been surrendered to 'Donny', i.e. the donor. So wiser will be the idea to educate these children so as to enlighten these communities but sadly there is no continuity of such as parents/guardians feel that the donor should continue with responsibilities he assumed earlier. On the other hand, the government which is already faced with other pressing commitments and the thin resources it has is not able to maintain the donor programmes.

In urban areas there is also a similar problem. For instance, some donors in some parts of the country have been involved with local communities in the community gardens initiative. The donor will help with fencing materials, boreholes, start-up seed etc. to the urbanites to ensure a soft landing of the project(s). Then the cultivation and monitoring will be done by the communities with the assistance of the donor focal people. At early stages there has been success as there have been improvements in diets for beneficiaries and a bit of income from sales. However, the problem became when the donors in most parts shifted focus to other projects. Most community gardens have since crashed despite the initial soft landing. Some of the fencing is being vandalised and plenty of tall grass is evident in a few remaining gardens instead of healthy plants. Several wards in Masvingo urban have had these donors driven programmes which later on simply died away.

Donor programmes in most communities in the country which have suffered this problem are countless. Even in small community environmental projects in which donors would give small tokens in programmes popularly known as 'food for work' targeting at reclaiming gullies and encouraging better environmental practices the outcome has been similar. Once the token vanishes with the donors, the environment with reckless abandon is left to degrade imposing danger to the communities the programmes intend to help.

In the cases we explored above, the main problem has been that of lack of ownership mentality among beneficiaries. Whether it is a result of the approach by donors in the examples we examined above it remains a subject of debate. The bottom line however is that as long as communities fail to own development programmes tailored to them by donors, millions of donor resources of type A aid will continue being thrown in a black hole in almost a similar fashion i.e. the programme only works a few months, later on it dies.

## Supply and Demand for Aid Cannot Be Manipulated at the Same Time

Government cannot say much on the supply of aid it will receive/request/beg for at any time, but can do a lot to control demand for it overtime. If only it was possible to do both then the streets of most developing states such as Zimbabwe could be littered with aid to solve their mountains of problems or even to use in irrational ways. Just a phone call or a simple email (mostly with attached files of hunger-stricken children and women) to benefactors would see loads and loads of aid extended to the requesting nation. It was going to be possible say for politicians (Recall that institutions for most developing countries are still very weak hence development is still centred on individuals) to place and receive orders of pizzas and sodas weekly for their respective constituencies after which their subjects will profusely thank them for a job well done and wish them many more years in office so as to guarantee more sodas and pizzas. If a government can control supply of aid, then it will also be possible for it to control the quality it will receive as well.

On the issue of supply of aid, the quality to be supplied is contingent on the giver and not the receiver in most cases. This is the predicament poorest countries suffer, the poorer the recipient country is. For example, a need like building factories can be pressing for an economy with huge amounts of idle labour but the aid patron can opt to support health of expectant mothers through building maternity homes to guarantee safe deliveries. A rational decision will be to opt for factories. Via the multiplier effect most industries will be created, hospitals and subsequent maternity homes can then be developed, thousands new jobs and general improvement in the GDP of the concerned country will be ensured. The second option is very noble. Lives can be saved. However, the only problem with that intervention is that more children will actually feed into a growing population, without corresponding efforts to absorb that supply of labour in future the concerned economy will plunge into more problems.

On the other hand, controlling demand for aid is possible for a country in the following way. The country has simply to develop itself sustainably backing this development through properly using plenty of available domestic resources. In Zimbabwe this could have been possible since there are vast amounts of resources including the hard working and gentle people. Honest and transparent hard work using local resources gradually helps a country wean itself from overdependence on type A aid and all its shortcomings.

South Korea is a fascinating example of what can be achieved if people put their heads together and think less of type A aid. Having had little room for foreign aid to develop her territory following a ravaging Korean War leading to the splitting into South and North Korea, domestic resources were mobilised. This became a starting point for her journey of miraculous transformation. From the tiny economy she was from the 1960s, she is now a huge economy belonging to the OECD group of countries. From a pariah state South Korea has become a major aid patron which has seen her extending her hand to numerous countries globally including Zimbabwe. Ironically, most of these countries especially in Africa were better than South Korea earlier on in GDP terms. These include, Uganda, Ethiopia among others. Thus, if an economy becomes inward looking to start with, once it gets the correct formula to develop its space then it will demand less and less of type A aid. In fact, with time it will be able to become a patron and support other countries in dire need of aid.

### Increases a Nation's Appetite for Begging

Continued overreliance will only lead to disturbing appeals for aid bail outs which at times will fall on deaf ears. A nation which is used to begging for its developmental needs may not be able to unlock its full potential to stand on its feet. Zimbabwe just like most developing countries especially in Sub Saharan Africa is sitting on riches, the flora and fauna, the hardworking people, culture and heritage, mineral wealth, convenient geographic position etc. to which there is a lot of hidden value which if properly unlocked there will be no need for her to be begging for support from the international community. For example, Zimbabwe has one of the richest deposits of platinum in the world alongside countries such as South Africa. More efforts at value adding of this mineral among others can actually be a game changer for development.

On the other hand, talents of Zimbabwe are scattered across the globe where it is recognised. Unique talents across the globe where they are rewarded better and receive conducive environments they tend to flourish even better. In the process they contribute better to development.

Once a country is used to begging then it tends to be content with mediocrity. Given that value in its vast endowments remains hidden there is no incentive to think outside the box to troubleshoot the myriad of challenges it may be grappling with. Rather it makes a country comfortable with begging and in the process disempowering itself and its people.

Taps of Type A are Slowly Drying up!

The world will never remain the same. Global problems in this broken world keep on mounting. While we live in a much-globalised village these problems will only threaten this connectedness. As this break in connectedness may be hard to avert, we are likely to see type A aid significantly facing challenges. One challenge can be its size and direction. Thus, how much to be given and to whom becomes a significant concern. Suppose an aid benefactor feels that they are benefiting less for her people despite them giving more as aid to others, is this worthwhile when the domestic economy itself is burning? The answer is likely to be 'No' because there may be less to benefit from this gesture.

The USA, one of the biggest funders of WHO has started processes of formally withdrawing from this global organisation. Things will thus never be the same for WHO especially the size of her purse. This move will be a big blow to most LDCs who are getting substantial assistance from WHO. While we cannot be certain of what will happen next but this move will affect budgets and directions of WHO's programmes given the significance of US support to this global body.

Taps of aid are therefore likely to dry as long as benefits accruing out of giving aid are outweighed by costs accruing out of the same action. What it then entails are that for a country used to getting aid if the taps are completely closed it will therefore come to a grinding halt as its development programmes will be starved of support.

#### 6.2.5.2 Type B Aid

This is aid which a country normally receives when there is an emergency. The main purpose being to avert a humanitarian catastrophe. Aid benefactors to Zimbabwe over the years to this cause include USAID, CHINA AID.

Zimbabwe has received numerous aid over the years in the wake of several environments induced calamities. Chief among them being droughts, and floods due to cyclones which are continuously recurring. Of late droughts and cyclones have become a regular phenomenon Zimbabwe has to contend with on her struggling economy. Is humanitarian aid bad then when vulnerable lives are having to be rescued? Should the levers of humanitarian aid be fastened? Honestly no. Lives do matter. Nations across the globe always feel the need to rescue one another when disasters strike. Loads of assorted items such food, clothing, toiletries, tents, medical supplies, building materials, are among items usually shipped to reach out to countries which may have been affected by disasters depending on nature of the calamity.

## Our Concern with 'Type B' Aid

### *Creates Lazy People's Representatives*

For most developing countries such as Zimbabwe where development of marginalised regions is still centred around individuals, with lesser roles being played by institutions, more and more aid only helps representatives of the people not to think through development problems in a much pragmatic manner. Instead, it breeds laziness among them. This is not to say development-oriented institutions are not there but are rather very weak to be relied upon for them to play a pivotal role in development.

In the book *Why Poor Nations Fail: The Origins of Power, Prosperity, and Poverty*, Acemoglu and Robinson (2012) cover extensively the issue of the role of various institutions in development. They explore specifically how weak institutions are an albatross to sustainable development of nations. For example, in Zimbabwe there are plenty of financial institutions but their role in financing development has been limited due to prolonged episodes of having to endure economic turbulence. The turmoil has actually claimed the scalp of many institutions as they fail to cope with high voltage turbulence. Financial intermediation remains very weak.

Type B aid mostly creates people's representatives who are lazy to think about real development for their territories and let alone the nation at large. Much of the energy is therefore expended at politicking and sloganeering. This is important in the following way. The more politicking and sloganeering the easier it becomes to stir confusion to divide especially the weak and vulnerable who at most are gullible. Those who fall in the wrong basket are easily ostracised and starved of type B aid despite the obvious need for it. The aid parcels will then be issued out to those who are 'disciplined'. The renegades are usually left in the cold, exposed and will be used as examples to others in future so as to make sure no one 'ill behaves'. In the end the society created will be that of powerful individuals who have no incentive to account much to their subjects on matters of real development but instead they are much comfortable to account for type B aid since it is an instrument to wield power and control.

So as a result, lazy representatives are created whose focus will be that of how much aid is distributed to people as opposed to how many development initiatives have been implemented. The representatives can therefore have the luxury to stay disconnected from their people for as long as they want and be erratically connecting with them as and when type B aid is available. Real development is a moving target it therefore cannot be achieved through this modus operandi.

## Type B Aid Ties the Poor and Vulnerable People to Cunning Politicians

In line with the above point explored, the lazy representatives an outcome of type B aid creates another problem. This problem now comes in form of a relationship which normally results out of the above condition. The weak and vulnerable subjects often become poorer as they do not have the capabilities to demand development goods from the lazy representative who will have become an elephant in the room.

On the other hand, the lazy representative has enough room to become more cunning as no one dares to challenge him/her to cause real development to the people. Even the more time he/she spends 'missing' no one is prepared among the weak and vulnerable poor will be willing to seek answers as their survival is dependent on the generosity of their representative on transmission of type B aid to them than creating development.

Given limited options to think on their own, the weak and vulnerable subjects will be bound to their lazy but cunning representatives and get stuck to them for years, creating a special relationship in which underdevelopment is an outcome.

### *6.2.6 Type B Aid Weakens Social Security*

Connected to the above two points is the fact that type B aid has the tendency to create vulnerable societies in which social security systems become weak. Robust social security systems allow cushioning of people even if type B is not readily available. This is very significant when hard times befall a society. Zimbabwe is a country in which peasant farming is still significant. During bountiful harvests it is common practice among rural folks to preserve mostly staple grain in well-sealed granaries so that during times of severe need these supplies can always be accessed so as to smoothen consumption. Taking a notch up, the whole community can have selected fields through which society members contribute efforts towards production of staple food which also be deposited and secured in the village granary whereby in most cases the chief will be responsible for seeing that vulnerable members of the society are cushioned in times of need.

Those who bear the greatest brunt of the hard times are mostly the elderly, the women and children and people who may be living with disabilities in general. When social safety nets are very weak, plenty of type B aid is an imperative or a society risks a catastrophe of unprecedented proportions as most of its weak will be exposed.

Whenever there is a humanitarian crisis, a gap is created which is supposed to be plugged by type B aid. So if this type of aid can be easily accessed from foreign donors for this purpose can an economy have the incentive to ensure sound domestic safety nets are in place? This may not be considered top priority especially when an economy is struggling. If, however type B aid is not easy to come by an economy can be forced to seriously consider putting in place a proper system of cushioning people in the long run. The simple village granary example we gave earlier opens our eyes to the importance of social safety nets on the entire economy. The next sub section delves much on how weak social security systems as a blunder contributed to turbulence.

### 6.2.7 Weak Social Safety Nets

In the 1980s and 1990s the Zimbabwean Government established a number of social safety nets designed to respond mainly to drought, malnutrition and agricultural produce loss. In responding to these the Government designed programmes such as Drought Relief, Child Supplementary Feeding and Agricultural Recovery in place (Munro, 2002, 2006). Although the previous programmes had a developmental role the adverse effects of ESAP in the 1990s also exacerbated the vulnerability of many people to different shocks and destitution hence the need to increase the number of safety nets to protect people. According to Mhone (1995a) ESAP badly affected the informal sector especially in the urban areas which heavily depended on the formal and modern sectors and as a result increasing the demand and cost of social services such as health and education.

As has been explained in previous chapters that Zimbabwe's economic prosperity took a different path after the first decade of independence, this prompted the government to take initiatives by introducing several social safety nets in the 1990s. Majority of these programmes aimed at thousands and millions of households who got impoverished due to a combination of the weakening economy and natural disasters such as droughts and floods. These categories of people were deprived of their livelihoods and were found to be unsure of what their next meal could come from. In the old Zimbabwean times poverty and vulnerability were predominantly a rural phenomenon and humanitarians used to steer away from urban intervention. This was because of the perception that the people living in urban areas were less pernicious since a wider range of opportunities were available to them compared to their rural counterparts whose livelihoods in most cases is heavily dependent on rain fed agricultural activities. However, by the turn of the millennium things took a different dimension as the urban population was also sinking in abject poverty as the doddering economy was slowly being shoved to the edge of a cliff by the mounting problems.

During old days (1990s) social safety nets were there on a transitory basis mainly targeted at the rural population vulnerable to both temporary and chronic food insecurity, the elderly and those living with disabilities. Nonetheless, with persistent economic collapse, soaring food prices, falling real wages, loss of employment over the years and Government's harsh actions and programmes including but not limited to *Operations Murambatsvina,* which negatively impacted urbanites and the tent of those in need had to be broadened to cater for more vulnerable groups regardless of their profile of living that is urban/rural (Munro, 2005, p. 6). In addition to the above, a lot of companies and industries closed their shops or moved to other countries at the height of economic and political crises resulting in many people being laid off from their jobs. Thus the target was no longer for the rural population and not restricted to combating temporary food insecurity, but had to be extended to urban populations and tackling of health, orphans who lost their parents due to AIDS, sanitation and unemployment. The continued deterioration of the economy over the years has also seen the middle class disproportionately vanishing, the working class being reduced to beggars and the number of those genuinely in need of social safety nets skyrocketing. Thus, giving a huge burden to the Government and donor community.

Despite the country having experienced significant progress in education, health, economic growth rate and other dimensions in the first decade after independence, poverty is still a pervasive and complex phenomenon in Zimbabwe. Eradicating poverty in all its forms has been a top priority for the Zimbabwean Government and strategies to eradicate it have always been embedded in most of the Government's development strategies and economic blueprints such as the 'Zimbabwe Agenda for Sustainable Socio-Economic Transformation' (Zim-Asset) October 2013–December 2018 over the years. Additionally, under the Sustainable Development Goals (SDGs) of ending poverty in all its forms is the goal of every member country of the United Nations. As part of its agenda to tackle increasing prevalence of poverty, Zimbabwe in recent past years launched a variety of social safety nets and incorporated them in the Interim Poverty Reduction Strategy Paper (IPRSP) 2016–2018 (Ministry of Finance & Economic Development, 2016). Although on paper poverty was a top priority for the Government, the reality on the ground told a shockingly different picture. According to Zimbabwe National Statistics Agency (ZIMSTAT, 2019, p. 42) in 2017, the number of people living in poverty was approximately 70% of the population. In terms of inequality as measured by the Gini coefficient, there has been growing welfare inequality and rising gap between the rich and poor as per data collected and statistics published in recent years for the total population in general and urban population in particular (ZIMSTAT, 2019, p. 40).

Evidence also reveals that the country was a middle-income country in the 1990s, income inequality and poverty increased over the years (Munro, 2005). The increase in the number of people sinking in poverty is also buttressed by the continuous fall of the human development index from 0.5 in 1991 to 0.425 in 2005. Zimbabwe being an agro-based economy with approximately 70% of the total population and 60% of economic industrial activities directly depend on agriculture land remains an important asset and treasure for people's livelihoods (Moyo, 1995, p. 95). The successive droughts in 1987, 1991, 1995, 2002–03 and 2005 means agricultural and industrial activities are disturbed making majority of the population more chronically poor, depressed and vulnerable to poverty hence the increased demand for social safety nets.

Despite challenges the land reform encountered in areas of food security in the country, economic growth, exports and employment, the programme helped in transforming livelihoods and lives of beneficiaries especially the rural population. The programme helped cushioning the rural population against chronic famine as they have been able to produce not just for their subsistence purposes but for sale as well. Since 2000 after the FTLRP the Government has been at the forefront helping poor farmers by providing them with subsidised agricultural inputs such as seeds, fertilisers through the Presidential Agricultural Inputs Scheme. The arrangement is another form of safety nets, but there have been problems of untimely disbursement of the inputs and sometimes they do not reach the intended beneficiaries due to a lot of problems to do with the management and implementation. In recent years since 2014 the Government in partnership with donors has been on an extensive drive to revive irrigation schemes around the country's dry and drought-prone provinces under the Smallholder Irrigation Programme (SIP).[1] Irrigation development is one way to cushion people from the vagaries of droughts and climate change and to mitigate people's vulnerability to hunger. If it is done in a proper way, irrigation development can ensure sustainability to smallholder farmers as they are enabled to do farming all year round and they can be able to produce for business and not just for personal their consumption. Additionally, irrigation development enables diversification in the agricultural sector as farmers will no longer depend only on rain fed to do their production. In some instances, farmers join hands with businesses to enter into commercially viable arrangements whereby the business supplies farmers with specific inputs to grow and in return sell their produce to enterprises. These are welcome developments since in most cases smallholder farmers get low yields and sometimes become food insecure because of facing a lot of barriers ranging from poor infrastructure, lack of access to inputs and farm implements and absence of well-functioning markets (Moyo et al., 2017). The inputs scheme and rehabilitation of irrigation schemes can go a long way in helping vulnerable households by cushioning their livelihoods against risks, maintaining their level of food consumption and making them food secure. They can also help households to build assets and prevent them from depleting their assets and adopting damaging coping strategies. However, due to lack of functional markets, poor infrastructure and weak linkages between agriculture and industrial sector the rural farmers are in most of the times on the losing side.

Safety net programmes are a part of the broader social protection agenda which aim to address risks, vulnerability and social exclusion. In East Asian and Latin American countries social safety nets played a big role by improving beneficiaries' livelihoods, economic opportunities, food security status and enhancing social inclusion through enabling participation in social events. In the case of Zimbabwe social safety nets have been very helpful since they minimise risks, social and economic exclusion and vulnerability to both the rural and urban communities. Through a means-tested basis beneficiaries are exempted from paying for health care and education (Basic Education Assistance Module), subsidies for basic goods for instance the current mealie-meal subsidy paid by the Government to cushion citizens from the rising price of maize flour.

Zimbabwe is an agro-based economy and in that regard Devereux et al. (2008) stress that the provision of social safety nets in agriculture alleviates liquidity constraints for farmers, stimulates the demand for agricultural produce, fosters income-generating projects as well as generates cobweb and multiplier effects to the rest of the economy.

Indeed, over the years, social safety protection and interventions have increasingly been considered very important in countering short-term social measures that can minimise the exposure of families to various transitory and permanent shocks as well as address present and future vulnerabilities. In some countries social safety nets have managed to create employment and enhance social inclusion and integration.

---

[1] http://www.fao.org/zimbabwe/news/detail-events/en/c/1195332/

However, according to Vivian (1994) social safety net programmes should not be used as the only solution to social impacts of adjustment, but it used to bridge the gap left by other developmental programmes.

In order for safety nets to be effective the programmes particularly project-based kind of interventions should empower the recipients not to make them vulnerable again if support is stopped. Adato et al. (2005, p. 4) stress that programmes ought to '(1) target infrastructure and resource deficiencies and focus on high-return investments, (2) be mainstreamed into cross-sectoral public planning, and (3) be flexible enough to respond to both chronic poverty and crises'. The beneficiaries from safety net programmes should also be involved during the early stages of projects and the whole planning process so that they own the project and ensuring sustainability and continuity. Besides having social safety nets to meet the immediate needs of vulnerable families, it is important for both government and the donor community to build a long-standing resilience that contributes to sustainability.

On another note, given that Zimbabwe has vast amounts of natural resources of which majority of them are non-renewable creating a sovereign wealth fund is a noble idea. The wealth is very useful in times of crisis hence creating a sovereign wealth fund is a must for the country. Although the donor community has been very helpful over the years the Government should not always depend on the donor community and this is misguided since sometimes the assistance is not timely provided and also there can be a rise in global demand for help as evidenced during the Covid-19 pandemic. In addition to creating a sovereign wealth fund, another possible area where the Government can protect citizens is to allow them to buy gold mints as a way to hedge the value of their money or savings against inflation or other assets such as cattle against drought. During hyperinflation many Zimbabweans who had saved their money in banks and financial institutions were forced into destitution. If the National Social Security or banks could allow people to convert their deposits or savings into interest earning assets Zimbabwe could not have an increased number of vulnerable people. In countries like Turkey citizens are free to buy gold mints to safeguard their money against inflation and even at their weddings they normally give gold coins or jewellery as gifts.

Rozanov (2005) is the first author to coin the term sovereign wealth fund. According to Sun et al. (2014) a sovereign wealth fund is a state-owned investment fund that is invested in real and financial assets. Harris (2017) also defines it as 'a mechanism through which countries make investments. A pot of money—often derived from oil or other commodities—that is then invested in shares, bonds, property or other areas of potential growth'. It is a state-owned investment fund or entity which comprises of pools of money derived from a country's reserves[2] which can be in the form of balance of payment or fiscal surplus, receipts from exports of resources, etc. These reserve funds are put aside for investment purposes that are meant to benefit the economy and citizens. However, these investments vary from one country to another. Many countries that produce non-renewable natural resources have sovereign wealth funds to preserve and invest earnings mainly from these natural

[2] https://www.swfinstitute.org/research/sovereign-wealth-fund.

resources. However, China has a lot of sovereign wealth funds whose earnings are not from commodities. By 2018 Norway had the largest sovereign wealth fund in the world in excess of US$1 trillion. Botswana has her own sovereign wealth fund called the Pula Fund and is one of the largest and oldest in Africa. The Pula Fund was launched in 1994 for the sole purpose of investing and preserving income from diamonds. In times of need the Government of Botswana draws money from the Pula Fund to help fund social welfare programmes.

Zimbabwe should create her sovereign wealth fund using the earnings from vast natural resources such as gold, platinum and many other minerals. The fund is useful for supporting government programmes that provide financial benefits or other aid including education and healthcare support, food aid or stamps and unemployment benefits to vulnerable individuals or groups that are not capable of looking after themselves. The creation of sovereign wealth fund can also ease the burden to taxpayers, reduce overdependence on donor support as well as allow vulnerable individuals to handle financial stress and poverty during hard times. In some cases, sovereign wealth funds can be invested in diversified assets or projects which can act as hedge against risks related to commodity price fluctuations. Countries that heavily rely on commodity exports are prone to earnings instability due to fluctuations in prices of commodities. The United Arab Emirates is such one country that over the years put part of her earnings from oil and devoted it to her sovereign wealth fund and diversified assets to shield against oil-related risks. Today, Zimbabweans in general and those in Manicaland, Marange in particular have nothing to show despite billions and billions worth of diamonds were mined in the area. If the proceeds from the mining of diamonds had been set aside for a sovereign wealth fund the aftereffects of Cyclone Idai that happened in 2019 in Chimanimani and other surrounding areas could have been mitigated. Given the unprecedented levels of corruption in Zimbabwe if the country is to create one sovereign wealth fund, an independent committee should monitor and oversee the funds otherwise politician can abuse the funds or even capture the system for their personal gains.

As indicated in this book, the informal sector now dominates the broader economic landscape of Zimbabwe. Most of the players are SMEs surviving on a hand to mouthy basis. This sector also has little if at all meaningful social security for people plying their trades in this sector. There are two main outcomes of this. One is that workers' compensation will be non-existent, the very issue social security should address when it comes to work. Furthermore, employees are likely not to get pensions out of this sector despite at times years of toiling. When they are past their productive years, workers from this sector are likely to live a difficult life exacerbated of cause by the inescapable companion of turbulence.

Finally, although social safety nets had notable successes in the lives of less privileged Zimbabweans it should be noted that they are not the answer to the current problems of Zimbabwe, but they just serve as temporary measures. Mhone (1995b) argues that due to structural adjustment measures which created enclave development as well as reinforcing poverty and inequality, safety nets are sometimes not able to have meaningful effect on the livelihoods of some beneficiaries. To come out of this predicament Zimbabwe should develop her economy through structural transformation targeting manufacturing sector. The starting point which is crucial for transforming the Zimbabwe agrarian economy is to embark on agricultural development. However, migrating from agrarian to industrial economy requires structural change in technology, innovation and product composition. Siyakiya et al. (2023) posit that African countries can realise high and sustained growth if they embrace technology and venture into capital-intensive manufacturing industries. In so doing, poverty in Zimbabwe can be reduced and at the same time markets are created. According to Lin (2012) in 1981 China had a staggering 84% of her population living in poverty, but by 2005 the rate had fallen to 16% which was well below the developing world's average. China transformed its agriculture and embarked on massive industrialisation. This is possible and it is not too late for Zimbabwe as well. Zimbabwe's resource abundance can be a blessing if good management of the resources is done. The resources must be saved for generations to come, and enclave rent capture must be avoided. Last but not least, part of the wealth generated from the resources must be used to facilitate and support structural transformation, industrialisation and manufacturing sector. The manufacturing sector has the most linkages with the rest of the economy and has high potential to generate income, reduce poverty and inequality and create productive employment.

#### 6.2.7.1 Why Robust Social Safety Nets Are an Imperative for Zimbabwe

Robust safety nets are important for Zimbabwe for the following reasons:

- Climate change is affecting food security given that the economy is largely agro-based.
- The informalisation of substantial parts of the economy a direct result of the struggling economy requires constant cushion of people as they mainly survive on hand to mouth.
- Rising poverty levels at households both among urban and rural households.
- Related to poverty levels are general low salaries across the economy making it very hard for people to making meaningful savings after consumption.

## 6.3 Nexus Between the Four Blunders

Demise of growth points, poor industrial clusters, overreliance on aid (both developmental and humanitarian) and weak social safety nets over the four decades of existence of Zimbabwe now act as serious blunders which saw the unpeeling of the jewel of Africa. Recalibrating, refreshing and restoring the settings so as to bring back the glitz and glamour of years gone is a mammoth task. It will take a great deal of honest hard work by everyone. Blunders created out of ignorance or carelessness over the forty years are numerous. However, from the four we have articulated above, the following concerns are notable:

- Growth points which have suffered many years of neglect, can they be adequately resuscitated for them to stimulate sustained growth, one way out of the turbulence?
- Robust industrial clusters have been proven to work elsewhere across the globe, so after forty years can we now give first order priority to proper clusters which meet international best practices to enhance our competitiveness?
- After four decades can we open our eyes to the reality that aid is simply supposed to 'aid' us along the journey but not to adequately sustain us as we pursue a journey of self-determination and that the true journey of sustainability lies within our reach?
- Weak social security systems, as long as they persist more turbulence fires are stoked for our economy. If we are to seriously consider robust social security, do we realise that we do have a starting point in form of our local endowments (Zimbabwe is a rich country) as the village example has shown?

What makes the aforementioned blunders significant in one way or the other is that they are intricately interwoven. We cannot have proper industrial clusters when our growth points which should act as special vehicles for regional development remain in bad shape and under resourced. On the other hand, we cannot have sound growth points when there is no emphasis on improving them riding on the concept of proper clusters. Through good and well-resourced growth points in which good clusters are embedded, manufacturing can then be enhanced. It is through manufacturing that regional economies can be boosted in the case of Zimbabwe since we have numerous comparative advantages which easily foster manufacturing in mining and agriculture for instance.

When regional economies tick, their contributions to development of their economies and subsequent national GDP is elevated. Through this, these little economies are also able to generate resources reasonably enough to allow creation and support of social security systems to cater for people. Well-functioning regional economies mean that significant people are gainfully employed in formal, organised and descent occupations which promote a culture of savings owing to availability of disposable income. This is good for the long run health of the broader economy as opposed to informal occupations mostly dominated by sporadic vending which has spontaneously sprouted across the greater part of the country, an outcome of turbulence of the years. The planned outcomes in turn also contribute to broadening of social safety nets of the country via their regional economies. What do good growth points anchored by healthy industrial clusters which lead to generation of resources for livelihoods including good social security entail? One implication is that with time, a country will be able to sustain itself and gradually weans herself eventually from type A and B aid burdens.

Conversely, if growth points for instance remain in their deplorable states, infusing the concept of robust clusters within them will be very difficult. No healthy industrial clusters will thrive when for instance infrastructure is nearly non-existent. Impossible.

Growth of firms towards full industrialisation and resulting agglomeration effects requires adequate infrastructure in respective regions. Experience from other successful global clusters has shown that even where comparative advantages do not exist in certain regions, through proper planning and modelling such areas can be improved when correct interventions are put in place. There are numerous places around the country with regions in which whatever exists in relation to growth points can be taken advantage of with infrastructure and other key interventions after which beautiful clusters can be achieved. Regional economies fronted by poor growth points cannot sustain robust clusters so as to generate enough resources for broad-based sustainable growth and development. This results in less favourable conditions for good welfare systems as resources become a major argument impinging on their sustainability. Catering for the vulnerable groups as indicated previously will become difficult resulting in the country extending its begging bowls for aid, a pill so hard to swallow. Thus, we cannot have robust clusters when growth points keep on deteriorating. Also, if the tide of turbulence is not tamed, fragile social security systems are likely to persist in which the economy will keep on bowing to external pressure through the desire to get its hands as much on type A.

## References

Acemoglu, D., & Robinson, J. A. (2012). *Why nations fail: The origins of power, prosperity, and poverty* (1st ed.). Crown Publishers.

Adato, M., Ahmed, A. U., & Lund, F. (2005). *Linking safety nets, social protection, and poverty reduction-directions for Africa.* https://ageconsearch.umn.edu/record/45767/files/ib28.pdf

Devereux, S., Sabates-Wheeler, R., Guenther, B., Dorward, A., Poulton, C., & Al-Hassan, R. (2008). Linking social protection and support to small farmer development. In *A paper commissioned food and agriculture organisation of the United Nations* (p. 59). Food and Agriculture Organisation of the United Nations.

Enright, M. J. (2000). Regional clusters and multinational enterprises: Independence, dependence, or interdependence? *International Studies of Management & Organization, 30*(2), 114–138. https://doi.org/10.1080/00208825.2000.11656790

FinScope. (2012). *FinScope MSME survey Zimbabwe.* https://www.finmark.org.za/system/documents/files/000/000/448/original/FinScope_Zimbabwe_Broch13FNL.pdf?1614943378

Government of Zimbabwe. (1991). *Economic structural adjustment program (ESAP).* Government Printers.

Harris, B. (2017). *What is a sovereign wealth fund?* World Economic Forum. https://www.weforum.org/agenda/2017/10/what-you-need-to-know-about-sovereign-wealth-funds/

Ketels, C. H., & Memedovic, O. (2008). From clusters to cluster-based economic development. *International Journal of Technological Learning, Innovation and Development, 1*(3), 375–392. https://doi.org/10.1504/ijtlid.2008.019979

Lin, J. Y. (2012). New structural economics: A framework for rethinking development and policy. *World Bank.* https://doi.org/10.1596/978-0-8213-8955-3

Mahuni, K., & Bonga, W. G. (2016). An explanatory analysis on the impact of industrial cluster strategy on industry growth in Zimbabwe. *Dynamic Research Journals' Journal of Economics and Finance, 1*(1), 22–32.

Mahuni, K., Taru, J., & Bonga, W. G. (2020). *Africa's incomplete cycles of development.* Peter Lang Publishing.

Mhone, G. C. Z. (1995a). *The impact of structural adjustment on the urban informal sector in Zimbabwe*. International Labour Office. https://citeseerx.ist.psu.edu/viewdoc/download?doi=10.1.1.610.1992&rep=rep1&type=pdf

Mhone, G. C. Z. (1995b). The social dimensions of adjustment (SDA) programme in Zimbabwe: A critical review and assessment. *The European Journal of Development Research, 7*(1), 101–123. https://doi.org/10.1080/09578819508426628

Ministry of Finance and Economic Development. (2016). *Zimbabwe interim poverty reduction strategy paper (I-PRSP) 2016–2018*. Printflow. Retrieved from http://www.veritaszim.net/sites/veritas_d/files/Interim%20Poverty%20Reduction%20Strategy%20Paper%20%28I-PRSP%29%202016%20-%202018.pdf

Moyo, D. (2009). *Dead aid: Why aid is not working and How there is a better way for Africa*. Macmillan.

Moyo, M., Van Rooyen, A., Moyo, M., Chivenge, P., & Bjornlund, H. (2017). Irrigation development in Zimbabwe: Understanding productivity barriers and opportunities at Mkoba and Silalatshani irrigation schemes. *International Journal of Water Resources Development, 33*(5), 740–754. https://doi.org/10.1080/07900627.2016.1175339

Moyo, S. (1991). *Political change and economic reform in Zimbabwe*.

Moyo, S. (1995). *The land question in Zimbabwe*. SAPES TRUST.

Munro, L. T. (2002). Zimbabwe's child supplementary feeding programme: A re–assessment using household survey data. *Disasters, 26*(3), 242–261. https://doi.org/10.1111/1467-7717.00203

Munro, L. T. (2005). A social safety net for the chronically poor? Zimbabwe's public assistance programme in the 1990s. *The European Journal of Development Research, 17*(1), 111–131. https://doi.org/10.1080/09578810500066654

Munro, L. T. (2006). Zimbabwe's drought relief programme in the 1990s: A re-assessment using nationwide household survey data. *Journal of Contingencies and Crisis Management, 14*(3), 125–141. https://doi.org/10.1111/j.1468-5973.2006.00489.x

Porter, M. (1998). Clusters and the new economics of competition. In *Harvard business review*.

Rozanov, A. (2005). Who holds the wealth of nations. *Central Banking Journal, 15*(4), 52–57.

Siyakiya, P., Erdoğdu, M. M., & Akay, E. Ç. (2023). Impact of industrialisation on economic development in selected African and Asian economies: The role of institutional quality and investment climate. *SN Business & Economics, 3*(12), 211–242. https://doi.org/10.1007/s43546-023-00585-3

Sölvell, Ö., Lindqvist, G., & Ketels, C. (2003). *The cluster initiative greenbook*. Ivory Tower Stockholm.

Sun, X., Li, J., Wang, Y., & Clark, W. W. (2014). China's sovereign wealth fund investments in overseas energy: The energy security perspective. *Energy Policy, 65*, 654–661. https://doi.org/10.1016/j.enpol.2013.09.056

Todorova, G., & Ilieva, Y. (2011). *Key motivational factors to locate within an industry cluster: The case of the Dutch flower cluster*. Aarhus University.

Vivian, J. (1994). *Social safety nets and adjustment in developing countries*. UNRISD Occasional Paper: World Summit for Social Development, Issue. UNRISD. https://www.econstor.eu/bitstream/10419/148791/1/862573750.pdf

Wekwete, K. H. (1988). Development of urban planning in Zimbabwe: An overview. *Cities, 5*(1), 57–71. https://doi.org/10.1016/0264-2751(88)90069-8

Wekwete, N. N. (1994). The status of women and fertility in Zimbabwe. In W. Muhwava (Ed.), *The demography of Zimbabwe: Some research findings* (pp. 5–28). Department of Socologogy.

Wolfe, D. A. (2009). Introduction: Embedded clusters in the global economy. *European Planning Studies, 17*(2), 179–187. https://doi.org/10.1080/09654310802553407

Zimbabwe National Statistics Agency. (2019). *Zimbabwe poverty report 2017*. http://www.zimstat.co.zw/wp-content/uploads/publications/Income/Finance/Poverty-Report-2017.pdf

# Chapter 7
# Sinking Further

## 7.1 Introduction

Will Zimbabwe's developmental puzzle be completely solved? It is now four decades of trying and testing this and that combination. Still the right kind of formula is yet to be found. What then will be the right formula and when will it finally arrive? Whatever the formula, it should allow the economy to move forward progressively, consistently and in a sustainable manner. Ordinary people should be able to eke a decent living with all the dignity in which they also have unfettered access to resources in their country and enjoying unalienable rights. Zimbabwe should be able to compete with other economies in the region and beyond. We showed in Chap. 5 how the jewel of Africa was trashed. Thus, hope out of the turbulence continues to be dashed. For how long should *economic recovery* be a phrase to be associated with the Zimbabwean economy? How many *recoveries* are needed for us to talk of a *recovered* Zimbabwe? A Zimbabwe which will in one day be able to extend this time not begging bowls, but Official Development Assistance (ODA) to other states? Nearly forty years of trying to recover is a painfully disappointing time period.

Unfortunately, however, the hypnotic forces continuously drawing Zimbabwe to the turbulence magnetic field, are of colossal proportions. They seem intractable. The country seems to be sinking further in turbulence, drowning into more and more problems. The internal environment itself has not been so kind to Zimbabwe just like the world economy at large.

Whilst there may be a semblance of 'normalcy' for Zimbabwe here and there in some sectors of the economy, the honest fact is that the challenges are still overwhelming. Stability has been difficult to sustain. Zimbabwe's economy has been fragile for too long.



K. Mahuni et al., *Zimbabwe's Economy*, Advances in African Economic, Social and Political Development, https://doi.org/10.1007/978-3-031-81588-1_7

## 7.2 Emerging Factors: A Long Road Ahead

In this Chapter we will dwell on the bulk of factors which are becoming a fresh source of problems for the Zimbabwean economy, they even add on to the fragility we just mentioned in the last paragraph. On top of factors we explored in Chap. 6 alongside issues which in part were highlighted in Chap. 5, the emerging factors we examine shortly are slowly gaining traction as strong arguments into Zimbabwe's difficult development journey. They are feeding into the already existing challenges. These factors include; millennial generation starved of opportunities, overdependence on primary commodities, climate change and corruption.

### *7.2.1 Disillusioned Millennial Generation in the Making*

Is entering into adulthood with too much hopes not creating a disillusioned millennial cohort in Zimbabwe? It's not uncommon in contemporary Zimbabwe to find a graduate hopping from one job to another or even working in a field completely unrelated to area of specialisation-if they are lucky of cause to find a job. The *jobs* are numerous ranging from vending, driving mostly of pirate taxis, private tutoring, brick moulding, public relations, marketing, selling insurance policies, selling drugs, transaction broking, illegal forex trading among a host of other jobs.

A 'special' category of jobs has to be highlighted at this point-there are those who are into *hustling*. Yes, we call hustling a 'job'. People are fending for families on it. Most activities under this category are predominantly done by millennials domiciled in urban setups. Activities they engage in are those that make them have a brush with law enforcement agents. They include pirate taxis operations, selling pirated discs, sand poaching, smuggling, forex trading in the streets, illegal fuel retailing and '*running*',[1]—they are plenty of runners around the country. Running mostly occurs at border posts and bigger cities around the country given volume of transactions which occur in various sectors of the economy. There are youths who act as conduits linking clients and officials in offices depending on what the clients want. The clientele base is diverse. It can be for instance border jumpers, smugglers, transport crews such as buses, truckers etc. Rarely do the client and the service provider (official) meet, but both know the runner whose task is to be efficiently running back and forth negotiating until a deal is struck. When this is accomplished, he/she pockets levies for his/her toils. Due to asymmetric information he/she enjoys the luxury of inflating the levies to the client on collection and deflating to the service provider on remitting, simply because these two parties seldom meet.

From the few above examples, we can conjecture that one unpleasant feature of the demography of Zimbabwe is the millennial generation which is continuously being starved of opportunities to express themselves and spread their tentacles in the mainstream economy. By so doing they are able to contribute to the greater success

[1] Some call it 'hustling'

of socio-economic and political transformation of the country. With very limited meaningful opportunities they then embark on some of the activities we explored above.

Who then are the millennial generation? The proper delineation of what a millennial generation is depending on the source you come across. For our context we refer to them as individuals born after 1980 through 2000. They make up most of the youthful segment of our population.

In this section we commit to explaining this *special generation* in that had it been afforded enough chances and opportunities in the development equation of this beautiful country, we could be talking of slightly different settings altogether. The coming of this generation coincides with the setting in of independence (i.e. in 1980) marking the birth of a sovereign Zimbabwe-to us this makes them a *special generation*, with a special assignment. Serious questions come to mind when we ponder over this special generation and a special task they have for the progress of this great nation. Have the millennials been given enough room to contribute? Overlooking this generation, what have we lost as a country?

It is a fact than within any generational regiment, there are disparities. Before independence, there was a generation too, but most of it fought the armed struggle and contributed in one way or the other to free the country from colonial shackles. This generation's contribution to shaping the history of the country cannot be overemphasised and will remain engraved in the hearts of many people. For the millennials, they ought to fight too—albeit a different war. A war against a *turbulent* economy is no easy feat. It's sad however how this 1980 onwards generation is often called the *born free*. Are they free? Really? Honestly to us they are not. By virtue of being thrust into the vortex of a turbulent economy they too have a couple of monkeys on their backs they should shake off. It's a heart-rending sight moving around ghettos of most big towns of the country when you come across idle millennials who despite massive potential but cannot find their way out as they are bound left, right and centre by chains of poverty to the tumultuous economy.

In the light of the above, millennials should be embodiments of the following three qualities;

- They ought to be change makers;
- They ought to be entrepreneurs of repute;
- They ought to be critical thinkers.

#### 7.2.1.1 Millennials as Change Makers

The first quality entails a generation which wishes to see the change they desire among others beginning with them. In Zimbabwe, this special generation yearns for change in society, a change that transforms them to the better. Change desired encompasses different sectors including education, religion etc. However, to see full consummation of this change they should actively participate especially given enough participatory space. They should be part of the change; with ample space they can cause this change to take place. For example, a very positive step in education in Zimbabwe has been a rethink on the inadequacies and shortcomings of the old education system. As such there is a revamp of the old curriculum so as to pave way for a new curriculum. Much emphasis of the new curriculum is to impart life skills in the life of the pupil/student beyond the classroom/lecture room. However, what irks most youth, the bulk of the millennials is that there hasn't been adequate consultation of them as a key constituency. As such they feel marginalised.

An encounter with a final year 23-year-old Engineering Student at the National University of Science of Technology located in Bulawayo, Zimbabwe's second largest city on how her thoughts as a millennial had this to say;

> I think as millennials we are not getting enough support we need from the government for us to be well equipped for our future career wise and in business.

Further with respect to her field of study she went on to say;

> Our learning institutions don't have resources for us to obtain knowledge we need for industry e.g. laboratory equipment. For final year engineering students, we tend to limit our ideas for projects because we can't afford to implement since we are sponsoring ourselves with chemicals and components.

This creative generation feels let down when it comes to their creations. The student further highlighted that,

> Added to that our work is not given the recognition it deserves. There have been many promises of commercialising projects which have not been done. Next thing you find your idea being implemented elsewhere.

As her last words she said:

> Generally, the future looks gloomy. There is not much to look forward to.

Connecting the above then, success of redesigning education remains to be seen, only time will tell and how it will have been embraced by the special generation.

We want to mention also another integral attribute this generation should embrace. Behavioural change is essential—it should be the bolts and nuts of the millennials. Out of it, virtuous, positively impactful and astute leaders rise and flourish. The present world, to which Zimbabwe is a subset is afflicted with numerous problems including disease, conflict, malice, drug abuse, greed, corruption, inequality, crime among other ills, this calls for change makers for it to be liveable—a special assignment for this cohort.

#### 7.2.1.2 Millennials as Entrepreneurs of Repute

The second quality entails millennials who ought to be entrepreneurs of repute. These should be able to create better and quality jobs which are capable of stimulating sustained development. Owing to unemployment levels which have obtained over the years in Zimbabwe, it is high time for current systems be it educational or other which nurture entrepreneurs who are able to also employ. Thus, this special generation should be afforded the chance to use for instance their tech skills for latent nurturing of entrepreneurial skills. It is disturbing to note however in Zimbabwe a growing tendency for the rise of a certain generation among the millennials of entrepreneurs whom most prefer to call '*tenderpreneurs*'. In this book we will not delve much into this category of entrepreneurs except for a few insights we would like to share about them.

Worth noting to the reader however is that this generation of 'business people' tends to increase the more the economic turbulence. Moreover, these tend to canvas for opportunities in the economy and these opportunities are called tenders. We are sure we can use them to gauge the health of our economy. A fully functional economy in which honest hard work is fairly rewarded is likely to have less of these ilk of business people. On the other hand, for an economy which is ailing it may not be much of a surprise to find tenderpreneurs choking every palatable sector of the turbulent economy. We can conjecture ten reasonable concerns about this cabal of entrepreneurs;

- What makes one a 'tenderprenuer' in Zimbabwe?
- What sort of sectors do they operate in the economy?
- Related to the above, why those sectors and not others?
- Do they eventually deliver goods/services (tenders) awarded to them?
- Are their projects/deals impactful to their communities to inspire other millennials in a positive manner?
- Are they desirable to an economy?
- Are they sustainable for an economy?
- Why are they so few in their numbers?
- Are there any barriers to entry/exit into their 'systems'/world of business?
- Lastly, with entrepreneurs such as those are they not an albatross to an already struggling economy?

#### 7.2.1.3 Millennials as Critical Thinkers

Last quality entails millennials who should proffer solutions befitting not only to their present circumstances but also into the future and beyond. Solutions range from issues such as climate change, ICTs, science and engineering, renewable energy, food security etc. For example, proper climate change programming so as to build resilient economies without millennials cannot be enough. If they are afforded enough space to actively partake and divert energies into all positive undertakings, they can catapult the country to dizzy heights of success through critical thinking.

The aforementioned qualities are the necessary paraphernalia the millennials should exhibit. Thus millennials in Zimbabwe and beyond have therefore a special task to be agents of hope in this broken world. An important question arises then, how can they be if they are so disillusioned, when most opportunities do not come their way?

According to Mahuni et al. (2020) in a book which explores a wide range of development issues plaguing the African continent titled, *Africa's Incomplete Cycles of Development* renowned Nigerian cleric, T B Joshua in one of his sermons once made a powerful comment regarding how the continent itself has and is continuously not doing much for the young generations. According to him, 'Africa has neglected her youths' (Pulse, 2017).

He explains further by saying that:

> Africa has abandoned the youths to themselves. Africa has failed to make provision for the youths, whereas tomorrow's Africa is the youths.

Failure to make the best out of this generation comes with a cost and the cleric is deeply concerned (this concern also resonates with the student we quoted earlier on her last words) when he further retorts that:

> When I think about the future of Africa, I have sleepless nights. Everything looks gloomy, frustrating, hopeless, dark, darksome, shadowy, shaded, dull, sunless and unilluminated.

One of the grievances among armed groups in the Niger Delta a region in Nigeria, a country where the prophet comes is that they feel sidelined from the mainstream economy. Moreover, they feel that companies involved in oil extraction are not compensating enough the environment. Isn't a genuine grievance? When we narrow this to relate to home, navigating out of the turbulent waters the millennials are the key, the hope and future for illuminating not only Zimbabwe but the world as a whole.

It is thus clear that the millennials of the continent are disempowered in a way by not getting adequate opportunities to thrive. Lacking all this is therefore fomenting frustration, gloominess, hopelessness as highlighted in the words of TB Joshua. In Zimbabwe therefore this generation is afflicted by numerous problems including being overburdened by an overdose of toxic politics, unemployment among others. For instance, youths are a strategic *apparatus* during election seasons, not only in Zimbabwe but entire continent since they constitute the majority of the population. They are apparatus in the sense that during election seasons they are normally patronised and cossetted by political parties for their own selfish interests with them not really benefiting much beyond free party t shirts, caps, occasionally a meal and cheap beer—this to us is a dose of toxic politics.

So if opportunities continue being elusive for the youth, should they stop surviving? No. They should find their way in this journey filled with turbulence. Where are they getting solace? In most ghettos in cities some are turning even drugs to drown their frustrations and doing even odd jobs not in tandem with their specialities. As Zimbabwe's turbulence implodes, over the years we have witnessed an interesting development on the religion front. There has been a growing number of churches of a Pentecostal nature, their key message being that, '*things shall be well*'. This is a tacit acknowledgement of turbulence being experienced. A striking feature of most of these religious movements is that they have majority of followers being our special generation-the millennials. The Herald Newspaper observes that:

> Prophecy has become central to Zimbabwe's social and economic transformation (The Herald, 2020).

We agree with the paper in that prophecy plays an important part for contemporary Pentecostalism. This has impacted on not only the socio-economic fronts as pointed by the tabloid but also the political landscape. Thus, another avenue where some of the millennials have sought refuge and solace is the church, much tendency has been towards Pentecostals as they deliver and unleash prophecies in line with their expectations. Much sought component of the prophecies has been miracles. We thus explain briefly growing Pentecostalism especially how it is impacting on millennials with the increasing of turbulence we have witnessed over the years.

### *7.2.2 Growing Pentecostalism in Zimbabwe*

As alluded to earlier increasing economic challenges have seen growing increase in a number of numerous Pentecostal churches in Zimbabwe. Ascertaining the actual number of Pentecostal churches especially after the year 2000 is not easy given that the environment of worship is not strongly regulated. Unlike in most traditional churches in Zimbabwe where you find mature audiences, Pentecostals are characterised by young people who are mainly *hunting* for immediate breakthroughs/deliverances/fortunes from their predicaments which are largely attributable to deteriorating economy. Chief among their issues include joblessness, search for financial breakthroughs, business success, travel documents among other issues of concern. The word 'hunting' has been deliberately italicised to emphasise the elusive nature of the targets being chased. For instance, the turbulence keeps on creating hordes of unemployed millennials, with some contemplating crossing borders purportedly to greener pastures hence the need to have proper travel documents. Sadly, getting a passport or any other travelling document is not so easy, just like obtaining most of other basic things in Zimbabwe.

Leadership of much of these Pentecostal movements has also been dominated by largely youthful preachers hogging limelight for one reason or another. With some it has been an opportunity to parade their wealth including motorcades, donning designer garments, flashy cars, body guards etc. as they minister to their largely gullible youthful crowds. To the reader, these authors are not in any way opposed to religion but are worried of how it is continuing to impact on thousands of vulnerable millennials in the light of unending economic challenges. The other interesting part of contemporary Pentecostalism has been the message peddled to the crowds by the preachers as we shall explore briefly.

#### 7.2.2.1 The Message of Hope and Miracles

Hope has been the central theme of most messages delivered on the pulpit. This is somehow not very new as even early Biblical prophets such as Jeremiah, Hosea, Isaiah among others at some point preached hope. This was so specially when there was growing turmoil and people needed that strength to cope, so the prophet's message of hope became very necessary. Hope is also a theme in the messages of the Pentecostal preachers we are exploring. The hope is largely motivated by growing turbulence.

Apart from hope carried in the messages of the preachers, an important component of Pentecostalism is use of miracles as a means of conveying a plethora of promises/deliverances to the audiences. Again, this is not new. Early Biblical times even through the New Testament miracles were performed. The miracles have been used to show power to followers, with some however branding these preachers 'showmen'. For instance, years such as 2013 the country witnessed a phenomenon in which congregants would find money stashed in their bank accounts, pockets and hand bags, the money was popularly known as miracle money. Can the miracle money be a part of the monetary policy by the exchequer? Can for instance printing of money be anchored on miracle money? Can we have for example an exchange rate of say 'X miracle money' exchanging for 1 USD? What will determine such an exchange rate? Undoubtedly, in the miracle money mechanics, the prophets may be instrumental in influencing the exchange rate among other determinants.

In some church sessions congregants would even have their mobile phones credited with airtime, electricity accounts recharged, gold dust raining in churches, miracle oil oozing among congregants' hands etc. It's not unusual to come across church sessions mostly punctuated by proclamations such as 'prophesy papa, I receive!!'There are two potential problems we see here.

Firstly, are we not creating a lazy generation of millennials who wait for milk and honey to be delivered on a silver plate? The '*I receive papa*' and '*prophesy papa*' generation is not restricted to millennials alone. However, our worry is that the impact on the millennials who ought to sweat it out and earn their stripes like those of other continents is likely to be harmful.

Secondly, are we not going to have a situation whereby the growth of churches will outnumber growth of industries in an economy full of potential? Slowly a region such as Bulawayo (Bulawayo over the years had been popular as a manufacturing hub of the country. It was once known by the moniker '*city of billowing smoke*', signifying presence of heavy industrial activity taking place). The country's second largest city has seen a number of churches occupying substantial spaces used to house several manufacturing companies. In conclusion, the extent to which these miracles and demonstrations of power would really rescue the millennials from the current disillusionment remains to be seen.

## 7.3 Primary Commodity Overdependence Dilemma

Early post-independent Zimbabwe has been known as the bread basket of Africa. Then she was able to feed her people adequately and even producing enough to also export beyond her borders. As a result, she was responsible for the Food Security Cluster of SADC region. Chapter 1 showed how vibrant agriculture was in early independent Zimbabwe. Buoyed by agriculture and manufacturing, we showed also how the exchange rate was among the strongest compared to most states. Key export commodities in agriculture included items such as flowers, tobacco, beef, maize, etc. Mining has been supporting the Zimbabwean economy significantly. The country boasts of abundant platinum deposits and among the best in the world.

The two sectors mining and agriculture thus have played a pivotal role in shaping the economic landscape of Zimbabwe over the years. Their contributions to GDP of the economy has been amazing. They have supported much of export revenues, taxes, employment and general well-being of the economy. In Chap. 5 we explained how the jewel of Africa was trashed, the other reason for this being underinvestment in the primary sectors of production. Mining and agriculture had massive potential to transform the economy of Zimbabwe and catapult it to amazing heights of prosperity. Closer to home is Botswana, diamond as a key export mineral has spurred inclusive growth and development of the economy through use of a transparent model of diamond mining. Further away from the continent, a country such as Israel transformed her desert like environment into a beacon of success with respect to agriculture. This has seen her advance to embracing precision agriculture which allows for efficient utilisation of resources such as water, fertilisers etc. As a result, Israel is well known for hi-tech agriculture in Europe and beyond.

What makes Zimbabwe's economy beleaguered is the overreliance on primary commodities in this complex global village of integrating Global Value Chains (GVCs). United Nations Conference on Trade and Development (UNCTAD), considers a developing country a Commodity Dependent Developing Country (CDDC) when it obtains substantial export revenues from two key sectors—mining and agriculture. Zimbabwe rightfully belongs to CDDCs. UNCTAD further reiterates that dependency is more severe in Least Developed Countries (LDCs).

### *7.3.1 Zimbabwe as a CDDC, Does It Matter?*

Is it important that Zimbabwe is a CDDC when we are examining what is inside her turbulence over the past 40 years? The major difference between LDCs and industrialised nations is that the former rely on export of primary products and raw materials. Conversely, industrialised nations export manufactured goods. Further they argue that this state of affairs has several important implications;

- The level of price competition is higher among primary goods exporters since they are largely many sellers and offering the same product.
- Export earnings for primary products are very volatile and are likely to be affected by e.g. weather vagaries such as droughts, famine etc. or some other shocks on the global market.

The above points are compelling when we explore Zimbabwe's economy. Owing to climate change, most countries in Sub Saharan Africa (SSA) are facing declining export revenues, declining incomes etc. as a result of poor performance of main export commodities. Malawi for instance, due to reliance tobacco exports accounting for 55% of export earnings production has been hampered by severe dry spells (Trading

Economics). Zimbabwe also exports tobacco, its production over the years has been gradually affected by El Nino induced dry spell causing persistent fiscal and trade deficits.

In line with the above, according to Feenstra and Taylor (2014) made an interesting observation about dependence on primary commodities from a study by two economists, Prebisch and Singer. The economists observed that prices of primary commodities tend to decline overtime and the studies became known as the Prebisch-Singer hypothesis. This was empirically observed for commodities such as wool, aluminium, tin etc. Given such circumstances, is Zimbabwe's turbulent economy safe? The predictive power of the hypothesis remains to be tested. The continued overreliance on primary commodities by Zimbabwe has important implications especially against the background of the unending turbulence besides what we have observed above. In particular, this terrible state of affairs means that the country will continue to miss out a number of opportunities as we explore briefly.

#### 7.3.1.1 Missed Opportunities on Integrating Global Value Chains

Increased globalisation has itself resulted in new relationships of connectedness among world economies. Those countries which are benefiting most are those that are able to network with better allies much to their advantage. GVCs have seen production and supply chains cutting across continents. The nature of goods which have dominated GVCs are mostly manufactured as well as services. So what national quirks can Zimbabwe bring to the globalisation table in the light of increasing connectedness of GVCs? Obviously she cannot bring the primary commodities. This is despite the fact that they are her life blood. As a result, she will remain a frustrated spectator on the terraces whereas other countries in the continent will be riding the tide of globalisation. Moreover, Zimbabwe can only hope that globalisation slows its pace so that by chance she can possibly catch up!

#### 7.3.1.2 Outsourcing Opportunities Lost

Related to the point on GVCs is outsourcing, a new form of international trade (Feenstra & Taylor, 2014). Further they submit that it is a trade in intermediate goods which is different from that of final goods as propounded by economists such as Ricardo and Heckscher–Ohlin. It involves provision by companies of a service or production of units of a good in several countries, then the final products will be made in another geographic location. For example, iPhone has some units manufactured in countries such as China. Several companies in the USA at times rely on companies in countries like India, Israel, etc. for outsourcing computer-related services. These will manufacture different parts and components which will then be assembled at a final destination to give a final product. India, China are among preferred destinations due to their cheap but highly productive labour. Outsourcing can be of materials or infrastructure depending on the company or nature of a good/service. Can Zimbabwe have a role to play in the global outsourcing market against the backdrop of increasing turbulence? For example, Zimbabwe is approximately 7 h ahead of the USA, this can present an opportunity for infrastructure outsourcing whereby US-based companies actually make use of Zimbabwean companies in sectors such as Information Communication Technology. This has succeeded for companies in countries like India. Given the encouraging level of education and literacy we showed in Chap. 2 this would be possible. The multi-million-dollar question is that is our turbulent economy ready to harness global outsourcing opportunities which the global village presents? Can we also curve a niche in the global outsourcing market? Is it not asking for too much?

#### 7.3.1.3 Opportunity to Arrest Deindustrialisation Lost

In Chap. 1, when we reviewed tabloids which have trended with the Zimbabwean story, one of the issues we came across was the impact the turbulence is having even on industries for instance falling capacity utilisation, power challenges as well as even relocation of other companies to other destinations as heat is turned on locally by the continued implosion. Deindustrialisation has been one of the effects of the turbulence. Manufacturing industries have been slowly declining in different sectors of the economy including textiles and apparel, steel, glass, cement, furniture, agro processing to mention a few. A city such as Bulawayo, the second largest in the country over the years was known as the manufacturing hub of the country boasting of big manufacturing companies. Then the City of Kings was also known as *kontuthu ziyathunqa*. This is a term which means smoke that bellows. It was a common feature as you enter the city of Bulawayo towards industrial sites when most firms were operating you would be greeted by smoke bellowing from manufacturing firms. Sadly, turbulence claimed the scalps of most of these manufacturing giants of this region. A cursory look at previous industrial sites in this city will only live one disturbed. Most companies closed shop, with some premises now having been turned into places of worship. For some still operating, the capacity utilisations are very limited. As a result, chances are very slim for the primary commodity dependent and turbulent economy to arrest the phenomena of deindustrialisation.

#### 7.3.1.4 Opportunities for Better-Quality Jobs Lost

Linked to the three points we explained above is missing of better-quality jobs. Overreliance on primary commodities has meant that most jobs are those in the extractive sectors. With minimum and little value addition the resulting quality of jobs is lesser than those in late stages of the value chain. For a number of More Economically Developed Countries (MEDCs) jobs in the manufacturing and tertiary sectors tend to dominate than those in the primary sectors. These jobs also pay much better than those in the primary sectors. Turning to Less Economically Developed Countries (LEDCs) such as Zimbabwe the burden of primary commodities is so overwhelming. The key sector for primary commodities is predominantly agriculture where you find most women. Global Fund for Women states that women are the backbone of agriculture and food production in Africa, supporting its population by producing 80% of its food.

With underinvestment being a key constraint in primary sectors of production like mining and agriculture, the resulting jobs in these two key sectors have often been low quality and with poor remuneration. For example, the mining sector especially for a mineral like gold has brought a myriad of problems in Zimbabwe including haphazard mining, gold wars among rival gangs, environmental degradation making it difficult to trace actual contribution to income and livelihoods of the chaotic artisanal mining. We may be at the maximum possible point on the Production Possibility Frontier (PPF) if artisanal mining was properly regulated? By remaining stuck with primary commodities better-quality jobs with better income levels will not be easy to conceive for Zimbabwe.

So in conclusion, the above overreliance on primary commodities by Zimbabwe has created much of problems for her than benefits. A lot is being missed by the economy as explained above. This problem is exacerbated the more turbulent the economy becomes. Given all the lost opportunities, can the country have a boost from turbulence or it will continue to sink further.

## 7.4 Climate Change, a Beckoning Reality

One reality global economies have to contend with is climate change. Due to it some places have become colder, whereas others have become hotter experiencing heat waves. On the other hand, others places are becoming increasingly drier with high incidences of droughts, yet others are receiving too much precipitation with increasing floods. Over the years floods and droughts have frequented regions such as Sub-Saharan Africa (SSA) resulting in losses of properties and livelihoods by the battered economies. Climate change has differential impacts on economies with the poor and weak suffering more damage. Can an already turbulent economy be spared of climate change wrath? Zimbabwe is in SSA where climate changed is also wreaking havoc and has seen droughts alternating at times with floods. Chapter 3 explored some of notable drought phenomena the country has experienced since 1980s.

### *7.4.1 Climate Change and the Zimbabwean Economy*

A number of concerns in the light of climate change against the backdrop of pressing economic challenges can be considered with respect to the Zimbabwean economy.

#### 7.4.1.1 Climate Change Burden Now a Global Problem

Climate change has been labelled as a 'new AIDS' for SSA in a paper titled *Climate Change 'Proofing' Sub Saharan African Women, A Step towards Sustainable Development* by Mahuni (2020). In the Amartya Sen award winning paper, the author explains how women especially of SSA are the most affected by climate change. While the author acknowledges early effects AIDS had especially on SSA and how it burdened the region, he switches on to explain how climate change is now the new challenge. He opines that, 'Climate change has thus taken over. It now the new problem set for the region which requires meticulous troubleshooting'. Gone are the days when developing countries would simply wait for support from advanced countries without taking much initiative. The world has since changed. Climate change knows no boundaries; global economies are reeling from its effects especially poor countries such as Zimbabwe. All the countries are affected by its impacts, the major difference being distribution of its effects on countries as we explained earlier.

MEDCs are now having to cut especially on aid to the developing world since they have to equally struggle with their domestic economies to deal with the burden imposed on them by climate change. Aid has been and remains a key intervention to reach out to LEDCs failure of which ensuing humanitarian crisis is usually dire. With no end to turmoil on the global economy, we are likely to see most economies inward looking as they to focus more on prioritising solving their own problems first without extending helping hands to foreigners. Donald Trump, the US President is well-known for his America first mantra implying that most energies have to be expended on ensuring comfort of Americans first then global matters such as climate change will follow later on his to do list.

#### 7.4.1.2 Agriculture Still the Mainstay of the Economy

In Chap. 5 we looked at critical blunders under the Zimbabwe's turbulent economic journey. One of it being underinvestment on the primary sectors of the economy-agriculture being one of them. Most peasant populations still subsist in agriculture for livelihoods to earn basic survival. One inescapable fact is that climate change will accelerate poverty. Masses especially those who live in the backward rural areas and have livelihoods which are tied to the land will be bear the greatest brunt.

#### 7.4.1.3 State of Preparedness with Respect to Climate Change Impacts Still not Enough

Zimbabwe's capabilities in dealing with large scale climate related disasters has always been put to test. Any environment related calamity always lives Zimbabwe badly exposed. Climate change requires well-functioning warning systems so as to be able to anticipate incoming disasters. Mitigatory measures will then be taken before the worst happens. Over the years, experience has shown that climate related catastrophes on Zimbabwe have left the country in need of massive support beyond her borders, a clear sign of inadequate preparedness to deal with this phenomenon. The effect will be simply to sink the country further in turbulence.

Weather extremes have not spared Zimbabwe in any way especially cyclones and droughts. Notable cyclone phenomena include Cyclone Eline (2000), Cyclone Japhet (2002) and most recently Cyclone Idai (2019) which we shall discuss in the next paragraph.

In March 2019, a powerful Cyclone, Idai swept through Mozambique and the greater part of Manicaland Province of Zimbabwe leaving a massive trail of destruction. A heavy battering from the cyclone induced floods added to turbulence of the economy also over the years. The province is well known for thriving timber processing and banana production supporting surrounding communities with livelihoods. Commerce was thus not spared by the cyclone. Chimanimani a region in Manicaland had road network severely damaged and over 50% of land for maize having been swept away. The paper further points out that a total of 17,608 people were displaced while 320 were killed by Idai. Properties and homes were swept away by the massive remains and scores of people remain unaccounted for.

The support from the international community to this humanitarian crisis has been overwhelming which saw food, clothes among other being mobilised so as to rescue the affected people. Temporary shelters were established in places such as Ngangu, Nyamatanda and Chimanimani Memorial gardens as people await further deployment to proper settlements. The disaster has been too much for an already struggling economy. Such a disaster will require greatest intervention by government to ensure a soft landing by the affected. Thus Zimbabwe still needs substantial amounts of intervention(s) as aid (humanitarian and others) for support to prop up the economy.

## 7.5 The Gangrene of Corruption: Getting More Cancerous

Corruption trumps everything. Not only in Zimbabwe has corruption become a cancer, the majority of the continent is not so clean, corruption has been allowed to take root in many spheres of life in the continent. This has actually added turmoil over the years in most parts of the continent as it has weighed down on prospects of turning around most economies in Africa. Corruption in the continent is in many facets include public, private sector or even interventions such as aid be it humanitarian or developmental have not been spared of this sickening ill. Zambian born Economist Dambisa Moyo in her book '*Dead Aid*' raises important concerns about weaknesses of aid as an intervention in the continent. She is very worried about developmental aid as it has failed to help the continent transform. One of the fate she raises which aid suffers is abuse and misuse due to *corruption*. To her, countries largely dependent on aid have been trapped in a vicious circle of corruption'.

In the book as she plunges deeper into the controversial aid discourse which has ruffled feathers among the donor world, she even probes as to why majority of SSA countries 'flounder in a seemingly never-ending cycle of corruption, disease, poverty and aid-dependency'. This disturbing position according to Moyo (2009) still obtains in the greater part of Africa notwithstanding the fact that aid over US$300 billion has been poured into the continent since 1970s. In this section we will not examine the causes of corruption in Zimbabwe, acres of space are required to do justice to this ill in the country. Earlier, we examined some of the high-profile scandals which have been in the public domain in the 1990s in Zimbabwe, little was done to address them yet so much harm was inflicted on the economy. Hence, corruption still stinks in Zimbabwe.

The figures show that corruption is becoming an albatross to Zimbabwe in as much as it has become to other countries in the region. So, for Zimbabwe over her turbulent journey has she done enough with respect to corruption or the decay continues due to this ill?

Ease of doing business remains a serious challenge owing to corruption in various sectors.

A very serious step towards dealing with corruption was establishment by government of the Zimbabwe Anti-Corruption Commission (ZACC) as a watchdog with a mandate to:

Its establishment was long overdue as corruption has been continuing with impunity in the economic landscape of Zimbabwe. Due to the backdrop against which ZACC was found, important questions at this juncture can be reflected upon;

- Cases of corruption are overwhelming in Zimbabwe, is ZACC adequately resourced to deal with them?
- Will ZACC have the much-needed 'bite' to decisively deal with corruption?
- How insulated is ZACC from any form of pressure to execute its mandate without fear or favour?
- How prepared is the public to report corruption to ZACC without fear? Are they safe?
- Who will 'police' ZACC?
- '*Catch and release*' is often a tag which of late has been associated with ZACC, especially by several media. Remember the role of the media we explained in Chap. 1? The actual meaning of this phrase is beyond the scope of this book. However, will ZACC shrug off this tag so as to gain the much-needed public confidence?
- Are we going to see an improvement in the Transparency International rankings on corruption by Zimbabwe? This is arguably one way of directly assessing ZACC's efforts among other measures the public can use.

In conclusion the gangrene of corruption requires collective and consistent effort by every progressive Zimbabwean for the efforts of ZACC to bring the much-needed hope out of the turbulence. If little and little is done to solve the corruption conundrum in Zimbabwe just like in other states in the continent, we are likely to see the country sinking further in turbulence. The burden of other problems we explored earlier in the book have already brought untold suffering to people, as other factors as discussed in this chapter.

## References

Feenstra, C. R., & Taylor, M. A. (2014). *International trade* (3rd ed.). Worth Publishers.

Mahuni, K. (2020). Climate Change 'proofing' sub Saharan African women, a step towards sustainable development. *International Economic Association (IEA).*

Mahuni, K., Taru, J., & Bonga, W. G. (2020). *Africa's incomplete cycles of development*. Peter Lang Publishing.

Moyo, D. (2009). *Dead aid: Why aid is not working and How there is a better way for Africa.* Macmillan.

Pulse, T. V. (2017). Cleric says Africa's future looks gloomy, hopeless. https://www.pulse.ng/communities/religion/tb-joshua-cleric-says-africas-future-looks-gloomy-hopeless/t9m0te4

The Herald. (2020). Miracles and prophecy, Zimbabwe's curse. https://www.herald.co.zw/miracles-and-prophecy-zimbabwes-curse/

# Part V
# Re-wiring Zimbabwe…Attempting to Make Things Work

# Chapter 8
# The Foot on the Pedal

## 8.1 Introduction

Despite turbulence being the dominant thesis of this book which dovetails with reality which has obtained on the ground for the greater part of the four decades, efforts at reconfiguring the economy to steer it out of the turbulence waters have always been visible. Key developments in various facets of the economy in which there has been 'walking the talk' is evident. One truth we have to contend with however is that there is plenty of hard work, in particular honest, sustained and focused hard work by everyone required for the economy to be reinvigorated to sustainable levels. Weaving the gigantic economy out of turbulence will not come cheap. The tsunami of multilayered problems overwhelming the economy are intertwined, more so they keep on becoming more complex.

Presently, Zimbabwe aspires to be an upper middle income by 2030, a much more realistic and attainable aspiration if positive energy is generated and directed appropriately. Rwanda is an example of what sheer hard work can bring to nation building. In spite of the negativity which the genocide of 1994 brought to her image, she was able to shrug off and look beyond that negativity. From ruins Rwanda has been able to build a fairly functional economy and has become a citadel of hope for most countries in the continent. These national gains however did not come on a silver plate.

We still maintain that Zimbabwe is beautiful. Yes! So beautiful and unique is Zimbabwe such that her success is a vital cog for the success of not only the southern part of Africa but the broader continent. Remember we are examining an economy once the *jewel of Africa* hence its transfiguration also helps to illuminate a significant portion of the continent. Her sustainable development will rub on to other states as positive spill overs. Not only that but it will also unlock potential and value embedded in other neighbouring countries also. Scanning across the length and breadth of the country, the desire to excite the economy is noticeable. The foot is still on the pedal.

 
K. Mahuni et al., *Zimbabwe's Economy*, Advances in African Economic, Social and Political Development, https://doi.org/10.1007/978-3-031-81588-1_8

Whether the correct foot is on the pedal or the foot is wearing the appropriate shoe, it does not matter.

Two concerns are nevertheless important here, i.e.;

- Whether the foot has enough energy which carries with it as it presses on the pedal.
- Whether the foot will be able to press on the pedal consistently so as to apply balanced pressure as the economy is steered out of the many challenges.

On the first concern, it is very noble to have enough energy reserves in all the efforts to pull the economy out of the turbulent waters. The required energy levels entail all the necessary assortment of resources, both material and human. As we explained in previous chapters Zimbabwe sits on massive resources, this is the energy which can power the economy. Furthermore, Zimbabwe has the people and the people have the talents. Also in the energy mix is the strong diaspora community of Zimbabweans which always has the energy to hold on to the ship's mast coming to the rescue of those back home when the tide rises, as it frequently does. For instance, Zimbabwe obtains diaspora remittances averaging USD 1 billion annually which sustain the economy. The sheer power of remittances should not be under appreciated as a vital cog in the revival of the Zimbabwean economy. A number of diasporians who have made it well in their respective destinations feel the need to also help the home country, this is the required energy. Together with the existing locals' ideas and resources, the combined efforts bring the much-needed energy to press on the pedal.

For the second concern, consistence is key. Sustained requisite pressure on the pedal is able to propel the *titanic* out of the turbulent waters. The two concerns are interlinked. The pressure can only be sustained when there are enough energy reserves. When the energy is far less than the required out of the turbulent tide, the engine of the titanic can stall mid journey. The next thing is for it to gradually sink. If you fail to swim, then you sink further. It is even much more punitive and catastrophic to sink in turbulent waters. Recall that in previous chapters we highlighted how in some instances Zimbabwe has had blissful moments which of cause did not last, the key lacking ingredient in all this being the energy to maintain the momentum.

Consistence of the pressure on the pedal helps to smoothen and balance the economy as it glides along. Pressing the pedal too hard can propel the economy with much speed, but maintaining this speed can be a great challenge. On the other hand, pressing weakly on the pedal can result in less than appropriate speed, a situation less desirable given that we now live in a globalised world. In this world whether or not you like it you find yourself in the fast lane in which your foot should be consistently on the pedal as you also trudge along in the midst of others, with enough *energy* of cause.

Setting aside the turbulence of the past four decades, Zimbabwe can be rewired to make her work again so as to give the much-needed hope to its massive expectant population. Sources of hope out of the turbulence are plenty in the economy, cementing the fact that the foot is on the pedal. There are a number of national projects and other projects/developments of note which can help the economy significantly.

Some of the projects and initiatives conceived way back but due to turbulence have been slow to be implemented or abandoned midway as turbulence took charge.

## 8.2 Attempting to Restore the Jewel

Under this sub-section we examine briefly a number of remarkable efforts especially in recent times to show some *efforts* to restore the economy.

### *8.2.1 Infrastructure Projects*

For any economy to be efficient in areas such as telecommunications, mobility, trade efficiency among other related aspects a sound infrastructure system is an imperative. Well maintained road and rail networks, communication systems help to enhance trade facilitation among economies. Furthermore, it goes a long way in reducing the cost of doing business. Much sections of the book have highlighted how early infrastructure of Zimbabwe was instrumental for its highly functional manufacturing industry then. Later on as the vice of turbulence tightened its grip around the comatose economy, infrastructure deteriorated rapidly. Railway network, for example, has seen a lot of vandalism and heavy cargo instead of it to be ferried by rail it is being transported by road, inflicting further damage on the country's road system.

The state of most roads country wide has deteriorated rapidly over the years. Huge potholes, unmarked lanes, missing road shoulders, etc. are among some of the features of the roads in most parts of the country. Owing to increased volume of traffic, the roads have seen massive carnage resulting in loss of lives, properties and increased damage of the same roads. While a combination of factors has been responsible for these accidents such as human error, the state of the roads themselves as a result of being poorly maintained comes in also as a strong factor.

Upon realising the importance of well-maintained infrastructure such as roads government is making a number of commendable efforts to rehabilitate trunk, primary and feeder road networks across different parts of the country. In 2018 through the Public Sector Investment Programmes (PSIP) and the Emergency Road Rehabilitation Programme (ERRP) a resource envelope amounting to $175 million was approved by government. According to The Chronicle (2018) the fund will focus on projects including bridges and roads dotted across the country such as Bubi Bridge in Matabeleland South on Lutumba Chikwalakwala Road, Chilonga Bridge in Chiredzi, Sango Road, Kawonga river bridge, Nyamangura River Bridge and Jeka river bridge in Mberengwa.

One big project currently underway at a macro level is the upgrading of the Chirundu Beitbridge highway amounting to USD 400 million. The highway is very key in that it links Zimbabwe and key regional trading partners such as South Africa,

Zambia. The project has been accorded the national status to show its significance to the economy. A number of reputable companies including Masimba Construction, Tensor Systems, Bitumen World among others are busy with work on the ground, each contractor is allocated a stretch of around 20 kms which they work on including widening the surfaces. On completion they move on to the next section as the works progress. Through use of modern techniques such as satellite technology and applying durable tarmac surfaces, the strategic nature of this highway is set to improve a lot of things for the country.

The current upgrade is important although dualisation could have been the most appropriate strategy as it accommodates huge traffic volumes and speeding up mobility. This work as we pointed early will be instrumental for enhancing trade facilitation as the country focuses on attaining Vision 2030. To complement this initiative revamping railway network is also crucial. Modern railway techniques, investment in new wagons are some of the important issues to be looked into for its contribution to be meaningful to the greater economy. Malfunctioning signals, old wagons, the characteristic of the present rail infrastructure only increases efficiency problems of the country in trade logistics. Much of what remains of the railway system is not adequate enough to support a fully functional modern economy. It still baffles logic to imagine that in the twenty-first-century rail network of an economy can be on the verge of collapse when in fact it should be instrumental for industry. The desire of the African continent through its Agenda 2063 is to industrialise the continent among other aspirations. Zimbabwe will need massive revamp of also the rail network as to meaningfully ride on this tide.

At a micro-level, efforts at infrastructure improvement in different provinces are also noticeable. Local authorities in particular rural authorities in collaboration with central government have embarked in projects such as construction of tarred roads feeding into main business centres. Moreover, this has seen a sizeable number of solar projects for street lighting being implemented. In a province such as Masvingo, districts such as Bikita, Gutu have shown significant progress in micro infrastructure projects.

On the other hand, in Manicaland, a province located on the eastern part of Zimbabwe, completion of the Tanganda—Checheche 100 km road is a timely intervention given presence of strategic industries such as tea and sugar cane in the province. Furthermore, in Manicaland road works currently in progress for the Jopa Kopa will be a boon for small-scale farmers in Chimanimani and Chipinge due to the importance of agriculture not only for this region but economy in general. A lot however is expected of infrastructure both at the macro and micro level for all these efforts to contribute meaningfully in transforming the economy which remains underinvested. To date in Masvingo province, Zimuto-Kapota has since been completed road, a very positive development.

#### 8.2.1.1 Developments in the Energy Sector

The pivotal role of the energy sector in transforming the Zimbabwean economy remains crucial. Industries need consistent and uninterrupted power supplies. Sadly, economic turmoil of the years has dealt a heavy blow to the energy sector. Under-investment has resulted in epileptic power supplies, starving not only industries but also domestic users. Power imports make up for huge power deficits existing in the economy resulting in massive foreign currency outflows for the fragile economy.

Major source of hydroelectricity power (HEP) for the country is Kariba dam which was constructed more than 50 years ago. Then it would significantly sustain domestic as well as industrial use. At the present against the backdrop of ballooning population which has increased demand for power both industry and domestic use with no other significant HEP projects to the magnitude of Kariba, energy has become a national concern. Efforts to increase power generation at Kariba have seen projects such as the 300 MW Kariba South extension being implemented with its full completion in November 2018.

Rehabilitation and expansion of Hwange thermal power station are also a key milestone in contributing to power improvement in the economy. Furthermore, opening up of the coal sector to more players is a boon for the economy. Coal sector remains important for the country's energy requirements. Recent coming in of more players such as Makomo Resources, Zambezi Gas in this sector helps not only to break down the monopoly by Hwange Colliery Company Limited but also to improve efficiency of the coal industry. Thus, domestic supplies will be added as well as boosting exports to other countries earning foreign currency for the country. Through value addition of coal to coke, the long run expanded coal value chain expansion will mean more jobs and export receipts for the country.

Efforts to tap into solar energy are also commendable. There is abundant sunshine in most parts of the country which can be utilised to power local economies and eventually the national economy. As we reiterated earlier, Zimbabwe aspires to industrialise—industries are sustained by power. Solar energy is a low hanging fruit in which proper investments can be game changers for the country's energy needs.

In Matabeleland South, the Gwanda 100 MW solar project is strategic. Efforts to iron out issues around its full implementation are important. Solar energy is clean and reliable in the wake of climate change. More efforts should be done so as to open up the energy sector to bring more players. Of importance is to also increasing licensing of reputable firms in solar and other related power projects for the benefit of the economy.

In line with solar energy, a clear-cut Renewable Energy Policy at a national level is pivotal. This will allow adoption of solar seriously as an alternative source of energy for the economy. For instance, in relation to urban and growth point residential houses development it can be made mandatory for households to install solar systems. Government will also try to subsidise all the necessary solar infrastructure to ensure its accessibility to the poorest people. The long run will allow the entire economy to benefit.

Micro power projects dotted across the country in which private sector as well as donor driven initiatives are taking place are notable in different parts of the country. In Mashonaland West's Nyabira 2.5 MW solar project is set to face lift the local economy. Similar projects can be rolled out in other provinces for benefit of the local people. What is also important is for local stakeholders to allow and give these projects a chance to be fully implemented. Haggling and tussling among stakeholders has often seen many projects taking longer for their implementation, a huge turn off especially for potential investors. Mini HEP projects in a region such as Manicaland has helped to change lives especially of rural communities. This has allowed communities to also enjoy electricity for household as well as small-scale agriculture irrigation has been enhanced. This has seen non-governmental organisations helping in the setting up of small HEP taking advantages of natural waterfalls.

#### 8.2.1.2 Recovering Agriculture

Agriculture as we reiterated throughout the book will always remain an integral part of Zimbabwe's economy. The abundant arable land and the fairly good climate still means that part of reconfiguring the economy hinges on developments in this sector. The more agriculture is revived the better the chances of also exciting other key sectors of the economy. Agriculture is key for food security of our economy and employs a significant size of our population. It's a fact that the more agriculture is enhanced for our economy the resulting multiplier effect will impact positively on the broader economy. For instance, agriculture during blissful years was contributing significant throughput for the manufacturing sector and other downstream sectors. For example, the beef value chain when the national herd was still sizeable used to be broader and supporting a lot of other industries. Due to decline of the national herd and other factors which shrunk the value chain a lot of other industries have been affected.

What is mind boggling of cause being why agricultural sector in general has suffered a lot of neglect over the years despite food for instance being essential for day-to-day survival of the people and the vast tracts of arable land and water bodies the country has. In agriculture lies the future and hope of the Zimbabwean economy. The threats to the sector are numerous. Climate change for instance remains a real challenge. One way of enhancing productivity in this sector is to employ modern techniques of agriculture which involves investment in appropriate technologies suitable for local conditions.

Of late developments in the education sector with an inclination towards agriculture are commendable. The new curriculum introduced in 2014 in the education sector focuses on producing a student who has better life skills in various facets of life. One of them is the realisation that Zimbabwe should exploit comparative advantages in agriculture. The Herald (2020) aptly captures this:

> The new curriculum aims to prepare learners for a largely agro-based economy and increasingly globalised environment; encourage life-long learning; and promote patriotism, participatory citizenship and sustainable development, among other objectives.

Other initiatives at recovering agriculture currently underway include mechanisation strategies. Close to 10 years ago a facility for helping farmers spearheaded by the RBZ was carried out. In 2020, John Deere a global manufacturer of tractors has since delivered tractors to government. The deal USD 50 million deal is set to help support mechanisation efforts by government (The Herald, 2020). The long run of this strategy is to improve productivity of land by farmers. Rain fed agriculture is increasingly becoming unreliable hence the government is embarking on rehabilitation of irrigation schemes around the country. This helps to improve food security in particular of disadvantaged households.

#### 8.2.1.3 Second Phase of the Ease of Doing Business Reforms

Mahuni and Bonga (2017) show that Zimbabwe still performs poorly on major indicators of ease of doing business. This is causing a subdued inflow of the much-needed FDI to the country hampering efforts at convincingly turning around the country. In the study, the authors highlighted a number of areas Zimbabwe should focus on to improve its ease of doing business. Mahuni and Bonga (2017) summarise these areas when they submit that;

> The study found that Enforcing Contracts, Paying Taxes, Getting Electricity and Dealing with Construction Permits are the significant indices to explain FDI flows in the country. The study recommends that; for FDI inflows to improve significantly in future, there is greater need to improve efficiency in the enforcement of contracts, fair distribution of electricity, improving taxes procedures and compliance enforcement and correctly dealing with construction permits.

Of late, the country is making commendable efforts to improve the ease of doing business which has seen the launch of the second phase of the doing business reforms by the government. At the time of writing of the above cited paper, Zimbabwe had no commercial court to look into commercial disputes. However, with the recent launch of the second phase a number of strategies have been considered including setting up of four commercial courts in major cities across the country. This is a positive step in the right direction. Among other strategies in the second phase is the reduction of bureaucracy regarding issues to do with construction permits. Overall success of these will also depend on how other visible all these efforts will be on the ground. Sprucing up the image of the country on the big stage is very critical for the country to come out of the turbulence.

## 8.3 Strong Economic Headwinds Ahead.........Not Out of the Woods yet!!!

Despite the foot somehow weakly on the pedal, strong head winds ahead show that the economy is not out of the woods yet. There is plenty of hard work required for the economy to be significantly reinvigorated. Fishing the gigantic economy out of turbulence will not come cheap. There is a lot of sacrifice required across the economy. The above few developments we explored affirm the desire by the country to move forward. For instance, infrastructure projects which have seen works on some major roads around the country are very welcome developments. Apart from this, other projects which have been accorded national status priorities are essential game changers set to drive the country forward. On the other hand, efforts on trying to have visible institutions and frameworks for fighting endemic corruption which has corroded the Zimbabwean society is much welcome.

Our message throughout the book is the need for consistence in all the positive initiatives aimed at tackling the turbulence which continuously engulfs the embattled Zimbabwean economy. For Zimbabwe, hurdles to be manoeuvred out of the turbulence still remain very significant. Despite all the commendable efforts for normalcy to return, a number developments threaten to reverse the gains. We have made a number of observations which we feel need serious attention or else the turbulence jinx can never be dismantled completely. Somersaulting out of the turbulence means that certain aspects have to be taken head on. For most sections of the Zimbabwean society the period such as 2007–2008 marked the climax of the economic turbulence because of the gravity of the problems. More than a decade after this debilitating crisis and all sorts of problems it brought to the people it seems similar challenges are beckoning and waiting to pounce relentlessly again on the feeble economy.

Zimbabwe is not out of the woods yet. The axe of turbulence still hovers grotesquely above the head and shoulders of the beleaguered economy, occasionally coming down to chop and chisel its various sectors with catastrophic consequences. When it comes down whether to chisel or chop, it leaves scores of causalities, a trail of destruction, many at times stirring more turbulence. In the following section, we will discuss briefly strong head winds gradually gaining traction, signalling that Zimbabwe is not out of the woods yet. These headwinds threaten to undo the few attempts at progress out of the turbulence, quashing once again the hopes on the people.

### *8.3.1 'Inflation Evil Slowly Working Its Way Back to the Economy'*

Inflation can destroy an economy. Zimbabwe's tumultuous journey has seen inflation reaching unprecedented levels experienced mostly by war torn nations. Record breaking inflation level of the year 2008 is a familiar path for most Zimbabweans, still fresh in the minds of many. Mere mention of the word alone invokes gory memories of losing lifetime savings for some, scrounging for basic food stuffs, empty shelves in supermarkets, long winding queues of bread, fuel among other essentials. Despair was written everywhere in bold print as marauding hyperinflation wreaked havoc in the country. Actual figures of inflation the country experienced are not easy to come by. In the book *When Money Destroys Nations*, Haslam and Lamberti (2014)

**Table 8.1** Average prices for December 2018 and June 2020

| Item | Average price as at December 2018 | Average price as at June 2020 |
|---|---|---|
| Bread | $0.99–$1.00 | $46.00–$60.00 |
| 2 litres cooking oil | $3.00–$4.00 | $220.00–$230.00 |
| 1 litre milk | $1.20–$1.50 | $50.00–$57.00 |
| 10 kg maize meal | $2.50–$3.00 | $70.00 (subsidised)<br>$250.00–$300.00 (unsubsidised) |
| 2 kg Sugar | $1.80–$2.00 | $200.00–$230.00 |

*Source* Authors' compilations

present a timeline of Zimbabwe's inflation dating back to pre-independence years. We will only pick a few years when the figures reached alarming levels, i.e. 2004–2008. Haslam and Lamberti (2014) show that in 2004 the country had already started experiencing three digit inflation of 133% reaching 89.7 sextillion by 2008.

Inflation for any country develops over time. If it is not nipped in the bud on time, it will implode to catastrophic levels which will cripple an economy. Over the period the printing press was running non-stop which saw the country having higher denomination notes such as $10 000 000 000 among others. With money supply growth not matched with enough productivity in the economy, it became a fertile ground for breeding hyperinflation until the sextillion mark was reached resulting in the relegation of the Zimbabwean dollar to the dustbin of history. A survey of a basket of prices of a few consumer basics approximately around December 2017 and June 2020 as shown in the table below speaks volumes on its own (Table 8.1).

While efforts are being made to normalise and flatten the turbulence curve, these adverse developments from the inflation front show that we are not done yet with the evil of inflation. Current estimates of inflation put it at around 700%. At this rate, the economy is slowly migrating towards hyperinflation. Serious efforts to curtail this disturbing trend of inflation related to a broader spectrum of cost drivers across the various sectors of the economy are thus called for or else the economy will further sink.

### *8.3.2 Developments in the Global Economy*

The global economy itself once it catches a cold, small economies usually bear the greatest brunt of troubles. Small economies themselves such as Zimbabwe by nature of their sizes cannot influence much the big stage. Their economies are too weak in the event of negative developments globally. For instance, when prices of primary products which they mainly export tumble, they cannot do much for the same prices to rise to sustainable levels for them to get fair values for their exports.

Zambia is Zimbabwe's closest neighbour we want to use to buttress what we have just pointed in the explanation. Zambia is the continent's second largest exporter of copper. Often when copper prices are depressed globally as a small economy, she is a price taker hence she accepts the price dictated by the world market. As such owing to unfavourable prices caused by decline in major consumers of copper such as China, the Zambian economy usually experiences trade and budget deficits. Closer to the budget and trade deficits of the economy is how the two are also closely linked to the exchange rate. When the trade and budget positions deteriorate, the exchange rate often weakens causing problems, frequently spreading to different sectors of the economy. In the few paragraphs to follow we will discuss a few developments from the broader global economy which on their own are strong undercurrents threatening to further submerge Zimbabwe in turbulent waters, sadly in the depth of the turbulent waters she will breathe less.

#### 8.3.2.1 Withdrawal of USA from the World Health Organisation (WHO)

Notice to withdraw by the USA from the World Health Organisation (WHO) will have a severe impact especially on small economies. WHO, a UN agency which has been in existence since 1948 and has membership of approximately 194 countries mainly focuses on promotion of health and serving the weak member states. Zimbabwe belongs to the subset of weaker states. The USA is a key benefactor of WHO, contributing approximately 15% of the agency's budget which is more than USD 400 million (BBC, 2020).

When the USA finally withdraws from WHO, there will gnashing of teeth and wailing for most vulnerable states. Most likely significant gains made in primary health care will be severely affected. For long countries such as Zimbabwe get significant support from WHO in helping to promote a healthy nation. It remains to be seen the extent to which weak states will be impacted by this move. While it may be too early to say what will happen once the USA succeeds in this move, weakest states will not remain unscathed if USA finally pulls out.

#### 8.3.2.2 Effects of the Corona Virus Pandemic

The global economy will not remain the same as the effects of the corona virus which has been declared a pandemic continues to wreak havoc. The pandemic has profound and differential impacts across economies around the world. The economy of Germany for instance is expected to shrink by 10.1% and full recovery expected after two years. Weak economies like Zimbabwe will arguably take a heavy battering as the virus continues to strangle and choke the global economy! Moreover, due to pre-existing conditions economies of weak countries are likely to take longer to recover. From a health perspective, Covid-19 is more severe to patients with pre-existing conditions such as respiratory problems, diabetes, hypertension among other related conditions. The same could be said about the economy of Zimbabwe. A number of pre-existing susceptibilities explored in much sections of this book due to the turbulence which has unfolded over many years only make Zimbabwe a patient in the intensive care unit (ICU) in the wake of this ravaging pandemic. Here is a look at some of these pre-existing conditions and how the advent of Covid-19 as of March 2020 only worsens Zimbabwe's turbulence.

Comprehensive social safety nets which continue to be weak have only worsened the situation especially of the poor sections of the society who have to grapple with what Indian Nobel Prize-winning economist Amartya Sen, calls 'raw poverty' in their midst. Efforts by government, the church and other external partners to help out people out of the turbulence caused by the pandemic are commendable. In various parts of the country, the elderly for instance have been getting food hampers to cushion them here and there. Government through its departments such as Ministry of Social Welfare has been active in trying to cushion vulnerable members of the society.

However, the challenge has been that food insecure households are getting more in numbers calling for more food assistance against a thin resource base. A 2019/20 report on Zimbabwe by Famine Early Warning Systems Network (FEWSNET) shows that official maize production estimates are about 30% below average. Since maize is a staple food accessible to most poor in the country food insecurity only increases. The government is overwhelmed with responsibilities, so coping with all this and other demands is not easy. Remember the cyclone Idai victims we explained briefly in the previous chapters, one year on they are still in need of support from the same thin resource purse.

At the time of writing of this book, Zimbabwe has had three seasons without reliable rains resulting in droughts. Climate change has not spared the economy which mostly depends on rain fed agriculture. The coming in of Covid-19 has further worsened food insecurity in not only Zimbabwe but the continent at large by affecting the agricultural sector. 30% of the continent's GDP comes directly from agriculture which employs over 60% economically active with most being women. Covid-19 has disrupted agricultural supply chains. Food prices are steadily on the rise living poorest in the cold. It is not only Zimbabwe of cause; other countries are in a similar corner. For example, Kenyan farmers popular for their horticulture products are still grappling with Covid-19 induced effects on agriculture, at the same time swarms of migrating locusts have invaded vast swathes of land dealing a heavy blow to the sector. Food prices are starting to increase.

Having too many people in informal employment is coming also as a vulnerability for Zimbabwe as the country grapples with trying to contain the spread of Covid-19. One measure has been to adopt lockdowns like other countries. However, the informal sector which largely has been an offshoot of a struggling economy than a product of proper planning has been bruised badly. Most individuals have been surviving from hand to mouth basis in this sector. With virtually little savings to smoothen consumption in times such as these, most can no longer breath, Covid-19 only locks them down to chronic deprivation and raw poverty. A welcome intervention by government has been to offer a cushion allowance to enable most affected people in this sector to cope. However, due to the inflation headwind we explored earlier on, the value of the allowances has been depleted by marauding inflation exacerbating the plight of the poor. So, a question is, how long will it take for Zimbabwe to fully recover from the effects of Covid-19? Only time will tell!

### *8.3.3 Artisanal Mining—Ensuing Gold Mining Wars and Environmental Carnage*

Gold is a strategic mineral for the health of Zimbabwe just like agriculture we explained in most sections of the book. Its contribution to the well-being of the country remains crucial. Generally, gold is regarded as a safe hedge asset especially in turbulent times. At the writing of this book the yellow metal has soared to $2000/ ounce, this alone is good news to economies properly producing the mineral.

In one of his addresses at the inaugural gold sector awards on 26 February 2016, the central bank governor, highlighted that gold contributes 30% to export receipts for the country. To show the relative importance of the sector to the economy, on 14 November 2014 a gold mobilisation technical committee was set so as to facilitate production of gold and subsequent deliveries to Fidelity, the main buyer of gold for government in the country. The sector also contributes a substantial chunk of royalties averaging USD 24–25 million to government coffers.

One commendable development three years ago in Zimbabwe was decriminalisation of artisanal gold mining. This declaration was premised on the anticipation that this would stimulate gold deliveries and subsequent generation of forex through exports. Artisanal mining would also help add on output already being contributed by small-scale miners who contribute 50% of output in the economy. Gold reserves available in the economy are estimated to be around 13 million tonnes, whereas as at 2016 year end only 586 tonnes have been extracted, (2016 Mid Term Policy Statement), with much concentration along the Great Dyke which stretches centrally towards north–south direction of the country. A huge chunk of the Great Dyke is in the Midlands province. Despite abundant reserves, gold smuggling in the country is still rampant. The country is losing about $200 million worth of gold on an annual basis[1], notwithstanding other leakages of the yellow metal which may go completely undetected.

Zimbabwe is endowed with gold. Small-scale gold mining sector is endowed with chaos. Gold is concentrated in three key different parts of the country including provinces such as Midlands in places like Shurugwi. In Mashonaland West areas such as Kadoma are rich in gold deposits. Matabeleland South areas like Gwanda have concentration of gold and as such there is hive of activity of small-scale mining. A number of regions in the country are endowed with mineral deposits, gold being one of them. These are only a few we have highlighted but the precious metal is abundant

[1] The Herald 16 May 2017.

in the country, however only few known reserves of gold have been exploited. Vast deposits still remain untapped.

Running battles among many artisanal miners, '*makorokoza*'[2] have become a regular feature in this strategic sector. Lives have been lost, properties destroyed when rival gangs mainly youths into mining of the precious stone clash. Most hordes of energetic youths with limited options of what to do have often thronged gold rich pockets of the country with the hope of laying their hands on the precious stone. Who doesn't want to strike a fortune in his/her life time? The reader should not however that the authors are not opposed to the young partaking in this sector just like in other sectors of the economy, the resulting chaos in this sector is the bigger problem. Often contentious issues among the groups are varying, ranging from ownership and control of 'rich' mining claims to trivial issues and long-standing disputes at times not related to mining of gold at all which are however settled in gold mining. Thus, running battles in gold mining claims have often been a feature. Surrounding communities have not been spared of the battles. Use of machetes, spears, stones, catapults, etc. have become common weapons in the gold wars. Media some of the headlines which have trended from papers concerning happenings in this sector include the following;

- Machete-wielding gangs hold Zimbabwe gold mines hostage (Business Day, 2020).
- Machete wars claim 105 lives (Newsday, 2020).
- Zimbabwe: Artisanal Miner Killed in Fierce Bubi Machete Wars (All Africa, 2019).
- ZMF to tackle machete wars (Mining Magazine Zimbabwe, 2020).

The last headline is tacit acknowledgement of chaos in the sector. ZMF is Zimbabwe Miners Federation which brings together miners around the country. A number of concerns have been raised by ZMF relating to chaos in small-scale gold mining. In one of the interviews the spokesperson for ZMF had this to say concerning on goings in this sector in 2019: '2019 ended on a bad note for us, especially given the fact that we failed to attain the set gold target and also an upsurge in violence and robbery cases within the mining sector' (Mining Zimbabwe Magazine, 2020).

In the midst of the gold wars, the biggest casualty has been the economy as little is realised from ensuing commotion despite the massive potential embedded in the sector. The chaos has opened floodgates for the mineral to be channelled outside the country through informal channels and little accountability taking place, prejudicing the economy of revenues which would otherwise sustain the economy. Moreover, aside from the smuggling the image of this sector and subsequently the country is slowly getting battered, mending it will not be easy so as to bring normalcy again. Thus, the chaos is a huge turnoff for real investors.

---

[2] Is an indigenous term used to describe small-scale artisanal miners found in most parts of Zimbabwe? The term is derived from another term, 'kukorokoza'. In street language it often refers to hustling. The terms were largely popularised at the height of economic implosion.

On the other hand, scanning the broader African continent the narrative of precious minerals in general is not so impressive. In most of the countries in the continent where the precious minerals are found unpleasant stories are abounding. Countries that come to mind include Liberia, Sierra Leon, both of these countries' diamonds have brought a lot tears for the people as chaos has often reigned supreme. Botswana is one example often cited in the continent where mineral resources of diamonds are being extracted and used in a fairly transparent manner.

### 8.3.4 *Revenue Leakages in the Economy—Smuggling and Corruption*

One result of the turbulence Zimbabwe has endured over the four decades is excessive leakages of revenues such as precious minerals, underpaid customs duty. While sources for these leakages are numerous, a lot can be said about smuggling on major border points as well as the vice of corruption as a conduit for revenue leakages. Smuggling has always been a point of concern in the economy especially at the country's busiest border post-Beitbridge. The border post links Zimbabwe and South Africa, the country's largest trading partner. Main challenges fuelling smuggling include ineffective border controls, customs loopholes. In 2019, a special audit by reveals 485 of irregular vehicles in which treasury was prejudiced of USD 70 million. This is just one example of how the country is haemorrhaged of revenues as a result of ills such as these. Other sources of revenue like exports remain depressed due to constraints in production, over dependency in primary products among other challenges.

## References

All Africa. (2019). Zimbabwe: Artisanal miner killed in fierce Bubi Machete Wars. https://allafrica.com/stories/201912040226.html

BBC. (2020). Coronavirus: Trump moves to pull US out of World Health Organization. https://www.bbc.com/news/world-us-canada-53327906

Busines Day. (2020).Machete-wielding gangs hold Zimbabwe gold mines hostage. https://www.businesslive.co.za/bd/world/africa/2020-01-02-machete-wielding-gangs-hold-zimbabwe-gold-mines-hostage/

Haslam, P., & Lamberti, R. (2014). *When money destroys nations*. Penguin UK.

Mahuni, K., & Bonga, W. G. (2017). Nexus between doing business indicators and foreign direct investment for Zimbabwe: A time series analysis. *Journal of Economics and Finance, 2*(2), 1–8.

Mining Zimbabwe Magazine. (2020). Zimbabwe Miners Federation (ZMF) to tackle machete wars. https://miningzimbabwe.com/zmf-to-tackle-machete-wars/

Newsday. (2020). Machete wars claim 105 lives. Report: https://www.newsday.co.zw/slider/article/51044/machete-wars-claim-105-lives-report

The Chronicle. (2018). Government pours millions into roads rehab project. https://www.chronicle.co.zw/govt-pours-millions-into-roads-rehab-project/

The Herald. (2020). First batch of John Deere tractors arrives. https://www.herald.co.zw/first-batch-of-john-deere-tractors-arrives/

# Chapter 9
# Critical Lessons for Other Post-Independent African States

## 9.1 Introduction

Zimbabwe's dalliance with a mixed economic history over the past four decades presents critical lessons to other post-independent African states. The journey has mostly been difficult turbulent as we explored in much of the book. It takes time for turbulence to manifest. It also takes a great deal of time and effort to wriggle an economy out of challenges caused by turbulence. Four decades of trying to find the right ingredients and formula to sustainable prosperity is quite a long time. There are invaluable lessons to be learnt by other post-independent African states. Specifically, rethinking on issues like land (e.g. how best should the land question be addressed), millennials, corruption, infrastructure, manufacturing, human capital development and general health of the economy at any given time is key. For example, for most countries in the African continent who fought armed struggles, land remains a contentious issue as most natives were disposed of their land when settlers took over. Zimbabwe is one such country, as such it has had its own unique experiences with land post-independence. The experiences will be valuable to others also (they will seriously think about *what to do or not to do* as far as addressing land related issues as Zimbabwe will arguably present a perfect example of the dos and don'ts in dealing with land).

In this chapter, we give a brief overview of some critical lessons which other post-independent African states can draw from Zimbabwe's experience. At the same time, Zimbabwe can also learn from its own experience and do even much better.



K. Mahuni et al., *Zimbabwe's Economy*, Advances in African Economic, Social and Political Development, https://doi.org/10.1007/978-3-031-81588-1_9

## 9.2 Fundamental Questions

The preceding chapters have explored Zimbabwe's four decades of development. The experience has been mixed and thus remains a very puzzling narrative. Whilst there have been some signs of transformation here and there in as much as progress is concerned, much of real development transforming lives of masses centred at the heart ordinary people is still to be realised.

Zimbabwe's unending woes implying and attention the country continues to get regionally and beyond means that the country has a special disposition to live up to these expectations. During the writing of this book, eight fundamental concerns in form of questions stood out during our analysis. These are;

1. Is four decades of facing almost recurrent problems frequently not too much in pursuit of sustainable transformation of an economy?
2. Will Zimbabwe be able to salvage lost decades of development?
3. Is the *First Economy* attainable again?
4. Turbulence is slowly becoming a vicious cycle for Zimbabwe. When will she break free from this trap which has become persistent?
5. Moving further away from the continent, a country such as South Korea for instance took approximately six decades to attain sustainable growth and development. Although conditions of the two countries are worlds apart. How many will it take for Zimbabwe to successfully transform?
6. How many more years does Zimbabwe need to catch up with other states which have registered *significant sustainable* progress?
7. Zimbabwe once the *jewel of Africa,* is she alive to the fact that she still has a special role to play regionally and beyond by inspiring sustainable progress?
8. In the next few years Zimbabwe will be turning fifty years. Zimbabwe @ 50 what will life be like for the ordinary Zimbabweans who have shouldered the crushing burden of difficult times?

Understanding the above questions is important not only for Zimbabwe but to other post-independent African states. For example, the last fundamental question is about what will be the life of an ordinary person be like when the country celebrates fifty years of independence. Any meaningful development and progress any country can make with no tangible results on the weak and vulnerable is not desirable.

The narrative of Zimbabwe helps other countries still trying to find their feet with regard to development. There is plenty of positives to copy from Zimbabwe. For instance, milestones such as in sectors like health and education during early independence stand out and can inspire other countries.

## 9.3 A Lesson from the 'Dream Team'

The phrase '*Dream Team*' is popular in Zimbabwean football circles. It was used to refer to the Zimbabwean football team in the 1990s under tutelage of German coach, Reinhard Fabish. The team was so good that during the days the team would perform well against continental heavyweights such as Cameroon who were also very good at the time. The team was a combination of talented as well as patriotic players as well as different stakeholders. These were directly or indirectly involved in the affairs of the team. Above all, the faithful supporters who would cheer on the boys made the team even much better.

The bigger lesson about the Dream Team here is, for the successful progression and real transformation of any economy, everyone should be involved. It is imperative for everyone to understand that they do have a role to play. No contribution is too small. As long as everyone is not involved, it is difficult to sustain any efforts towards *real transformation* for posterity.

It is misplaced to think that politicians will be the ones to solely deliver as well as sustaining developmental goods. This is not only misplaced, but it simply shifts blame and focus entirely on them yet in the tent of progress, everyone should fit. Fit well for that matter. Remember as we reiterated in the Preface that this book is not about *sinners* (to borrow words from Lebanese Economist, Badaro (2020)). There are certain behaviours which have however become pervasive (we can term them *sins* as in Badaro's terminology) on the broader economy of Zimbabwe. These include;

- Wanton and reckless dumping of litter in most settlements (has become common site in major towns)—Creates unpleasant environments.
- Drug addiction (especially among the young people)—The country will lose out on future leaders to steer the economy well.
- Proclaiming/preaching malicious falsehoods about the country—Creates further polarisation which contributes less to national development.
- Vandalism for instance on public infrastructures such as railways, motorways—The whole economy loses out.
- Black market activities such as basic commodity hoarding, overcharging, exchange rate manipulation and other related ills. These are mostly a result of the problems largely discussed in most parts of the book—The problems on the economy only worsen.

However, the problems (sins) listed above are only part of the problem set. They are in fact innumerable. But by the end of the day, they only contribute even to bigger sins such as looting and corruption which have become entrenched in the broader economy. Furthermore, all this will result in peeling of the jewel we aim to preserve. Countries, such as South Korea for example, have shown how progress can be attained if a shared national vision exists in which everyone plays a part. It can be said also of countries like Japan. In Africa, countries like Rwanda have made significant strides through patriotism and focus. Burkina Faso lately is clearly showing how the national vision can be driven if national interests are put first. On the other hand, the example of Libya serves as a reminder to a majority of African states that absence of national unity can decimate a potential development state.

## 9.4 Crisis Begets a Crisis

One thing which an unresolved problem does is to give birth to other problems. When these problems keep on mounting there will be even more problems. Long-standing economic problems can be a breeding ground for complex problems. For instance, a problem such as corruption in the continent which remains difficult to fight for years resulted in the economies losing billions of revenues in different sectors. Estimates from organisations such as Transparency International show that Africa loses over USD 50 billion annually through corruption linked financial flows. This is a huge chunk of resources which can help to uplift the continent from poverty. For Africa owing to untamed corruption, accountability has become a problem rampant in the public as well as private sectors. Moreover, due to high corruption levels in the continent attracting private sector investment for instance remains a big challenge. Flows such as FDI prefer destinations in which corruption is minimum. Besides these problems just discussed due to long-standing corruption, there has been a problem of increasing cost of doing business in general in the continent.

Zimbabwe has a challenge of corruption as demonstrated in the book. In fact, it has matured to a crisis level by remaining unresolved. It has instead brought about other problems including weakening of institutions as well as stunting of development.

## 9.5 Endless Challenges and Arrested Development

Endless challenges have fuelled more problems consequently arresting sustainable development. They in fact overshadowed the glory of the early days of independence. For instance, the *bread basket of Africa* years is long deeply buried. Scars of economic turbulence still run deep arresting sustainable development.

It is a great learning point to other countries that economic problems being faced at any given time require immediate attention failure of which the price to pay will be unprecedented-development will be arrested. The engine of economic growth stalls mid journey. What remains for such an economy? Problems and more problems. Continued problems graduate an economy to crisis level as correctly observed by a Lebanese economist Roy Badaro in reference to the crisis in Lebanon, once prosperous leading regional centre for finance and trade. He is quoted in the New York Times saying:

> "There are many sins and many sinners," Further he goes on to say that, "The sins of the past have to be paid for today and in the future, so there is a distribution of pain to cover the costs." (New York Times, 2020).

In the book, we explained numerous problems for example the hyper inflationary episodes a part of the problems experienced in the turbulence. With little solutions to stabilise general price level what started as single-digit inflation rose to astronomic levels almost bringing the economy to a grinding halt, the resulting pain and suffering especially of the poor was profound. Hyperinflationary years for an economy suffocate development by making a country unattractive for investment as returns may not matched with invested capital. No serious development takes place as the atmosphere will not be rewarding much especially honest hard work. Development is thus one of the major casualties when inflation rears its ugly head on an economy.

From Zimbabwe's narrative it seems when an economy finds itself in a path of turbulence there is a tendency for many regulations/laws/controls/strategies to be imposed in the economy in attempt to douse the turbulence flames. The resulting numerous restrictions do not help much for the long run of the economy. Cosmetic changes brought about by the strategies only help to give temporary reprieve to the economy but mostly it reverts to its turbulence trajectory. Any *progress* registered in the process will be undone by the pre-existing turbulence. During Zimbabwe's hyperinflationary years one of the monetary measures adopted by the central bank was to slash 'zeros' for the local currency as the local unit had ballooned to notes as high as trillions for a single note. The monetary crisis masking the deep underlying economic turbulence did not end with the slashing of the zeros, rather the zeros bounced back with much gusto. In February 2009, due to the continued depreciation of the local currency, the local unit could not help any longer and the market's message was very deafening. As a result, the local currency was abandoned and marked the beginning of dollarisation.

There are many examples globally which we can pick to show how long-standing problems can stall development. They include, countries such as Yemen, South Sudan, Syria, Venezuela and others. Briefly we profile Venezuela to draw parallels which we can draw and relate to the economy of Zimbabwe.

### *9.5.1 Lessons from the Case of Venezuela*

Venezuela is known to have one of the largest reserves of oil in the world. The country due to her massive dependency on oil revenues has seen 95% of her receipt exports being generated directly from oil. When oil prices were buoyant before the year 2014 things were flowing well for the country. The period after 2014 saw plummeting of oil prices resulting in the exposure of the Petro state. Plummeting oil prices became a main factor pushing the economy to the edge. An imploding economy became infested with challenges, one after the other as summarised by one report from CNBC (2019):

> Venezuela's crisis has been marked by corruption, hyperinflation, one of the world's highest homicide rates, food and medicine shortages and the largest exodus "in the recent history of Latin America," according to the U.N. Refugee Agency.

Ever since, the economy has been on a nose dive with reports showing that between 2013 and 2017 the economy contracted by almost one third. In 2018 Venezuela declined further by 18% (Sabga, 2019).

Other problems for the embattled economy also included power cuts crippling many sectors of the economy. While they could be attributable to general under investment in the energy sector, adamant politicians have blamed the outages on the USA by engaging in a 'demonic' plot by carrying out an 'electromagnetic attack' on the country's electricity system (The Guardian, 2019). Venezuela obtains 80% of its hydro electricity from Guri Dam built around the 1960s. Frequent drought episodes has caused dam levels to deplete causing power generation problems for the economy.

Once an economy gets in trouble, most of its sectors are not spared. The monetary sector took a battering also which has seen hyperinflation putting pressure on the bolivar, the country's currency. With no respite from the oil sector the local unit continued to depreciate in value. Attempts to arrest hyperinflation induced depreciation of the bolivar was done at some point through slashing away five zeros in 2018. Other strategies were also carried out to try and win back the deteriorating economy, but to no avail.

An environment littered by problems we have just highlighted does one thing to the people. It drives them away en masse as they scrounge for survival outside their borders. Venezuelans have sought economic refuge from neighbours such as Brazil, Peru, Ecuador and Columbia. Who are these people? It is mostly the professionals, the bulk of them being economically active middle-class Venezuela urgently requires to have the economy back on track. The professionals include specialists such as engineers greatly needed for the oil sector among others. United Nations shows that approximately 4.8 million Venezuelans have left the country since 2014 as they could not withstand the debilitating challenges.

Most problems highlighted in the Venezuelan example have a striking resemblance to Zimbabwe's narrative over the course of her turbulent journey. The countries share almost a similar template of economic problems. A thorough exegesis of the two countries can only be equated to the following words: same strategies is equal to same outcomes. The hyperinflation, currency crisis, power outages, mass emigrations of professionals and general shortages of basic supplies have been the major highlights defining the turbulent journeys of these countries.

With respect to hyperinflation an IMF official Maurice Obstfeld, comparing Zimbabwe and Venezuela remarked that 'We're seeing a hyperinflation that is rivalled only by Zimbabwe', (PBS News Hour, 2018). Hyperinflation of Zimbabwe was explored in this book in Chap. 5. Zimbabwe also had currency issues, slashing zeros was adopted as a strategy, but they bounced back. This was of little use as it did not address the underlying economic challenges.

The issue of power outages Venezuela has been grappling with are not new to Zimbabwe. There has been a companion of most Zimbabweans due to deteriorating infrastructure which has constrained power generation and ravaging climate change effects lowering major water reservoirs. Just like Venezuela has Guri Dam as a major hydro power source, so is Zimbabwe with its Kariba Dam as the main power source.

The dams were built approximately similar periods (Guri 1960s whereas Kariba 1950s). Both economies have been hit by droughts which has caused a knock-on power generation in the two economies. In Zimbabwe at the time of writing of this book, there has been a marked improvement in power availability due to efforts by government to ensure its availability. A lot still remains to be done in investment in other alternative sources of energy, which could have been done a long time ago with forward planning.

The challenges in Venezuela's case have driven an estimated 4.8 million people to other countries, so is the case of Zimbabwe. Over millions of people are believed to be in the diaspora (exact figures are difficult to get. But Zimbabwe's diaspora community contributes over billions in remittances annually). Countries such as South Africa, Botswana, Namibia, UK, USA hosting a number of Zimbabweans looking for economic respite. The middle class making the bulk of professionals has been depleted by turbulence over the years. Professionals lost to other countries for both countries will be difficult to win back unless sound and convincing progress is visible.

While there is no magic wand to fish out these economies out of the storm of turbulence, Zimbabwe lately is trying to turn a leaf in trying to normalise things. It remains to be seen however the extent to which the economy glides out of the turbulent waters-recall that in the next ten years, half a century of independence will be celebrated. Currently, for Venezuela however, it is still game on.

In conclusion, as we have seen from the above case of Venezuela the problems over the years. We can safely maintain that in the history of economies, there are surely no new challenges. Rather it is all history repeating itself albeit in a different context. The causes and outcomes as we have seen above are pretty much the same, a great lesson for other economies.

## 9.6 Dazzling in Borrowed Ill-Fitting Robes: 'The Residuals Effect'

Most countries especially those which were colonised in Africa had something to *smile* at as soon as they became independent—the economies they inherited. In some instances, the settlers had made fairly remarkable improvements in aspects such as infrastructure, industries although it was largely oriented for their comfort. There was a special relationship which existed between the respective colony and the coloniser. For example, the colony would act as a source of raw materials to the coloniser. A country such as France immensely exploited West African states as this allowed her access to resources as well as labour.

Most of the improvements were *basic* creating economies which aimed largely at maintaining a master and colony umbilical code. Other colonies however offered favourable conditions in relation to climate, land, etc. not only for business for the settlers but also, they provided fairly good conditions for habitat with respect to climate, land, etc. This saw some settlers permanently shifting base from their places of origin to make the new colonial spaces their new homes. As a result of this motive, some colonies were developed fairly well in terms of amenities so that they become as liveable as possible. Under this section, we are largely concerned with economies fitting into this dimension.

Zimbabwe is one such country which was *lucky* to be fairly developed as her environs were pretty favourable for settlement- vast tracts of arable lands, untamed flora and fauna as well as good climate. This saw the proliferation of standard infrastructure such as roads, rail (some still standing up to now) across the length and breadth of Zimbabwe accompanied also by industries promoting huge manufacturing catapulting her to *jewel of Africa* status. Administrative structures were established across many parts of the country allowing the settlers to have a firm grip on the levers of the economy alienating natives in the process. These improvements brought some modicum of decency to the British colony resulting in a robust economy. In short, Zimbabwe was dazzling!

However, colonial rule did not last forever. Liberation fires across the continent were ignited starting in the 1950s allowing most states to gain independence. States such as Ghana, Nigeria, Tanzania were among the pioneers of independence in the continent. The newly found sovereignty entailed also freedom by the majority to manage the economies and resources previously owned by the settler minority in ways they saw fit. How easy was this? It was not.

The greatest challenge for most independent states became that of maintaining the *glory* of the residual economies they had inherited from the colonisers. The fresh infrastructure did not go very far to support the new states. Like morning dew, the glory that had been enjoyed earlier on did not last. The *dazzle* due to very little effort to maintain it, began to lose its lustre for most economies. As we mentioned earlier, for the case of Zimbabwe just like in several countries in the continent the glory of the days gone by was to be obscured later by fresh problems which set in for the new economy. The newly found independence gave the country the opportunity to dazzle as it was associated with the *glory* of the inherited economy. To us this was a mistake. Dazzling in borrowed robes became the genesis of fresh problems for the country. Not only were the robes borrowed, but they were ill fitting as well. It was only a matter of time before problems began to implode.

The hard-won independence brought through sacrifice by blood and sweat was *over celebrated*. A lot of work lay ahead. Focus was not supposed to be on the residual economy which we now had unfettered control all over-the factories, land, infrastructure, etc. A new futuristic model of the economy was required once we hit the ground running. New approaches which would anticipate that one day new and fresh roads would be required, new industries were needed, population especially of the millennials was growing exponentially yet opportunities were declining, climate change would soon become a strong argument in modern economies dynamics, robust manufacturing was supposed to be maintained for a country to remain competitive were all supposed to give us a home work of what lay ahead.

For example, for an economy with ambitious targets of delivering development goods to its people as evidenced by the numerous economic programmes and policies in Chap. 2. For instance, power supply from Kariba Dam as a major source was not going to be enough to power industry and for domestic use. Population of the 1960s was approximately 3 million, the power then was almost enough to cater for the country. With fairly good rains then hydroelectricity was reliable. Years later the population ballooned with 2020 estimates indicating that it is over 15 million inhabitants. Coupled with underinvestment in other alternative energy sources, climate change has adversely affected power generation by Kariba Dam. In part it explains existing power challenges by the economy. The same could be said of road infrastructure, industries, etc.

The newly found freedom ought to be an opportunity to invest in the future of the millennials as they will be vital cogs for real transformation of the continent. In turn this will allow the economy to maintain/keep pace with other countries as far as progress is concerned. By and large, the millennials have been missing the greater part of the four decades serve for only a few years in which very thorough and committed efforts have been made at enhancing their capabilities. Briefly we will explain what the residual economy did to Zimbabwe, a great lesson for countries in a similar predicament.

### *9.6.1 'The Residuals Effect'*

In this context, we define residual economies as the left-over economies which natives inherited from settlers as soon as they attained independence. Most of these left-over economies had the basic industries, infrastructure and amenities. These gave the new states a *false hope* of things which are *well* now that we are in charge. As pointed earlier independence celebrations took centre stage at the expense of real business of growing economies and taking everyone on board. A country such as Tanzania before John Pombe Magufuli's administration took over normally had independence celebrations often characterised by pomp and fanfare consuming significant state resources. The coming in of Magufuli resulted in the celebrations being greatly narrowed to allow much resources towards revamping the giant east African economy.

In closely analysing the history of Africa as a developing continent, we observed two distinct paths followed post-independence by most countries. Despite being different paths, the outcomes have largely been the same. The outcomes are what we call the 'residuals effect'. Several countries failed to escape the residuals entrapment, breaking free now is even harder unless drastic changes happen.

The first path was that of fighting over the left overs (residuals). This became a preoccupation and a perennial problem for most states in the continent as highlighted by Mahuni et al. (2020) as they vividly describe the fighting over residuals in parts of Africa:

> The period of leftovers was often chaotic and difficult to manage. Economies were quickly run down through mismanagement or people would fight over control of resources. This saw a number of coups being the order of the day in the continent.

Furthermore, the authors cite Wangome (1985) who also analysed this intense fighting starting from 1960s as people tussled for control of the leftovers manifesting as vicious coups, Wangome (1985) notes:

> The period between 1960 and 1970 and slightly beyond has generally been called the *decade of coups* in Africa. Once coups started in Africa they became like a wild African bushfire. They swept through the entire continent at an alarmingly high speed. They leapt through national borders as if those boundaries did not exist anymore.

On the other hand, the second path has been that of those that fought little but largely *sat and marvelled at what the white man had left behind.* Not much was done to take economies to the next level of progress. More could have been done to drive economies forward. Focus was mostly on downloading the residuals with benefits trickling only to a few people magnifying inequality legacy bequeathed to most colonies. Improvements made however were piecemeal without contributing much to real transformation of lives of the people. So, in both paths' economies were starved of their full potential. The results have been catastrophic.

On 1 October 2020, Nigeria turned 60 years as an independent state from British rule. While many Nigerians expressed mixed feelings about this milestone, a twit '*Nigeria @ 60 and useless*'. touched our hearts. From the words, there is not much hope implied vin the twit. Africa's most populous state has not lived up to expectations. The state has disappointed in much instances. The coups and stinking corruption have run deep for the giant African state obscuring any glory brought about by self-rule, arguably prompting twits such as the above. For Nigeria the path after independence was to fight and continue fighting for the control of left overs. Development lost in the years of tussling may never be recouped.

On the other hand, Zimbabwe mainly followed the second path in which she relaxed and felt at ease savouring the left overs chunk by chunk. The reader should remember that the country earned the moniker jewel of Africa for the beautiful left overs she had boasted of. A terrible mistake was that of doing little in improving and upgrading the bulk of the residual economy. In later years, this was to catch up with country manifesting as turbulence as we shall explain below.

### *9.6.2 The Ill-Fitting Robes*

Early post-independent Zimbabwe dazzled. This is irrefutable. She however shone on the borrowed robes. Not only were they borrowed, but there was one disturbing anomaly—the robes were ill fitting. In fact, an ill-fitting garment has two sides to it. It is either too small or too big for the frame trying to put it on. In the end whoever puts it on will appear awkward in it. For instance, if a young person puts on an oversized garment, he/she is often mistaken to a grown-up person. This is not uncommon. On the other hand, for a grown-up adult putting on a small sized garment he/she will appear more like a very young person.

Zimbabwe inherited a fairly functional but too small an economy. Remember Zimbabwe is a giant with respect to huge potential she has and what she owns. The *jewel economy* she had was too small to sustain the humungous and pregnant expectations brought about by the independence euphoria we described in Chap. 1. There was a vast mismatch between what the jewel economy offered and the oozing expectations of the masses.

The too small jewel economy was akin to a small sized garment we described above, its main result is to ill fit whoever wears it. The outcome is for that person to appear awkward in that rob. Normally a garment too small usually makes it difficult for its owner to move around comfortably, for instance they may risk the seams unknotting lest they are left uncovered for the eyes of the onlookers to feast.

Zimbabwe took the second path as described earlier on. She spent too much time marvelling at the crumbs left both implicitly and explicitly by the former colonial masters. Sadly, the population for instance was growing rapidly. Recall improvements in health sector highlighted in Chap. 2 meant that in future labour supply would outstrip the few jobs available anchored by the industry which colonial masters left behind.

Also, the infrastructure of the years gone by especially in urban settlements in as much as it was fairly standard it was reasonably adequate for the numbers available then. For example, sewer, clean water, housing then was at least available and accessible. However, with passage of time these deteriorated resulting in serious service delivery challenges. It is not uncommon to come across pothole roads in most urban settlements as well as burst sewer pipes or even clean water gushing out across the country. Most infrastructure is too old to sustain a modern economy.

Across other parts of Africa, a challenge of infrastructure such as the one we pointed is very common. Places such as Lagos, Nairobi, Johannesburg in the continent has similar challenges owing to a similar challenge to that of Zimbabwe.

Having overstretched facilities such as infrastructure against the backdrop of bulging populations is no different from an ill-fitting rob. As a result, Zimbabwe cannot progress sustainably just like the adult putting on an undersized garment cannot move around in comfort. Owing to the turbulence of the years resulting in the peeling of the jewel, the economy of Zimbabwe shrunk over the years against ballooning expectations and bulging populations.

In conclusion after donning ill-fitting robes, Zimbabwe stole the thunder and earned herself the moniker jewel of Africa. With little due care like most newly independent states from the continent, she voraciously devoured the *crumbs* of the newly inherited residual economy. The dazzle of the post early independent Zimbabwe did not last, like the early morning dew it vanished. She failed to convincingly maintain the thunder; hence turbulence took over. Upgrading and reinvesting in the small jewel economy inherited was supposed to be given first order priority to create a model of an economy which would move in tandem with demands of modern times. Sadly, for Zimbabwe and other similar developing states there were so carried away with marvelling at what the white men had left behind at the expense of creating a fresh economy with a new lease of life.

## References

Badaro, R. (2020). *Lebanon's economic crisis explodes, threatening decades of prosperity*. The New York Times. https://www.nytimes.com/2020/05/10/world/middleeast/lebanon-economic-crisis.html

CNBC. (2019). Venezuela hyperinflation hits 10 million percent. In *'Shock therapy' may be only chance to undo the economic damage*. https://www.cnbc.com/2019/08/02/venezuela-inflation-at-10-million-percent-its-time-for-shock-therapy.html

Mahuni, K., Taru, J., & Bonga, W. G. (2020). *Africa's incomplete cycles of development*. Peter Lang Publishing.

New York Times. (2020). https://www.nytimes.com/2020/05/10/world/middleeast/lebanon-economic-crisis.html

PBS News Hour. (2018). https://www.pbs.org/newshour/world/venezuela-knocks-5-zeros-off-its-currency-will-anything-change

Sabga, P. (2019). What brought Venezuela's economy to ruin? *Aljazeera*. https://www.aljazeera.com/news/2019/02/brought-venezuela-economy-ruin-190201152238535.html

The Guardian. (2019). Venezuela blackout: what caused it and what happens next? https://www.theguardian.com/world/2019/mar/13/venezuela-blackout-what-caused-it-and-what-happens-next

Wangome, J. (1985). Military coups in Africa: The African neo-colonialism that is self-inflicted. In *Global Security Organization [Site]*. URL: www.globalsecurity.org/military/library/report/1985/WJ.htm. Accessed: 14.03.2016.

# Chapter 10
# Migration, Empowerment and Zimbabwean Women

## 10.1 Introduction

The role of women in Zimbabwe has been discussed in earlier sections. Of importance has been significant strides in making sure that they participate in the mainstream economy through various government interventions over the past four decades. However, owing to increasing deterioration of the economy, one copying mechanism of Zimbabweans in general has been through migration. Destinations often travelled include; United Kingdom, South Africa, America, Botswana, Mozambique, South Africa and others. Zimbabwean women especially travelling to South Africa are increasingly becoming visible in Zimbabwean migration literature. In some cases, the journeys can be irregular. This is an important discourse in Zimbabwe's forty-year journey. It cannot be ignored. One other aspect which makes it important is the fact that, empowerment issues have a history with respect to Zimbabwe. Government has done a lot towards empowerment of women in the economy.

Learning from other contexts, we seek to answer the following questions with respect to migration phenomenon in Zimbabwean migrating women in response to socio-economic drivers.

What are the indicators of women empowerment across migration literature? What factors stimulate migration of women resulting in their empowerment? Role of government and societal dynamics—how do they affect empowerment of women in relation to migration? In the process, we attempt to situate the theme of women and empowerment through harmonizing growing body of migration literature we encounter to date. Furthermore, we will propose key interventions to help the problem of outward migration by women from Zimbabwe informed by literature. This is a special chapter[1] reflecting on the issue which has been part and parcel of Zimbabwe's journey of four decades.

[1] The chapter is a special contribution by Kenneth Mahuni, Associate Professor T.S. Ramessur, Moses Changa.



K. Mahuni et al., *Zimbabwe's Economy*, Advances in African Economic, Social and Political Development, https://doi.org/10.1007/978-3-031-81588-1_10

## 10.2 What is Empowerment?

Clearly defining women empowerment is difficult like explaining the phenomena of migration itself (Alvi et al., 2023). At times it may depend on the context (Gaye & Jha, 2011; Malhotra et al., 2002). As a result, empowerment in relation to women has thus gained interest among migration scholars. Empowerment can be thought of as a process of providing women with the necessary resources and opportunities to exercise their rights, participate in decision making and take control of their lives (Reshi & Sudha, 2022). The authors add that women empowerment implies increasing women's social, political and economic power. On the other hand, it can also be understood as allowing self-expression in women, enhancing their education, status, awareness as well as education (Bayeh, 2016; Mosedale, 2005).

In this section, therefore, we define empowerment by incorporating ideas from Sen's Capability Approach. The Capability Approach is premised on two ideas; (1) the notion of *freedom* to attain well-being and (2) the idea that attaining the well-being should be understood in terms of people with capabilities (CMI, 2020).

Thus, for us empowerment when related to women with respect to migration refers to the '*ability*' of women to '*decide*' and '*participate*' without *hindrances* in the migration decisions affecting them from '*time to time*'. In a nutshell, we therefore posit that an empowered woman in migration should be the one who is capable enough (ability) to have a say (decide and participate) in discourses to do with their migration decisions. Besides, our definition also implies the importance of hindrances with respect to decisions by women to migrate. Women's migration decisions are largely not easy. Furthermore, in our definition we underscore on the centrality of time in these decisions also. This definition thus acknowledges that empowerment is not a static concept. Thus, also women empowerment is also evolving with times.

## 10.3 Women Empowerment Indicators in Literature

Given that it is difficult to properly define empowerment in relation to migration as alluded to earlier on, it also follows that it is also not easy to partial out measures/ indicators which have been used to delineate women empowerment in literature (Alvi et al., 2023; International Organisation for Migration, 2024). On the other hand, Malhotra et al. (2002) cited in Gaye and Jha (2011) shows that issues of data limitations make it difficult to effectively measure empowerment of women. In addition, the author points out that behavioural and normative boundaries which change with time also constrain how empowerment can be measured and hence the complexity of the indicators.

So, while we may come across several tools on empowerment of women in literature, this study will only focus attention on the Women Empowerment in Migration Indicators (WEMI). It is one of the tools developed to date to specifically look into empowerment of women in migration. However, the theme of empowerment of women is not an easy phenomenon, hence we will also go further and look at other domains we encounter in literature.

## 10.4 Women Empowerment in Migration Indicators (WEMI)

This measure is given by Alvi et al. (2023) based on work carried out on 1019 women migrant returnees in Bangladesh. The measure is centred on the notion of *agency* of migrants (i.e. intrinsic agency, instrumental agency, and collective agency) in the process of migration. In the method, the authors tried to improve on earlier measures of empowerment; Women's Empowerment in Agriculture Index (WEPI) and the Project-level Women's Empowerment in Agriculture Index or Pro-WEAI to give an enhanced index primarily focusing on migration.

Alvi et al. (2023) made use of several indicators of empowerment in constructing the index based on the three agency dimensions. The indicators include; access to training, freedom of mobility, group membership, access to finance, land ownership and other assets.

WEMI index assigns scores to each individual indicator. In the process, it helps to elucidate more on women and empowerment in migration by providing a quantitative measure on issues pertinent to women with respect to migration. WEMI however is not exhaustive in its analysis of the issue of women empowerment. Briefly, we examine other empowerment domains we encounter in literature which are not captured by WEMI.

## 10.5 Other Domains of Women Empowerment in Literature

There are a number of other manifestations of empowerment of women we come across in literature. Briefly we explore some of them.

### *10.5.1 Women Participation in the Phenomena of Migration—A Sign of Empowerment*

Partaking of women in different migration typologies has been growing over the years. Thus Hugo (2000) posits that migration is both a cause and consequence of empowerment. Increase in volumes of women participating in migration is in fact a sign of empowerment itself. Miller (2019) also supports this. Bachan (2018) in

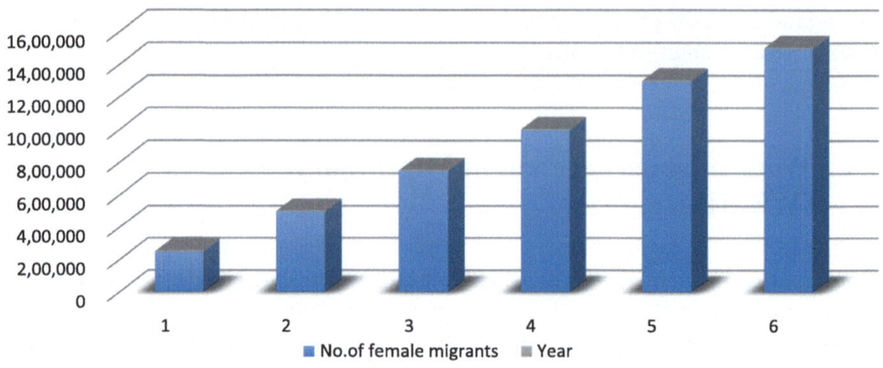


**Fig. 10.1** Number of female migrants in South Africa, 1990–2020. *Source* Authors' illustration based on UNDESA (2020)

reference to migration of women in Senegal posits that it is viewed as an '*aspiration for emancipation*'.

As a result, increasing number of women taking part in migration has actually led to the birth of the term, '*feminization of migration*'. However, the term 'feminization' when applied to migration has its own controversies. Donato and Gabaccia (2016) observe that there are many interpretations from scholars of the term when applied to migration. They posit that other scholars define it as rising number of women participating in migration between two or more time periods. On the other hand, the authors note that other scholars define it as increasing of women in migrant populations, or simply the increase in the population share of women in among migrants.

Empirical evidence to show increase in women in migration in different contexts can be encountered in literature. For example, United Nations Department of Economic and Social Affairs (UNDESA) shows that between 1990 and 2020, female migrants have been increasing in South Africa as given below (Fig. 10.1).

On the other hand, International Organisation for Migration (2024)[2] shows that 55% of 4 million Caribbean migrants in the USA were women by 2013. For instance, one island from the Caribbean, Barbados was shown to have 60% of migrants being female.

### *10.5.2 Power of Decision-Making at Household Level*

Decision making at household is key in migration studies (Stark & Bloom, 1985). This is important for empowerment of women also. Power dynamics which in turn

[2] Available at: https://rosanjose.iom.int/en/blogs/empowering-caribbean-women-through-migration#:~:text=Migration%20and%20women%27s%20empowerment%20are,in%20terms%20of%20household%20tasks.

affect social location of women differ in households across societies and consequently their empowerment. In Asian societies such as Bangladesh, women decisions on migration are not made independently. Women have to get approval from a male figure head of the family. For example, a husband, brother or father. This has also affected status of women on empowerment and inequality (Pickering & Powell, nd). Conversely, in other societies migration can actually be a norm with women having a voice on their mobility (Gaye & Jha, 2011).

Doss et al. (2022) show that in Asian countries such as Nepal, family aspects such as extended families, joint households in fact constrain women (specifically daughter in law empowerment). In addition, they also show that dynamics such as social location within a family set up is also an argument on whether women will have power of decision making at household level. For example, the authors show that for the case of Nepal, daughters in law have minimal say on property rights in families they are married than mother in laws. In sum, depending on society, power of decision making thus becomes also an important domain of women empowerment as discussed in the preceding paragraphs.

### 10.5.3 Women Authority and Enhancement of Their Value

Related to the above, Cities Alliance (2024) shows that improvement in women authority and their value is also an indicator of empowerment. In addition, they posit that as a result of enhanced value and authority women will then be able to challenge status quo as well as roles largely been viewed as traditional. With this new status, women are able to also build on a number of competencies including skills, assertiveness and expertise. This view is also echoed by Chowdhory et al. (2022). They submit that for example, women following migration which may allow them to gain education and new employment chances they attain empowerment.

### 10.5.4 Labour Force Participation/Labour Market Outcomes

Some studies highlight that women status can sometimes change at household level resulting in them being empowered. This can also depend on the respective context. de Brauw et al. (2021), for instance, show that evidence from China supports women empowerment with respect to participation in agriculture production following migration of males from the household. For the authors, de Brauw et al. (2021) they examine this phenomenon with respect to agricultural production of the cash crop jute with respect to Bangladesh. Their findings show significant women empowerment at household level due to production of the crop.

On the other hand, Eryar et al. (2020) show that empowerment of women in a study of Turkish women has resulted in a number of important labour outcomes. These include, for example, accessing and participating in high income labour markets like in regions such as Istanbul.

## 10.6 Factors Stimulating Migration of Women Resulting in Their Empowerment

Literature highlights several factors. There are both positive and negative. Positive factors in fact empower women whereas negative disempower women. Interestingly, in literature we also encounter situations where women who will be a 'disempowered position' get empowered due to migration experience in a destination country. However, later on the same women can also find themselves in a position of disempowerment in the country of destination.

### *10.6.1 Migration of Men*

Migration literature shows that migration of men can actually be a cause of women empowerment depending on context. Levitt (2001) asserts that migration provides an environment for the reconstruction of gender norms and negotiations of the dynamics in couples. In some cases, women can enjoy some degree of autonomy due to migration of their husbands. In the 1990s in an Egyptian village, spousal migration freed women from supervision and increased their ability to make financial decisions (Brink, 1991). In addition, evidence from Doss et al. (2022) posits that migration of men from rural Nepal in fact helps to empower women at family level. Due to migration of men, women are left to make major decisions in the home thereby getting empowered. A number of studies from across the world, for example, in Bangladesh (Hadi, 2001), Mexico (De Snyder, 1993), Morocco (Radel & Schmook, 2009) demonstrate that migration of men can be an avenue for women empowerment. Migration of men creates a void which women step in to fill so as to make sure that decisions are made.

On the flip side, the authors show that migration of men can also create a vacuum which in turn dampens women agency to migrate resulting in mixed effect of male migration on women empowerment. In some contexts, men can still retain control over household resources and decisions even when they are abroad (Lopez-Ekra et al., 2011). In Egypt, erratic remittances made it difficult for women to make household decisions (Brink, 1991). Women left behind can still experience difficulties in trying to be independent due to strict policing from extended family members (McEvoy et al., 2012). Empirical research on women left behind by Menjívar and Agadjanian (2007) in Armenia and Guatemala shows that migration of men further reinforces gender inequality within households. What is clear from these studies is that empowerment of women through migration of men depends on a number of factors and therefore must not be amorphously treated as a homogeneous experience.

One such factor is the nature of the destination country. For example, in Egypt, women whose husbands migrated to Arab countries were more likely to experience strict control from their husbands on return, further exacerbating existing gender imbalances and discrimination (Samari, 2021). This is due to the fact that Arab countries have fewer egalitarian norms and more restrictive gender norms for women (ibid).

It should be noted that empowerment of women due to migration of husbands or men can be temporal or long term. In fact, United Nations World Survey[3] shows that, some gains on empowerment by women through migration can only be limited and may not extend to other spheres. For Yadav (2021), this is mainly because change does not take place in a vacuum but takes place within situated constraints and limitations that determine the nature and pace of gender transformation. Temporal empowerment entails that which can be reversed when men come back from the battle front or other destination countries. The benefits that women would have accrued in the absence of men can be reversed and challenged. Menjívar and Agadjanian (2007) noted that in Guatemala and Armenia any power women left behind gain in decision making and mobility is lost when the husbands visit home or moves back. The duo also noted that women left behind in the two countries give their husbands a passport to infidelity to maintain an inflow of remittances and to maintain their status as married women. Thus, their economic insecurity as women left behind is a source of disempowerment. Literature also points to the fact that the physical absence of men does not necessarily result in empowerment of women. Patriarchal control can even be exercised over the phone. Rashid (2013) found that women in Bangladesh received instruction pertaining to debt, migration of sons or a daughter's marriage over the phone. Other female family members could be sought for advice when the husband is unavailable.

### *10.6.2 Conflict*

Migration literature attest to conflict and wars as driving forces for women to migrate to other countries. The outbreak of conflicts and violence push women to seek refuge in other countries perceived as relatively peaceful. To exemplify, women in Syria migrated to Europe, with the highest number to Berlin, German fleeing from the precarious living conditions induced by conflict since. Most of these women were irregular migrants who made a tough decision to migrate after having lost their relatives, housing and a safe environment. It is important to note that women can move to areas that can further push them into serious vulnerability especially if they move to countries where gender discrimination is prevalent. For example, Syrian

[3] https://www.un.org/en/development/desa/population/migration/events/coordination/3/docs/P01_DAW.pdf.

women who fled to Libya, Egypt, Sudan among other countries were susceptible to gross human rights violations such as forced marriages, domestic violence and other forms of abuses whether in camps or urban housing (Zetter & Ruaudel, 2014).

While wars and other forms of conflicts might be destructive (Berry, 2018), it should be noted that they can offer new windows for women empowerment both during and after conflicts (Andrabi, 2019). As pointed out by Yadav (2016, p. 171), women are not just victims but are also beneficiaries of war and displacement due to the 'rupture in restrictive gender norms. The civil war in Nepal, for example, enabled several women to cross the gender boundary and enter into previously male dominated jobs. For example, due to displacement from Kathmandu in 1993, most women became tempo drivers (a tempo is a three-wheeled electric vehicle that carries up to 12 people) (Yadav, 2021). The increased participation of women in the driving profession changed the Nepal people, both men and women's perceptions of women. Women also participated in community developmental projects and other community affairs. This provided an opportunity for them to participate in the politics of the country after the war for example in the 2017 local elections 41% of women joined local governments and 98% of deputy majors were women (Yadav, 2021).

Conflicts can force men to be away from home fighting at the battle fronts. This temporal absence of men can contribute to women's increased exposure to the public sphere and thus can be a vehicle for empowerment (Asaf, 2017; Tripp, 2015) (Berry, 2018). For some women, especially those who can escape gender-based violence, the flux created by such instability may create chances of mobility and new social roles that would not have been otherwise possible, and thereby are empowering. For example, among displaced communities in Burundi and Sri Lanka, it was observed that displaced women took on more and different roles as protectors and providers of families, and drew confidence and determination from these experiences. As a result, both their agency and their political participation were strengthened. Literature reviewed above does not present conflict as a positive event. Rather, the conditions that are created by conflict for example, the temporal absence of men from home can provide a basis for women empowerment. Thus, for Yadav (2021) conflicts create room for the exercise of reflexivity that can significantly result in the transformation of gender relations.

Women take advantage of the freedom prevailing in destination countries to empower themselves as individuals, communities and subsequently the entire nation. Thus, migration does not only empower the migrants per se, but also empowers those that are left home. This of course can result in high divorce rate as the discourses of freedom and emancipation come head on with restrictive patriarchal norms especially in the rural areas (McDuff, 2015).

However, literature also points to a number of cases where women can be disempowered and face multi-layered forms of oppression in the host countries. Hlatshwayo (2019), for example, posits that the desire for emancipation and empowerment by Zimbabwean migrant women to South Africa violence and discrimination are always associated with their lives. Migrant women experience multiple forms of discrimination constructed around their identities as women, non-citizens, black African and poverty stricken (Hlatshwayo, 2019). This is further corroborated by Mutambara and Maheshvari (2019)'s study which revealed that most women migrants in South Africa experience gender-based violence in all its forms. Despite their ability to endure all forms of oppression, women's agency is thwarted by their financial insecurities and in most cases structural factors such as legality, positions migrant women as victims of xenophobic gender-based attacks (ibid). Thus, in most cases, life-changing opportunities through employment is overshadowed by the migrant women's lived realities as they are perceived as 'others' and are exposed to a multiplicity of insecurities in South Africa. Empowerment of these migrant women therefore is contextual and depends greatly on their resilience capacity.

#### 10.6.2.1 Increase in Demand for Domestic and Care Work

Domestic work is largely gendered with 83% of global domestic work being women (Jayasuriya & Opeskin, 2015). The demand for domestic and care work overseas stimulated many women and girls to migrate from their home countries in search of jobs in the sector. The International Labour Organisation (2015) estimates that the number of people who migrated in search of domestic and care work internationally was 11.5 million. Women and girls constituted 75% of these migrants. For O'Neil et al. (2016) the demand for domestic and care workers was increased by a ballooning ageing population and entrance of women in the labour market in greater numbers. This is also confirmed by Kuschminder and Siegel (2014) who opine that almost three-quarters of migrants were moving in search of employment in Ethiopia. Poverty is also key in explaining migration by domestic workers although it is not the only factor. The massive migration of women as domestics and care workers created a 'global chain of care' which for example pushed many Ethiopian women to the Arab countries.

Literature on this form of migration show that it can both be empowering and disempowering. On one hand, domestic work is generally less socially valued compared to other jobs (O'Neil et al., 2016). This feminisation of domestic care work implies that women still maintain their low status even when they earn some income. This type of work also further confines women and girls in the private sphere and thus exposing them to sexual abuse, discrimination and ill-treatment (see (Temin et al., 2013)). On the other hand, migration can raise women to the status of a breadwinner in the transnational family. In Ethiopia, for example, the money sent back home by migrant women boosted their voices and acceptance in their home communities. This has resulted in shifting power dynamics in families (O'Neil et al., 2016).

#### 10.6.2.2 Gender-Based Discrimination and Structural Inequalities

Women sometimes migrate in order to flee from discriminatory practices and structural inequalities in their home countries. A study by Yeoh et al. (2010) for example reveals that Southeast Asian women migrate specifically to escape forced marriages.

In sync with these findings, Erulkar et al. (2006) as cited by Ferrant et al. (2014) assert that 23% of the adolescent migrant girls from Ethiopia migrate to also escape early marriages and fear of and sometimes experience of gender-based violence. Women are therefore likely to be attracted to countries with less restrictive gender norms and where the legal systems protect and advance women's rights (Ferrant et al., 2014) for example, most women flock from countries where Female Genital Mutilation is practised to Belgium where such practice is strictly prohibited. Georgian women also migrate from their home country to London in search of freedom from oppressive gender regimes. In a study by Curro (2012), most Georgian women believed that migration to London offered them an opportunity to be independent and charge of their lives. They could now depend less on relatives and friends to make decisions with regards their own lives. Migration helps to revisit gender norms and values.

The central question revolves around whether women migrating from countries or regions where there are serious restrictive gender norms can be empowered through migration. Extant literature points to the empowering dimension of migration, albeit with different magnitudes depending on context (McDuff, 2015). However, some scholars believe that the outcome of migration processes are not always predictable. Women fleeing from harmful gender practices such as female circumcision can actually encounter some disempowering experiences in host countries. While women from countries where FGM is practised can gain social status within their families and countries, they can lose that status and recognition in other contexts such as Belgium.

From the literature reviewed above, one can note that empowerment of women through migration is contingent upon a number of factors. These include, but are not limited to the context of migration, type of migration (whether it is legal or not), characteristics of the migrant woman and age of the migrant woman (Hugo, 2000). He reasons that empowerment is likely to occur in the context of legal migration, urbanisation, when the migrant is separated from the family, when the migrant is working in the formal sector in the destination country and when the migrant woman stays in the destination country for a long time. A clear understanding of the role of migration in empowering women thus requires one to unbundle the concept 'women'. This is in line with the postmodern feminist view of women as a heterogeneous rather than a homogeneous entity (Abbott et al., 2006). Migrant women vary remarkably in terms of age, social class, educational status, skills possession and ethnicity. Considering the multifarious nature of migrant women, it becomes obvious that empowerment is experienced differently depending on their standpoints.

In line with the above, irregular female migrants are likely to accrue little economic returns than regular ones. This is primarily because they rely on recruitment agencies for their migration since they have limited resources and information. In the Philippines for example, about 1200 licensed recruitment agencies are there to assist migrants. These, however, charge exorbitant fees pushing women into huge debts that are difficult to pay off since they earn less compared to men (Ghosh, 2020). This results in the economic disempowering of the migrant woman.

## 10.7 Government and Societal Dynamics in Relation to Women Empowerment in Migration

Given the diverse experiences and outcomes of migration on women and their empowerment or as espoused in the literature above, it is unequivocally clear that migrant women require social support before, during and after migration. This enables skills retention and a sense of empowerment on return (Bachan, 2018). Thus, there is need for institutional support at national, regional and international level. At the national level, the government must play a key role in safeguarding women's concerns in migratory flows. Government is a key player in any economy through its influence on policies. As a stakeholder, the government determines the potential of migration to empower women and consequently to contribute to national development. Increased support from government also results in increased chances of empowerment of migrant women while lack of support can have a disempowering effect.

It should also be noted that migrating women encounter government in two spaces, i.e. at origin and destination. Each interface at either space there has an effect of either empowering or disempowering as we will show in this section.

### *10.7.1 Government Role Through Direct Programmes and Policies Impact in Relation to Migration*

The Senegalese government under the leadership of Macky Sall instituted a number of immigration-related policies in the areas of protection, security, migration and development, diaspora involvement, and migrant return and reintegration (United Nations, 2007). One such programme is the Investment Support Fund for Senegalese Abroad which among other things, funded Senegalese migrant projects abroad and upon return. Through this fund, many Senegalese women particularly those in the diaspora were able to engage in farming, handicrafts and information technologies. This promotes skills development and economic empowerment of women. In addition, the Help of Migrants (HOM) platform was created. This is an online programme designed to promote interaction between migrants abroad and those left behind in Senegal. Information sharing through this platform promoted empowerment and skills exchange.

### *10.7.2 Regulations on Migration*

Literature shows that governments come up with regulations which in turn have a bearing on women migration. It should be noted that some regulations can be in countries of origin which facilitate women migration or can hamper their efforts at migration. On the other hand, other regulations can be in destination countries which can have similar outcomes as well depending on country. Outcomes in this dimension can be mixed as we shall highlight.

In some countries, mobility of women in general and married women in particular is legally restricted. The World Bank Group (2015) noted that in 30 countries women are not free to choose where to live. The same study found that in 19 countries women are required by law to respect their husbands. In countries like Iraq, Iran, Qatar and Saudi Arabia women have to get the permission of their husbands to travel internationally. The situation is worse in Syria where men can prevent their wives from migrating by listing their names with the Ministry of Interior (Amin et al., 2013). These restrictive laws are compounded by unequal citizenship rights in some contexts. In 2013, for example, the Lebanese ministerial committee rejected a proposal that allows Lebanese women married to foreigners to pass citizenship rights to their spouses and children. This is despite the fact that men in the same context married to non-nationals are granted such rights (Reuters, 2020).

In contexts where there are no legal restrictions on women migration, restrictive laws can still function to thwart the benefits of migration. Some laws for example prohibit women who migrate to join their spouses or family members to work. For example, until 2005 the law in Germany prohibited migrant spouses from working for one year and later on required proof that their employment will not culminate in unemployment of European Union citizens. This is also the case with the United States where visas for spouses restrict employment and education. According to the Women, Business and the Law data some 100 countries have laws that restrict women from doing the same job as men and this confining them to the low paying, feminine jobs (The World Bank Group, 2015). In this case women who flee from gender restrictive norms at the workplace in their home countries will never be empowered by such environments marked by gender hierarchies that are skewed in favour of men. All these government policies and laws on migration affect the degree to which women are empowered by migration. These can as well enhance or stifle the migrant woman's agency.

In literature, governments have been shown to play a brokering role liaising with other governments or Non-Governmental Organisations focusing on women through numerous programmes. These will be aimed at ensuring that women's empowerment through migration is enhanced. Sasikumar and Thimothy (2012) highlight that pre departure programmes are common in South Asian countries which have been flocking to the Gulf. The express purpose of these have been to reduce vulnerability of women and promoting their empowerment.

Jayasuriya and Opeskin (2015) show that Sri Lanka is one country which has long encouraged domestic labour at a higher scale to most Middle East states as early as the 1980s. Thus, government has acknowledged contribution of this sector through remittances and welfare improvements to the domestic economy. On the contrary, Jayasuriya and Opeskin (2015) submit that regions such as the Middle East have in part stifled women empowerment despite initially empowering them with opportunities for work. The migrant women through work opportunities they get, they are empowered. However, the authors show that in most instances, the same women through restrictive visa regimes by the hosting countries, they are not able to have their families to join them. In the process they are therefore disenfranchised and disempowered of their rights to be with their families reunite with them.

The Guardian (2024)[4] reports that in the Gulf States, a practice known as *kafala*[5] which has blessings of governments has resulted in the enslavement of women by their employers. In fact, the system empowers employers (sponsors) to have much power and control over their employees. For instance, it is illegal for one employee move to another employer. Further, should an employee decide to terminate their employment, they should pay the remainder of the employment period to their employee. Besides that, the employee will not be released. This is rampant in domestic work. Countries such as Qatar have tried to revisit this system so as to make it favourable to women labourers. However, countries such as Jordan, Lebanon and other Gulf States including Kuwait, Saudi Arabia still practise this system (The Guardian, 2024). Kafala system has largely taken away labour rights of women and giving too much power to employers. This is further worsened by the fact that for domestic work, an employee will be confined to the home of the employers. This further escalates disempowerment.

In a recent development in Laos, the government through the Ministry of Labour and Social Welfare plans to issue visas to illegal foreign workers (Vietnam+, 2024).[6] In addition, those with legal permits will also be extended. This move is meant to ease shortage of labour in the country as well as dealing with illegal migrants (Vietnam+, 2024). The outcome of this will be to enhance empowerment of foreign labourers such as women and men working in factories in Laos as well as other sectors.

### *10.7.3 Human Development Strategies as Part of the Broader Macroeconomic Governmental Goal of Development*

Migration literature also shows the instrumental role government also plays in ensuring that supply of labour especially for domestic work is guaranteed (Jayasuriya & Opeskin, 2015). This practice they argue is commonly found in a number of labour sending developing states. They show that governments can in fact investment in human development sectors such as education and health with a long run goal of making sure that skills of their people are improved as they prepare them for work in better economies. The authors show that in the early 1990s, Sri Lanka had highest number of female migration per capita with 3 female departures for every 1

---

[4] Available at: https://www.theguardian.com/global-development/2024/apr/25/kafala-labour-system-gulf-women-talk-about-life-as-a-domestic-worker-in-the-gulf.

[5] It refers to a legal sponsorship system which spells out the relationship between employers and employees. Mostly it has been practised in the Gulf States to ensure control of labour supply.

[6] Available at: https://en.vietnamplus.vn/laos-speeds-up-granting-licences-to-foreign-workers/285044.vnp.

male departure and government had invested highly in making sure that a guaranteed stream of labour was available.

In addition, literature also shows that governments can also carry out outreach programmes in destination countries. This can be in partnership with hosting government, civic organisations and other stakeholders to directly empower migrant women with much-needed information. Newswire (2024) shows that as of year 2023 the government of Sri Lanka has been involved in critical awareness programmes through various outreaches to its women domestic workers in Singapore. In 2024, an outreach was held for 200 women targeting key thematic areas for migrants including welfare, safety and security. On completion, all participants were given certificates (Newswire, 2024).

### *10.7.4 Societal Norms and Practices*

United Nations World Survey[7] shows that existing hierarchical social relations in any context are key. They shape experiences of the actual actors involved in migration and their experiences affecting their empowerment in the process. For example, the same survey shows that female labour supply is in fact an outcome of existing norms which often confines women to whether they can be empowered to migrate or restricted. The survey shows that if expectations about reciprocity by females in relation to ploughing back once they start getting income in their family are high after they are subjected to migration experience, their empowerment is enhanced. Different migration typologies we highlighted have also important implications on women empowerment. Migration for marriage and work can be strongly influenced by already existing norms and practices at origin with outcomes which spill into the destination country. United Nations World Survey shows in some instance women can migrate following their spouses. Once they are in the destination, suppose they start a small venture, for female counterparts due to existing norms and practices they can find themselves working without remuneration stifling their empowerment (United Nations World Survey).

## 10.8 Major Interventions to Help Empower Women Migrating from Zimbabwe

Informed by the above, the following can help to promote safer migration by women from Zimbabwe as well as empower them.

---

[7] https://www.un.org/en/development/desa/population/migration/events/coordination/3/docs/P01_DAW.pdf.

- Zimbabwean government can consider empowerment programmes (both at origin and destination) targeted at women such as offering training. This helps to raise awareness in women about issues such as their rights as migrants. Also, empowerment at home country can be a tool to discourage migration.

  Interactions with stakeholders such as Empower Bank[8] have shown that empowering women improves livelihoods. Challenges indicated by the institution is lack of security, experience and general support in beneficiaries. Women can be assisted; this empowers them helping to reduce migration especially in communities where it is rife. Places such as Honde Valley have succeeded in this regard according to Empower Bank in the same interview.
- In addition, women require also support in terms of equal access to assets such as land, properties and others depending on contexts. For instance, Zimbabwe, like other countries such as Ethiopia are largely agrarian. As such empowerment in terms of access of assets like land cannot be ignored.
- Collaborations between sending and receiving countries is also important in relation to empowerment of migrating women. As we saw in other contexts, this can go a long way in promoting safe migration (especially those who may be irregular migrants). Their empowerment is enhanced through working together of countries.

  Engagements with key stakeholders such as Beitbridge Support Resource Centre[9] dealing mostly with receiving deportees from South Africa highlighted the importance of efforts at combating especially irregular migration between Zimbabwe and South Africa through multi stakeholder collaborations. Among problems facing migrants like women during the interview were lack of documentation, trafficking, family separation, crime among others.

In sum, we have situated the theme of women and empowerment as we encounter in migration literature. We harmonised the various literature which has delved into this complex discourse as it relates a lot to Zimbabwe's experience over four decades with respect to the economy.

## References

Abbott, P., Tyler, M., & Wallace, C. (2006). *An introduction to sociology: Feminist perspectives*. Routledge.

Alvi, M., Ratna, M., Sufian, F., Khan, M. H., & Ringler, C. (2023). *Development and validation of a Women's empowerment in migration index (WEMI)*. International Food Policy Research Institute (IFPRI).

Amin, M., Bin-Humam, Y., & Iqbal, S. (2013). Mapping the legal gender gap in accessing business environment institutions. In *Women, business and the law note*. World Bank.

[8] Interview 24 July 2024.

[9] Interview, 26 July, 2024.

Andrabi, S. (2019). New wars, new victimhood, and new ways of overcoming it. *Stability: International Journal of Security & Development*, *8*(1), 3. https://doi.org/10.5334/sta.665

Asaf, Y. (2017). Syrian women and the refugee crisis: Surviving the conflict, building peace, and taking new gender roles. *Social Sciences, 6*(3), 110. https://doi.org/10.3390/socsci6030110

Bachan, A. (2018). An exploration of the gender-migration-development nexus. *Consilience, 20*(20), 1–22. https://www.jstor.org/stable/26760100

Bayeh, E. (2016). The role of empowering women and achieving gender equality to the sustainable development of Ethiopia. *Pacific Science Review b: Humanities and Social Sciences, 2*(1), 37–42. https://doi.org/10.1016/j.psrb.2016.09.013

Berry, M. E. (2018). *War, women, and power: From violence to mobilization in Rwanda and Bosnia-Herzegovina.* Cambridge University Press.

Brink, J. H. (1991). The effect of emigration of husbands of husbands on the status of their wives: An Egyptian case. *International Journal of Middle East Studies, 23*(2), 201–211. http://www.jstor.org/stable/164237

Chowdhory, N., Sabur Ali, M., Kaur, R., Kajla, M., Kumari, N., Tiwari, B., & Ishaq, S. (2022). Gendering migration: Evaluating empowerment of single migrant women. *Social Change, 52*(1), 24–39. https://doi.org/10.1177/00490857211068569

Cities Alliance. (2024). Migration, gender, and women's empowerment. https://www.citiesalliance.org/migration-gender-and-womens-empowerment#:~:text=Successful%20urban%20migration%20can%20bring,develop%20self-esteem%20and%20capacities

CMI. (2020). Amartya Sen's capability theory approach. https://www.cmiuniversal.com/en/amartya-sens-capability-theory-approach/

Curro, C. (2012). National gender norms and transnational identities: Migration experiences of Georgian women in London. *Slovo, 24*(2), 114–131.

de Brauw, A., Kramer, B., & Murphy, M. (2021). Migration, labor and women's empowerment: Evidence from an agricultural value chain in Bangladesh. *World Development, 142*, 105445. https://doi.org/10.1016/j.worlddev.2021.105445

De Snyder, V. N. S. (1993). Family life across the border: mexican wives left behind. *Hispanic Journal of Behavioral Sciences, 15*(3), 391–401. https://doi.org/10.1177/07399863930153008

Donato, K. M., & Gabaccia, D. (2016). The global feminization of migration: Past, present, and future. *Migration Policy Institute, 1.* https://www.migrationpolicy.org/article/global-feminization-migration-past-present-and-future

Doss, C. R., Meinzen-Dick, R., Pereira, A., & Pradhan, R. (2022). Women's empowerment, extended families and male migration in Nepal: Insights from mixed methods analysis. *Journal of Rural Studies, 90*, 13–25. https://doi.org/10.1016/j.jrurstud.2022.01.003

Erulkar, A. S., Mekbib, T.-A., Simie, N., & Gulema, T. (2006). Migration and vulnerability among adolescents in slum areas of Addis Ababa, Ethiopia. *Journal of Youth Studies, 9*(3), 361–374. https://doi.org/10.1080/13676260600805697

Eryar, D., Tekgüç, H., & Toktas, S. (2020). Does migration contribute to women's empowerment? Portrait of urban Turkey and Istanbul. In *Women's empowerment in Turkey and Beyond* (pp. 30–51). Routledge. https://doi.org/10.1080/14683849.2018.1495566

Ferrant, G., Tuccio, M., Loiseau, E., & Nowacka, K. (2014). The role of discriminatory social institutions in female South-South migration. In *Organisation for economic co-operation and development.*

Gaye, A., & Jha, S. (2011). Measuring women's empowerment through migration. *Diversities, 1*, 1–13. https://newdiversities.mmg.mpg.de/fileadmin/user_upload/2011_13-01_Gaye_Jha.pdf

Ghosh, J. (2020). Migration and gender empowerment: Emerging issues. *Governance and Labour Migration*, 134–162. https://doi.org/10.4324/9781003157175-6

Hadi, A. (2001). International migration and the change of women's position among the left-behind in rural Bangladesh. *International Journal of Population Geography, 7*(1), 53–61. https://doi.org/10.1002/ijpg.211

Hlatshwayo, M. (2019). Precarious work and precarious resistance: A case study of Zimbabwean migrant women workers in Johannesburg, South Africa. *Diaspora Studies, 12*(2), 160–178. https://doi.org/10.1080/09739572.2018.1485239

Hugo, G. (2000). *Migration and women empowerment*. Moving Beyond Oxford University Press.

International Labour Organisation. (2015). *Migrant domestic workers across the world: Global and regional estimates*. https://www.ilo.org/sites/default/files/wcmsp5/groups/public/@dgreports/@dcomm/documents/publication/wcms_436343.pdf

International Organisation for Migration. (2024). *Empowering Caribbean women through migration*. https://www.iom.int/resources/empowering-caribbean-women-through-migration

Jayasuriya, R., & Opeskin, B. (2015). The migration of women domestic workers from Sri Lanka: Protecting the rights of children left behind. *Cornell International Law Journal, 48*, 579.

Kuschminder, K., & Siegel, M. (2014). *Migration & development: A World in Motion Ethiopia country report*. Maastricht University and United Nations University.

Levitt, P. (2001). Transnational migration: Taking stock and future directions. *Global Networks, 1*(3), 195–216. https://doi.org/10.1111/1471-0374.00013

Lopez-Ekra, S., Aghazarm, C., Kötter, H., & Mollard, B. (2011). The impact of remittances on gender roles and opportunities for children in recipient families: Research from the International Organization for Migration. *Gender & Development, 19*(1), 69–80. https://doi.org/10.1080/13552074.2011.554025

Malhotra, A., Schuler, S. R., & Boender, C. (2002). Measuring women's empowerment as a variable in international development. In *World Bank workshop on poverty and gender: New perspectives*, Washington, D.C.

McDuff, E. (2015). Women's voices from the Zimbabwean diaspora: Migration and change. *Ìrìnkèrindò: A Journal of African Migration, 8*, 10–52.

McEvoy, J., Petrzelka, P., Radel, C., & Schmook, B. (2012). Gendered mobility and morality in a south-eastern Mexican community: Impacts of male labour migration on the women left behind. *Mobilities, 7*(3), 369–388. https://doi.org/10.1080/17450101.2012.655977

Menjívar, C., & Agadjanian, V. (2007). Men's migration and women's lives: Views from rural Armenia and Guatemala. *Social Science Quarterly, 88*(5), 1243–1262. https://doi.org/10.1111/j.1540-6237.2007.00501.x

Miller, J. (2019). More choices, more power: Opportunities for women's empowerment in labour migration from Viet Nam. *International Labour Organization Publication*. https://www.ilo.org/wcmsp5/groups/public/---asia/---ro-bangkok/documents/publication/wcms_738372.pdf

Mosedale, S. (2005). Assessing women's empowerment: Towards a conceptual framework. *Journal of International Development, 17*(2), 243–257. https://doi.org/10.1002/jid.1212

Mutambara, V., & Maheshvari, N. (2019). The human security implications of migration on Zimbabwean migrant women in South Africa. *African Human Mobility Review, 5*(3), 1774–1796. https://doi.org/10.14426/ahmr.v5i3.891

Newswire. (2024). Outreach programme organized for Sri Lankan migrant workers in Singapore. https://www.newswire.lk/2024/05/03/outreach-programme-organized-for-sri-lankan-migrant-workers-in-singapore/

O'Neil, T., Fleury, A., & Foresti, M. (2016). Women on the move. Migration, gender equality and the, 2030.

Pickering, S., & Powell, R. (nd). State of evidence: Women and irregular migration. In *Migration displacement & briefing note series*. Oxfam-Monash Partnership.

Radel, C., & Schmook, B. (2009). Migration and gender: The case of a farming "Ejido" in Calakmul, Mexico. *Yearbook of the Association of Pacific Coast Geographers*, 144–163. https://doi.org/10.1353/pcg.0.0027

Rashid, S. R. (2013). Bangladeshi women's experiences of their men's migration: Rethinking power, agency, and subordination. *Asian Survey, 53*(5), 883–908. https://doi.org/10.1525/as.2013.53.5.883

Reshi, I. A., & Sudha, T. (2022). Women empowerment: A literature review. *International Journal of Economic, Business, Accounting, Agriculture Management and Sharia Administration, 2*(6), 1353–1359. https://doi.org/10.54443/ijebas.v2i6.753

Reuters. (2020). Lebanese citizenship law strips women of identity and property. https://www.reuters.com/article/world/lebanese-citizenship-law-strips-women-of-identity-and-property-idUSKCN0YH03O/

Samari, G. (2021). Coming back and moving backwards: Return migration and gender norms in Egypt. *Journal of Ethnic and Migration Studies, 47*(5), 1103–1118. https://doi.org/10.1080/1369183x.2019.1669437

Sasikumar, S., & Thimothy, R. (2012). *Migration of low skilled workers from India to the European Union.*

Stark, O., & Bloom, D. E. (1985). The new economics of labor migration. *The American economic review, 75*(2), 173–178. http://www.jstor.org/stable/1805591

Temin, M., Montgomery, M. R., Engebretsen, S., & Barker, K. M. (2013). *Girls on the move: Adolescent girls & migration in the developing world.*

The Guardian. (2024). https://www.theguardian.com/global-development/2024/apr/25/kafala-labour-system-gulf-women-talk-about-life-as-a-domestic-worker-in-the-gulf

The World Bank Group. (2015). *Women, business and the law 2016: Getting to equal.* World Bank.

Tripp, A. M. (2015). *Women and power in post-conflict Africa.* Cambridge University Press.

UNDESA. (2020). Population division. 2020. *World population prospects 2022: Summary of results.*

United Nations. (2007). *Indicators of sustainable development: guidelines and methodologies third edition.* Economic and Social Affairs.

United Nations World Survey. https://www.un.org/en/development/desa/population/migration/events/coordination/3/docs/P01_DAW.pdf

Yadav, P. (2016). *Social transformation in post-conflict Nepal: A gender perspective.* Routledge.

Yadav, P. (2021). Can women benefit from war? Women's agency in conflict and post-conflict societies. *Journal of Peace Research, 58*(3), 449–461. https://doi.org/10.1177/0022343320905619

Yeoh, S. A. B., Hoang, L. A., & Lam, C. F. T. (2010). Effects of international migration on families left behind.

Zetter, R., & Ruaudel, H. (2014). Development and protection challenges of the Syrian refugee crisis. *Forced Migration Review* (47).

# Chapter 11
# Further Issues

## 11.1 Introduction

The greater part of this book explored Zimbabwe's journey for the past four decades' post-independence extensively examining issues from 1980 to 2020. From the small achievements attained over the years by the country, problems are also becoming complex. This chapter briefly looks at further issues. These issues add on to the multi-layered complexities examined throughout the rest of the book. Thus, we maintain that, attaining sustainable development for Zimbabwe will also be dependent on addressing these issues fully. They indeed affect the country's aspirations.

## 11.2 Pervasive Problem of Drug and Substance Abuse

Drug and substance abuse is not only a problem in Zimbabwe, but most countries in the continent and beyond. Even island countries such as Mauritius,[1] Seychelles,[2] the problem is also a cause for concern. In Zimbabwe, the Ministry of Health and Child Care (MoHCC 2023) shows that the problem is common among the young people, 15–19-year-olds. What is most disturbing is that, youths are the foundation of the future of the country. Out of upright and sober youths, comes astute leadership to stir the nation forward. On the contrary, with drunk youths, there will be a number losses inflicted on the economy. One of them is lack of leadership as well as productive people. There are also costs to the economy in dealing with drug and substance abuse. For instance, maintaining proper rehabilitation facilities comes at the expense of the tax payers. Besides this, mental health issues linked to drug abuse are slowly

[1] See: https://www.aljazeera.com/features/2023/10/4/kids-whose-insides-are-destroyed-the-return-of-drug-abuse-to-mauritius.

[2] See: https://www.afrobarometer.org/publication/ad819-seychellois-want-more-government-action-to-curb-the-countrys-drug-epidemic/#:~:text=In%20Seychelles%2C%20a%2.



K. Mahuni et al., *Zimbabwe's Economy*, Advances in African Economic, Social and Political Development, https://doi.org/10.1007/978-3-031-81588-1_11

coming up in the society. There is also a strong link to escalation of HIV/AIDS due to increase in drug and substance abuse (MoHCC 2023). All this costs the economy precious resources.

## 11.3 Institutional Reforms

Robust institutions are key for sustainable growth and development of any economy as we highlighted from Acemoglu and Robinson (2012) in earlier sections of the book. Over the years, institutions in Zimbabwe have played a limited role to champion growth and development of the economy. Instead, the experience of Zimbabwe's institutions more often has been failure to operate independently without having to succumb to political pressure. The greatest casualty has been the economy. One institution which has played significant role in the Zimbabwe's economic landscape and is recognisable even by the ordinary man, has been the Reserve Bank of Zimbabwe (RBZ). In 2019, International Monetary Fund (IMF) warned that failure by Zimbabwe to have an independent central bank was only escalating risks of high inflation (The Zimbabwe Independent, 2024). The IMF observed that the RBZ as a key institution has largely failed to operate independently. This has resulted in a number of problems including excessive printing of money which has directly fed into inflation pressures (e.g. during the 2008–9 period).

Relatedly, in the same report, IMF (2019) notes the failure of an institution such as parliament to play its oversight role in monitoring government borrowing. Instead, the IMF laments the fact that the role has been largely relegated to civic society. This has resulted in government excessive borrowing accumulating a huge debt stock.

Another area of concern with respect to the RBZ has been in its involvement in quasi fiscal activities over the years. This has taken many forms including; support of agriculture, food security and allocation of basic commodities (through BACOSSI programme). All these interventions led to excessive printing of money which did not help matters.

## 11.4 Informal Economy

Informalisation of substantial parts of the Zimbabwean economy over a few years ago has largely been attributable to the challenges the formal economy has faced. Much discussions on the informal have been made in previous chapters. However, we avow our fundamental concerns about increased informality as follows;

- Informalisation is unfolding at the expense of quality jobs in the economy. The argument around increased informality in political circles in Zimbabwe is that employment opportunities are being created. While this may be true *quantitatively* to some extent, the worry is about the *quality* of jobs generated. The contribution

of manufacturing sector of Zimbabwe has declined from 23 to 9% since 1980 to 2023.[3] This translates to a lot of jobs lost as well as closures of a lot of companies thus impacting downstream industries as well. So, can informality effectively contribute to generation of real jobs which used to exist?
- The experience of Zimbabwe with informal economy is that substantial transactions which occur in this sector do not pass through the formal channels of the economy. For example, several players in this sector prefer keeping sums of money in the home (popularly known as *mattress/pillow banks* in local language).
- The informal economy has often made it easier for black market activities such as illegal fuel sales and foreign currency exchange to thrive. With respect to currency, it has often made it easy for driving monetary inflation.

The informal economy makes the economy of the country complex with multilayered problems. For example, how should it run alongside the formal economy which is struggling? More so, the informal economy mostly conducts transactions in cash and occasionally use mobile money platforms. This gives challenges for example on issues such as tax collection by Zimbabwe Revenue Authority. Without robust tax systems, there is a lot of revenue leakages via the informal sector.

## 11.5 The Weak and Vulnerable Members of the Zimbabwean Society

Under normal circumstances, the state should shoulder a substantial burden in terms of looking after the weak and vulnerable in society. However, Zimbabwe's challenges have largely diminished the state's capacity to effectively look after the weaker members of the society as evidenced in other countries. Instead, the economic challenges which have resulted in the state facing financial difficulties to fund critical social sectors of the economy have led to widening gaps between the poor and the rich in the country. For example, the health sector has seen increased emergence of private healthcare providers who mostly cater for the elite in well-resourced facilities. In the absence of National Health Insurance to at least cater for everyone, the majority have to contend with poorly equipped public health institutions. The same could be said also of sectors such as education. In the process, this has increased social inequalities.

Zimbabwe spends averagely 0.4% of its GDP on social protection. This is 1.5% below the Sub-Saharan average (UNICEF, 2021).[4] The net effect has been to increase vulnerability of both rural and households. The situation is dire on the disabled, albinos, child headed households, the elderly, unemployed as well as people

---

[3] See Newsday: https://www.newsday.co.zw/theindependent/business-digest/article/200028261/zim-manufacturing-sectors-contribution-to-gdp-declines#:~:text=The%20report%20shows%20that%20in,2023%2C%94%20the%20report%20reads.

[4] See UNICEF: https://www.unicef.org/esa/media/10216/file/UNICEF-Zimbabwe-2021-Social-protection-Budget-Brief.pdf.

living with chronic illness. Ideally the state should intervene to rescue in these circumstances.

## References

Acemoglu, D., & Robinson, J. A. (2012). *Why nations fail: The origins of power, prosperity, and poverty* (1st ed.). Crown Publishers.

International Monetary Fund. (2019). Zimbabwe. https://www.imf.org/-/media/Files/Publications/CR/2019/1ZWEEA2019003.ashx

Ministry of Health and Child Care. (2023). *Drug problem from US to Zimbabwe*. Retrieved from https://www.mohcc.gov.zw/?p=6843

The Zimbabwe Independent. (2024). Zimbabwe manufacturing sector's contribution to GDP declines. https://www.newsday.co.zw/theindependent/business-digest/article/200028261/zim-manufacturing-sectors-contribution-to-gdp-declines#:~:text=The%20report%20shows%20that%20in,2023%2C%94%20the%20report%20reads

UNICEF. (2021). 2021 Social protection budget brief. https://www.unicef.org/esa/media/10216/file/UNICEF-Zimbabwe-2021-Social-protection-Budget-Brief.pdf

# Chapter 12
# Conclusion

## 12.1 Introduction

This rest of the book has shown how 18 April 1980 ushered in a new state called Zimbabwe in Southern Africa. The independence itself created a *bubble pregnant with hope* for the masses. A lot lay ahead in terms of expectations and hope implying that the government had a plate full of responsibilities to deliver this hope to its people, a hope which would be sustained not by turbulence but with orderliness.

Early post-independent Zimbabwe was indeed a jewel. The then model economy had a lot to offer not only to itself but to other economies in the continent as well. It is logical that when you share a neighbourhood with a neighbour who strives to do his/her best, chances are high that you will be inspired to also take a leaf. By 'copying and pasting' all the good deeds you can also improve the neighbourhood you share in general and yourself in particular. Thus, Zimbabwe by being a jewel she was obliged to have her star shine to plenty of economies in the process millions of people would be improved. For instance, aspects such as education system, health care, agriculture among others were fairly robust as discussed in Chap. 2. Despite a few challenges emanating from the colonial past, this ought to give the country a solid start.

Agriculture then coupled with good climate meant that the country would sufficiently feed not only its people but other countries in the region and beyond through exports. Sound infrastructure of post early independent Zimbabwe helped also to maintain a buoyant manufacturing sector creating the much-needed impetus for *quality jobs* as well as supporting exports. Quality jobs are crucial for any economy as they result in better and higher incomes and eventually improve standards of living for the generality of people. The experience with most advanced countries has shown that as fortunes of an economy improves, contributions to GDP of sectors such as manufacturing tend to be enhanced, and this is also accompanied by rising incomes. What is critical is to sustain these jobs, this will then define whether an economy registers sustainable progress or not.

 
K. Mahuni et al., *Zimbabwe's Economy*, Advances in African Economic, Social and Political Development, https://doi.org/10.1007/978-3-031-81588-1_12

Against the backdrop of fairly reasonable early development indicators of post-independent Zimbabwe articulated above, a number of milestones were achieved. The economy had to open more opportunities so as to accommodate previously marginalised groups such as women so as for growth and development to be more inclusive. Moreover, enhancing the capabilities of marginalised groups would itself be a stimulus to create development with a human face for a state seen as a model economy. Thus, a number of initiatives in which focus has been on vulnerable people such as women have been witnessed.

Milestones in sectors such as health ensured that the HIV/AIDS deadly pandemic was also brought to manageable levels. A number of programmes related to management of the pandemic allowed the country to succeed in the fight against the disease. Since the disease was taking its toll mostly on the economically active, its management is worth celebrating. On top of those few gains in the health sector, successes in education have also been remarkable allowing the country to be ranked among the best in the continent in terms of educational indicators such as literacy rates. A lot though needs to be accomplished so as to improve the quality of education throughout the broader economy so that it creates reputable entrepreneurs as opposed to wide eyed job seekers.

## 12.2 Turbulence: A Confluence of Problems

Throughout the majority of chapters of this book, *Zimbabwe's Economy: Four Decades in Perspective: (1980–2020)*, Zimbabwe's experience as an economy can be described as *mixed* and has often been *turbulent*. At a time when other countries are enjoying a decent modicum of prosperity and progress, Zimbabwe's problems over the years remained stronger. More over at a time when other economies are creating quality jobs for their people, turbulence has seen the wiping clean of the very industries supposed to be a source of good quality jobs plunging thousands into unemployment, migration and informal economy. Turbulence of the years has in effect offloaded multitudes into the streets where they scrounge hand to mouth for basic survival. The informal economy as we highlighted in Chap. 2 has been largely an outcome of turbulence rather than an offshoot of orderliness in which proper dictates of planning are religiously observed. As an example, the level of haphazard vending across the cities and towns of the country alone is unprecedented, speaking volumes about an unwell economy as people struggle to make ends meet.

The bubble of hope was thus burst by the turbulence experienced in phases over the past four decades by the economy. The tumultuous journey is testimony to an economy saddled with many challenges which have become endemic.

## 12.3 The Cost of the Challenges to the Broader Economy

The unending challenges we have examined for most parts of the book have had a bearing on the economy. The challenges come with costs. These are not borne by the current generations only but future generations are also not spared as well. We briefly examine some of them.

### *12.3.1 Disruption of Economic Growth and Development*

Economic growth and development which can be sustained should encounter the minimum of disruptions. Turbulence is coming as a strong argument impinging on proper transformation of Zimbabwe. What it has largely done is to disrupt development momentum by disrupting proper take off. On taking off, an aeroplane requires a certain speed along the runaway, once it reaches this critical speed, up it leaps into the air. It is important that it maintains this power once it is airborne to the desired altitude until it reaches the final destination. The same logic is important for an economy. Half-hearted attempts to develop will not work the real magic for a country, progress will be derailed. With turbulence overpowering Zimbabwe for greater part of the four decades, the little momentum Zimbabwe garnered here and there lost steam, resulting in the transformation completely disrupted.

Chapter 5 of this book has been explosive. It delved much on some of the major issues defining the history of our country post-independence. While some may have helped in a way on building Zimbabwe, the majority of them contributed to the woes of Zimbabwe which punctuated its 40-year journey which has seen most people disenfranchised of means of survival and drowning in a cesspool of poverty. In the process the greatest casualty was development.

Related to the above, Chap. 4 explored much of the policy experience of Zimbabwe. Plenty of noble policies/programmes are failing to yield much positive results, the net effect of this being lukewarm growth and development as opposed to robust and impactful transformation. The economic growth and development which we are discussing here is not that of mere GDP figures, but real development in which people's lives and capabilities up to the lowest person are enhanced as propounded by the renowned economist and Nobel Laureate, Amartya Sen. Policies and programmes which inspire growth and development in an economy call for undivided commitment from all stakeholders in an economy. This is not easy to achieve if an economy is always in the eye of a storm.

In Chap. 6, we also encounter the numerous blunders committed by the economy in its turbulent journey either out of sheer ignorance or carelessness. Each commission in turn led also to the disruption of growth and development of the economic space which would be sustained. For example, ignoring the potential the growth point concept had and still has in territorial development had a knock-on development also. On the other hand, overdependence on Aid did not do the country much good. Aid, the experience of poorest countries is to corner them in a trap in which they ignore to mobilise domestic resources towards meaningful progress. In essence, Aid with its numerous problems as highlighted by Moyo (2009) tends to disrupt development for most less developed countries.

### 12.3.2 Loss of Incomes

One other thing which turbulence has done to the people is to rob them of incomes. For example, several inflation episodes experienced during the course of the turbulence meant that most people could not salvage savings especially monetary denominated in local currency. Moreover, due to inflation, the marginal propensity to save especially the local currency diminished as its value was depreciating by each day. The inflation evil had a toll on firms also as it caused closure of firms as the full wrath of inflation was felt across most industries. The effect was also to force masses into unemployment. With no meaningful work to do comes no income when social security is in shambles. With virtually nil significant safety nets to cushion people as explained in Chap. 6, poverty levels escalated.

### 12.3.3 Infrastructure Burden

Sound infrastructure for any economy which aspires to be competitive in modern times is crucial. Energy, water, transportation and logistics, internet connectivity, etc. which are modernised buttress the standing of an economy in aspects such as manufacturing, trade among others. Continuous upgrading of all these is also critical, failure leads to an economy failing to catch up with modern trends.

The chaos of the years has not done any good to the stock of infrastructure of the economy. Current existing stock of infrastructure does not add much impetus to an economy which was not only the jewel of Africa but aspires to be among the best in the continent. The current stock of infrastructure has resulted in the economy missing out on opportunities. For example, rail network across the country is in a deplorable state, yet it is a critical enabler of especially the manufacturing industry. Efforts to rehabilitate especially major roads as we showed in Chap. 8 are laudable. However, sectors such as railway network also require similar attention resources permitting. Countries such as Ethiopia, Zambia, Kenya through assistance of countries such as China are making encouraging efforts to develop rail infrastructure to boost connectivity and hence trade. Energy is still in short supply in the economy so as to power industry, this makes it difficult for new investors to flock into the country. The cost and availability of energy in any economy are crucial barometers investors use to gauge the health of an economy. Powering industries with generators is currently untenable due to constraints such as high prices of fuel.

As long as infrastructure remains in short supply or in a sorry state, the burden will be passed on to the next generation. Owing to turbulence, the deplorable infrastructure means that supporting sustainable development is almost impossible. The future generations as long as they inherit decayed infrastructure it means they will have a heavy burden to carry on their shoulders. Any meaningful transformation not fully anchored on robust infrastructure will be a futile adventure.

### *12.3.4 Loss of Human Capital*

A strong human capital base is vital for development of any economy. Asian giants such as South Korea were supported by investments in human capital (SaKong & Yoh, 2010), a process which happened overtime through the course of its six decades of growth and development. The decent education system of Zimbabwe which we traced in Chap. 2 has been instrumental in developing a strong human resource base. Zimbabweans are talented as a people as we highlighted in Chap. 4. Zimbabweans have skills which make them employable globally owing to educational policies which developed gradually. The churning of over 30,000 graduates annually means that there is plenty from the labour supply side as far job seekers are concerned. However, economic challenges have nearly collapsed especially the formal job market to absorb all these graduates, stifling labour demand. For scores of the economically active, one option has been to look beyond the borders for opportunities. Zimbabwe has lost a lot of skilled labour via migration to countries within the region such as Namibia, South Africa, Mozambique and to faraway lands. Professionals going out included lecturers, nurses, teachers, doctors, engineers among others where remunerations have been better besides even better job prospects. The study explored also how issues of empowerment can be responsible in accounting for migration of women.

Once professionals migrate to other countries, the resulting human capital gap is difficult to plug. The losses in terms of training of those professionals by the government will run into millions. Furthermore, recouping investments made into those professionals may not be easy, as a result our economy will act as some big training facility for other countries which would then tap into this talent with the minimum of costs. In conclusion, the turbulence of the years has resulted in a convergence of problems. Economic development has been disrupted and incomes lost. The infrastructure burden it has inflicted on the entire economy just like the human capital losses caused will complicate progress.

## 12.4 Overloaded Bus Metaphor Revisited

The overloaded bus metaphor we used in Chap. 1 has a strong resemblance to Zimbabwe's situation. Given the striking similarity especially among countries in the continent, the imagery we used is easy to relate to other countries also, except for one outstanding difference—the colour of the bus. Here and there, there might be slight variations in the colours of the buses but the general functioning is the same. Thus, there are many countries in the continent of Africa with similar experiences as Zimbabwe. With the forty years post-independence the journey has in fact been overwhelming. Understanding very well the load the bus is carrying is important.

## 12.5 Trumping the Challenges

Various socio-economic challenges Zimbabwe has faced over the past four decades have created a huge black hole for the economy. Inside the hole are the obstacles we have explored, in particular in much of Part III and IV of this book. The challenges are making it difficult for the economy to sustainably progress. Several efforts we have witnessed throughout the book are reasonable attempts at filling the hole. However, completely healing the economy from its complex problem set will not come on a silver plate. The truth is that there are no easy solutions to these problems. Crawling out of the black hole and weaving out the economy out of turbulence requires what Dambisa Moyo terms, '*a generous dose of honesty about what works and what does not as far as development is concerned*'. Zimbabwe needs this also. Simple.

For instance, we saw how numerous programmes and policies in Chap. 4 failed to work the magic through the economy. The deeply entrenched problems of the years in which industries have been pushed to the brink of collapse and decay of infrastructure implies that there may be no quick fixes to the mix of problems. Consistence is key to a sustainable recovery for Zimbabwe. As long as an insatiable appetite for taking a deep plunge and remaining submerged in murky and turbulent waters remains, then attaining progress for the economy may remain a field of unfulfilled dreams.

The book presented important lessons to be learnt by other countries from Zimbabwe's economic history from 1980 through 2020. How to then trump the challenges is crucial. While the array of solutions is targeted to countries in similar predicaments, a lot is still expected of Zimbabwe as a former jewel of the continent. Besides consistence we explained above, more still can be done by the economy. It is not necessarily about giant steps, but those small well calculated consistent single steps are game changers for the economy. Rwanda has written a beautiful script on emerging from the throes of a turbulent past to be one of the most sought investment destinations in the continent by turning a new leaf. Zimbabwe still sits on abundant potential which requires latent nurturing. Unity of purpose countrywide is called for. Every progressive Zimbabwean should partake in the rebuilding of the economy;

every effort is worthwhile. Mere politicking and sloganeering will only divide citizenry more, fuelling more turbulence. The opportunity cost of this is unbearable, Zimbabwe may fail to catch up as she still languishes in the lowest rungs of the development ladder as a perfect member of what Collier (2008) calls the *bottom billion countries*. Human resources the country has are instrumental in changing the turbulence script. The millennials the country just like other economies in the continent boasts of deserve a big chance to leap frog the country into dizzy heights of success! The millennials are the gems which define our tomorrow, if however, they are underused or misused the opportunity cost again is profound.

It's high time also Zimbabwe should wake up from the slumber. Dazzling in borrowed robes should now be a thing of the past. Residual economy inherited from the colonial times is just temporary, as long as focus is not beyond these left overs, there is a price to pay by the entire economy-one of them is turbulence, the remainder is obvious.

Successfully gliding out of the turbulence waters also entails serious design rethinking in sectors such as education as it is the foundation upon which a sound human resource base is anchored as explored also in earlier. On top of all this hard and soft infrastructure, supporting modern economies are vital cogs for real economic development. Through a sound infrastructure a robust manufacturing base can be established. No economy can prosper without significant manufacturing.

The policy environment upon which economies are nurtured is critical. Policy somersaulting are recipes for economic disasters. The book gave an overview of some of the numerous beautiful programmes with good intentions which have been carried in the economy, sadly most of them yielded little to douse the turbulence fires. Policies should not only be crafted but should also be religiously followed for the betterment of economies for effective implementation. Also 'copying and pasting' all that is good by other economies is critical for learning. Despite differing domestic circumstances, economies in modern times are so linked by globalisation such that what happens next door will also affect your well-being either positively or negatively. We still maintain that trumping the turbulence for Zimbabwe will not come cheap.

With everyone's hands on the deck…Zimbabwe can retrace back the steps and reclaim the jewel of Africa status. The future ahead is still bright. We see plenty of light!

## References

Collier, P. (2008). *The bottom billion: Why the poorest countries are failing and what can be done about it*. Oxford University Press.

Moyo, D. (2009). *Dead aid: Why aid is not working and how there is a better way for Africa*. Macmillan.

SaKong, I., & Yoh, K. (2010). *The Korean economy: Six decades of growth and development*. Korea Development Institute.

The manufacturer's authorised representative in the EU is Springer
Nature Customer Service Centre GmbH, Europaplatz 3, 69115 Heidelberg,
Germany. If you have any concerns regarding our products, please
contact ProductSafety@springernature.com

Printed and bound by CPI Group (UK) Ltd, Croydon, CR0 4YY
01/10/2026
02225954-0018